ANIMAL TRAINING
101

ANIMAL TRAINING
101

THE COMPLETE AND PRACTICAL GUIDE TO THE ART
AND SCIENCE OF BEHAVIOR MODIFICATION

JENIFER A. ZELIGS, PH.D.

MILL CITY PRESS

Mill City Press, Inc.
322 First Avenue N, 5th floor
Minneapolis, MN 55401
612.455.2293
www.millcitypublishing.com

ISBN-13: 978-1-63413-066-0
LCCN: 2014915921

Cover Design by Jenni Wheeler
Typeset by James Arneson

Printed in the United States of America

"For Sake, who has ever been my inspiration."

CONTENTS

CHAPTER 5: COMMUNICATION - OPERANT CONDITIONING / 95

THE BASIC PROCESS FOR TRAINING A BEHAVIOR / 99

THE SIX BASIC OPERANT TECHNIQUES / 107

FOREWORD

By David Lichman

5 Star Parelli Natural Horsemanship Instructor

Figure 1: David Lichman and horse Thirteen.
(Photo credit: Jay Mather.)

What I love about Jenifer is her dedication to discovering the practical truths about animal training and her passion for sharing them. My mentor, Pat Parelli, defines a true horseman as "someone who can get a horse to do anything within the realm of possibility, without offending the horse in the process." I would extend this to all animals in Jenifer's case. She has experience with everything from chickens to jungle cats. In her current position she manages a group of California sea lions, some of the most highly trained and enthusiastic animals I have ever witnessed. Anyone who trains animals for a living knows that although the communication systems vary, the one thing that keeps us up at night is how to motivate these animals to do more, jump higher, move quicker, and be generally excited and enthusiastic about doing AND learning. This is the art, and Jenifer is a consummate artist. The dedicated student will also study Jenifer's brilliant implementation on the accompanying DVD. Her superior timing and unbridled enthusiasm are evident in both the training and the results.

The other reason I love Jenifer's teaching is that she takes each of the six techniques for communicating a concept to an animal, and outlines in detail the benefits and drawbacks of each. Her openness to use whichever technique fits best for the situation is a rare quality. What does this technique accomplish? What does it cost? Can I minimize the cost and still reap the benefits? We all love positive reinforcement, because, let's face it, we love the animals and it feels good to reward them with something they like. But other techniques may be, in the end, a better deal for both the animal and the trainer. Blind dedication to a single approach ignores the benefits offered by the others. Benefits that would make it easier on the animal and therefore more strengthening to the relationship.

As a great example of this, Jenifer achieved Level 3 in Parelli Natural Horsemanship with her Morgan horse, Smitty. Smitty was a very challenging, dominant animal, and Jen's willingness to become skilled in the Parelli system only enhanced her relationship with Smitty. With the inclusion of a strong education in bridge and target training - Smitty became a superstar who helped many of her students advance in their learning about a variety of species.

Jenifer's dedication to the relationship is paramount. She often says that in a crunch situation, such as a movie set, you can get an additional 20% effort from the relationship points alone. Even when you are out of treats and the animals are tired - they will give you that extra effort. In the horse world we call that "heart and desire." Jenifer Zeligs is learned, talented, creative, entertaining and caring. She and her animals are supreme examples of what "heart and desire" is all about.

"Animal Training 101" opens the door to this world in a clear and well-organized fashion, that makes it a "must have" reference for anyone serious about improving their understanding of the psychology and training techniques, and their own relationship with animals. The book is divided into two main concepts: Communication and Motivation. Simply put, Communication helps the animal to understand what we are asking, and Motivation helps her to want to do it. If an animal doesn't understand what we want, no amount of motivation will help him to figure it out. If we explain it so the animal understands, how do we build great motivation to do it? When I think of a motivated animal, I think of one that asks, "Can I do it again? Please?!!!!"

When encountering a training problem, Jenifer first teaches to ask, "Is this a communication problem, a motivation problem, or a little of both?" This book is a wonderful guide to the process of answering that question - with tips and techniques for both recognizing what is happening (reading the animal) and how to move the training forward based on the answer. "Animal Training 101" will give you a much greater understanding of what to do and how to do it, because Jenifer clearly explains the underlying psychology. This deeper understanding of the process is so much more powerful than any step-by-step guide could ever provide.

ACKNOWLEDGMENTS

I would like to state up front that many, if not most, of the concepts that I discuss here have been explored in whole or in part by my mentors and my colleagues and our predecessors across many disciplines. I fear I will not properly be able to thank the many people with whom I have learned, debated, and addressed these concepts over my thirty years of interest in this subject. So in advance, I want to appreciate for their insight and assistance, the dozens (hundreds!) of students and colleagues with whom I have engaged these ideas. But a few individuals require special recognition for their involvement in my education and ministrations on this subject.

My mentor, Kayce Cover, provided the essential foundation and perspective around which my entire behavioral philosophy is based. To her I owe the greatest debt of gratitude, not only for the invaluable insight, but also for the incredible patience and inspiration she provided to that ten year old kid who I was when she first took me under her wing. I can only marvel and wonder at what she must have seen in me that could have possibly made it worth putting-up with me all of those years ago.

My partner, colleague and best friend, Stefani Skrovan, has had the dubious distinction of having to debate and evolve these concepts with me over a twenty year (and counting) period. To her I owe the ultimate gratitude, for without her wisdom and collaboration I might have long given up the subject years ago. And it was she who finally assisted in every way to help me get this book into print!

I must thank my parents, who may never have understood my interest in this seemingly inconsequential, certainly unusual, passion of mine. They nevertheless supported me unfailingly. I have endeavored to conduct myself to the highest standard and find a way to pursue my strange enthusiasm to the most honorable end. I hope I have made you proud.

I am grateful to several friends and colleagues who were generous enough to help me edit this book: Beau Richter, David Lichman, Nicolette Canzoneri, and Maxine Easey. Thank you for your support and effort. I hope you enjoy how it turned out!

Finally, all the many animal partners with whom I have been blessed to share moments and bonds of collaboration throughout my life have been my truest teachers. Chief among those is my beloved Sake - a most remarkable individual by any standard - sea lion or otherwise. It is to her that I dedicate this book, for it is because of animals like her that this discipline has continued to captivate me throughout my winding career.

ANIMAL TRAINING
101

CHAPTER 1
OVERVIEW

Figure 2: The author working with a sea lion,
free-released in the open ocean for research purposes.

(Photo credit: ATR International.)

The art and science of behavior

The purpose of this book is *to explain how to get an animal (of any species) to both understand and to choose to do what you want,* a process otherwise called 'behavior modification.' The focus will primarily be on species with whom conversational language is not a viable means of communication. Nevertheless, an understanding of animal training and behavior analysis is directly relevant to a wide range of potential human applications including education, business, economics, and history. People who are talented in behavior modification can easily leverage this ability to increase their success in many other areas, especially teaching. Thus the discipline of animal training should not be considered a narrow or arcane field, but one of potentially great value to a wide range of daily applications.

How much of this discipline is an art and how much is a science is hotly debated among animal behaviorists, psychologists, zoologists, educators and those in any way responsible for the challenging task of animal care and training. I see merit in both perspectives, and will attempt to explain and combine elements of both practices in this text. It is my earnest intent to reflect on the complex gray areas that must, by nature, dominate any discussion of a subject as complicated as the workings of the brain. It is my belief that the brain is the single most elaborate system currently known to mankind. Yet, it is still governed by definable scientific principles. Unfortunately, at our current level of understanding, we are decades, if not centuries away from being able to make consistently reliable and reproducible predictions of behavior in the natural environment.

What we do know are general overarching truths that tend to guide learning and, therefore, behavior. This knowledge is the science of animal behavior. Since there remains a great deal yet to be scientifically determined about behavior, we must therefore often rely more on the art form as we look to apply what we know about the science of behavior to the practical purpose of animal behavior modification. *This book will attempt to consolidate the art and science of behavior, in order to provide a guide for the practical goal of behavior modification in animals and, by extension, humans.*

A practical and yet comprehensive approach

This text offers a fundamentally practical approach to the science and art of behavior modification. It is designed for those actively working with animals (including humans) toward a specific, desired objective. I have attempted to inform without advocating either an overly simplified and limited dictate of techniques or an unwieldy mass of theoretical scientific considerations, which often result in challenging practical application. However, this is basically a reference book on animal training, and as such, it will not always be limited to the simple, dogmatic discussion more common to the animal training field.

Unlike most texts of this type, I will endeavor not to limit the reader to specific preferred techniques or to use a cookbook approach. This is not an instruction manual. Other training references may choose to offer a formula of approach out of a genuine loyalty to a particular methodology or out of a concern for possible disadvantageous outcomes of certain techniques, especially in the hands of inexpert practitioners. These are valid perspectives that I do not share. I value the flexibility of all the training tools in my tool chest too much to withhold any from discussion. Ultimately, in my long career, I have seen that there has been a time and place for each tool, regardless of my personal biases. Therefore, *this text is designed to be more informative than instructional.* I hope it will provide a deep and thoughtful reference to all aspects of this discipline, regardless of the reader's application and preferences.

Behavioral science and the real world

There are volumes of insightful behavior analysis work evaluating what can be proved in laboratory experiments. Where possible, I will refer to and rely on these resources, without burdening the reader with too much psychological jargon and technical referencing. I have included references to any claim I make in this book at the conclusion of the text, but do not find it helpful to weigh down the discussion with constant citations. This is not that kind of text. Indeed there are many more detailed references than this, if the study and theory of behavior is your fascination. It is my experience in the real-world environment, however, that these sterile psychological manipulations often fail to provide sufficient savvy and finesse for routine practical application. Perhaps this is due in part to the truth that at its heart, behavior is the result of the interaction between the singularly most complex known system in the world (the brain) and a chaotic, varied and cumulative environment. As a result, *many people feel hopeless about attempting* to understand the origins or meaning of their own behavior, much less that of others.

This complexity has resulted in a number of classifications which attempt to categorize and analyze behavior from certain philosophical viewpoints: structuralism, functionalism, behaviorism, psychoanalysis, as well as humanistic, cognitive, evolutionary, and sociocultural psychologies. While each of these doctrines may add considerable value to conceptualizing the brain's processes and functioning, they have, at best, an indirect effectiveness on modifying behavior. As proof, I point out that, while they can offer counsel, psychologists have yet to rule the world!

I find the attempt to confine complex behavioral mechanisms to a particular doctrinal viewpoint disadvantageously restrictive, especially for the practical outcome to which this book is directed. Too many of these theories involve understanding complex and restrictive terminology that often has relevance only in the laboratory setting. As a result, few practicing animal trainers have thoroughly studied the scientific literature on the subject.

The typical trainer's reference

Instead, the field of animal training has seen the pendulum swing radically in the other direction. There is a myriad of different training systems, specialized methods, and texts with rather limited, cookbook approaches for solving all your behavior modification needs. Most of these systems do not have or do not offer much of a studied understanding of the underlying processes. While these systems may be useful, they are often applicable to a limited range of species, in limited scenarios. And generally, they serve to perpetuate a beginning level audience by limiting the understanding of the underlying processes and the choices available. *I am aware of no behavior modification system or text that attempts to summarize and unify the entire discipline, both as it is practiced and through an understanding of the underlying science.*

Neither a cookbook nor a textbook

I will attempt to unify these approaches and provide the reader a solid foundation in the psychological sciences and the practiced art of animal training without being married to a particular discipline or school of thought. I will try to limit the jargon to the minimum needed for clear and accurate communication without holding too much allegiance to the less practical laboratory origins of the ideas. You will find a full glossary of terms at the end of this text. Please refer to this glossary if you are struggling with any of the terminology as you are reading.

This book offers a *new* option to those who are interested in the subject of animal behavior modification: neither a cookbook nor a scientific textbook. I hope to instead provide something more flexible, complete and pragmatic than either of these traditional approaches, while combining a bit of both methods.

The dedicated amateur and the seasoned professional

As an animal behavior enthusiast, I am not merely content to teach at an entry level or keep everything simple and safe. Although this text is designed to be comprehensive and thorough, I hope that it *will serve both the dedicated amateur and the seasoned professional.*

Novice and intermediate trainers

Novices will find some of the material quite challenging. This is the reality of dealing with behavior. It is a mistake to assume that there are simple and universal solutions to every situation. Additionally, the purpose of this text is to serve as a complete and accurate summary of the discipline. This requires a thorough grounding in the *science* of behavior modification, married to the daily practical application of animal training. I hope that this book will serve as a solid reference to all aspects of this field, to inform and expand the reader's understanding, at all levels of expertise.

I have indicated where the concept is more advanced to help the reader understand the areas most appropriate to their own expertise and interest. *Please do not be discouraged if some things are difficult to grasp.* Particularly for those at an entry or intermediate level, I recommend that you read the book from start to finish. The material builds on itself as you journey through the text, and the information in the earlier chapters supports an understanding of the later ones. The final chapters are particularly designed to help those beginning level practitioners focus on getting started and utilizing the most reliable techniques.

Ultimately this field is one of *apprenticeship*. You cannot expect to become an excellent animal trainer by reading a book. I know of no one who has done so. To become competent at any of these techniques, a person should be mentored through hands-on workshops and instruction. If you are interested in my personal approach, my laboratory offers internships ranging from a single day to years of apprenticeship (www.animaltraining.us). I have also created a DVD to accompany this book, which will aid in visualizing some of the concepts. There are many others similarly offering seminars and live tutoring. If you are a beginner and truly fascinated by behavior, my advice is to embrace the process and find a mentor(s).

Pushing the boundaries of the discipline

It is my hope that by embracing the entire complex art and science of animal training, we can push forward new understandings and practices so that each generation of practitioners surpasses the previous. I don't believe that providing a limited view could accomplish this goal. Thus, it should be stated at the beginning that this text will contain *many 'dangerous' ideas* and tools that others feel are for advanced practitioners only (or in some cases - techniques to be largely or entirely avoided). I will outline these concerns in each case to warn the reader of possible pitfalls, while attempting to give a fair and unbiased view of each tool. It is important to realize that transitioning to any of these advanced or risky methodologies must be done very slowly and carefully. Rushing into the use of challenging techniques may easily cause failure and frustration. Some of the techniques in this book are very difficult to utilize properly without prior experience and expertise. So please use this information wisely and judiciously.

To those who might criticize my inclusive approach, I would point out that ignorance of a thing does not insure its abdication, and further that even the 'best' techniques can lead to disaster when used poorly. Since neither ignorance of, nor the simplicity of a tool can protect against a potentially damaging error, it is my resolve to explore all subjects thoroughly. This, I believe, will offer the discerning practitioner a truly *informed reference to this challenging and fascinating discipline.* There is always more to learn, however, and I welcome correspondence and ideas from others who are similarly fascinated by this subject.

Communication and motivation

Another distinguishing characteristic of my approach is the simplified central philosophy that I propose and have found useful. My framework is quite simple. Directing behavior in any individual comes down to two fundamental principles: 1) *explaining what you want done* and 2) *convincing your subject to feel the same way.*

This philosophy stems from the idea that an individual, within their capability, will fail to do something for only two reasons: the first is that they do not understand how to do the thing and the second is that they do not feel entirely convinced to do so. So it follows by this logic, that there are two tasks animal trainers must master: *the first is to be able to explain what it is we want the animal to do and the second is to convince them to do it.* Mastery of these two components and the associated techniques will result in success regardless of the underlying process. Using this framework, I will attempt to categorize, simplify and coalesce all the practical techniques that I am aware are used or have ever been used to modify behavior. I will do so while *supplying the reader with a cost/benefit analysis of each technique* to enable a personal, needs-based assessment of all options.

Communication

The first subject is the rich tapestry of what I am calling *communication*. This is genuinely the fun tool bag that most people conceptualize as animal training: *explaining what we want done*. While I must profess a great fondness for this component of the art form, the truth is that this aspect of training is by far the least challenging and most open to varied successful interpretations of the imaginative trainer. Truly there are many ways to "skin a cat"… or rather, in this case, to "train a cat." Since there are many successful and different ways to do so, anyone trying to sell you a particular system of communication is, at best, pointing you in a highly successful direction, and not "the one true path." As I have promised, I will not attempt to sell you a particular logic or system to follow, but rather open the tool bag and explain how each tool works. Using this approach, I hope that you will have the opportunity to invent your own unique and successful way of 'cat whispering' or 'iguana whispering' or 'human whispering,' depending on your application.

As soon as you mention cats, many people are often quite surprised at the notion that it is even possible to really train a cat. This widely held perception is directly related to the second, and admittedly much more challenging, component of animal training: the subject of *motivation*.

Motivation

It is not that cats cannot be trained, nor is it that cats do not understand. The problem of training cats lies in the difficulty of *convincing them to want what you want*. The perception that dogs are "man's best friend" comes from the fact that they are so easy to motivate. In fact, we have bred dogs to view human beings as primary motivators, making our very presence desirable to the dog. You can confirm this yourself, as practically every dog you meet will greet you as a long-lost friend, even on first introduction. This endearing quality has made dogs, in my estimation, the easiest animals to train on the planet, owing to the front-loaded ease with which they can be motivated. While it is true that we have similarly domesticated cats into a preference for human company, this motivation is not nearly as universal. Cats can still more easily adapt to living a feral lifestyle without people. This is partly due to the fact that cats, unlike dogs, have retained a great deal of their more primitive motivations and action patterns (which can be challenging to change, for reasons I will discuss).

Some of the reasons that cats can be more challenging to train than dogs result from the pervasive nature of two special subcategories of motivation: desensitization and aggression. *These four subjects (communication, motivation, desensitization and aggression) make up the foundational elements of this book's presentation of behavior modification analysis.* Techniques and theories for each of these categories will be discussed individually and then brought together at the end of the text, to pull the material into a practical perspective.

Desensitization. *Desensitization* issues are the special motivational case where an animal fails to comply with the trainer as a result of *direct opposition from stronger, personal motivations.* These competing motives can be on either end of the spectrum: attractive things the animal wants or things the animal is trying to avoid. The solution to desensitization related problems lies in neutralizing the value of the competing motivations and/or in increasing the value of what the trainer is offering. But of course, that can be easier said than done, making desensitization issues some of the hardest training problems to solve.

Aggression. *Aggression* issues, for the purposes of this discussion, are situations in which the competing motivation is an intent by the animal to violently control the situation with an undesirable, *physically threatening behavior directed at a human being.* Since this book is focused on the practical subject of animal behavior modification and not merely on the general subject of animal behavior, I have placed human-focused aggression in its own category. In this case, the animal's behavior may, by design, result in harm to the trainer. Therefore these types of behaviors can cause overwhelming disruption to the training process and, as a result, need to take special priority. While it is true that there are also inter-animal aggression problems, these motivations functionally fall into the category of desensitization issues.

Motivation is the key to success

Motivation is the genuine challenge of animal training. There is no comparison between working with someone who is trying to do what you want and someone who is not. If the animal is focused on cooperating and achieving your goals, that assistance will make up for enormous shortcomings on your part. Contrast that with the alternative. The most perfect explanation will be wasted on the animal who doesn't care. For this reason, all successful training strategies will involve successful motivational strategies. Thus *the competent trainer will carefully weigh the net effect on the motivation of the animal, when making any decision regarding their care and training.*

This principle is the third part of the approach that I am offering in this book. As I outline each technique, *I will attempt to evaluate the benefits and drawbacks of the method.* I will focus this analysis from the perspective of how each decision can be expected to affect the current and future motivation of the animal to perform for the trainer. This motivation is partly described by how strong the relationship is between the trainer and the animal. Or in cases where there is no direct trainer relationship, the motivation attaches to the scenario instead, and might represent the animal's 'attitude' while on task.

The relationship bank account. The value the animal perceives the trainer and his or her actions to have can be described as the *relationship* between the two. It will directly affect the animal's motivation to perform. This relationship will be based on a history of personal experiences and species-specific affinities. All interactions between the trainer (and by generalization to a certain extent, all humans) and the animal can be conceptualized to have one of three values: reinforcing, punishing, or neutral. Thus, every interaction can be seen to add, subtract or have no effect on the relationship 'bank

Figure 3: Tova Lichman and her horse, Jasmine.
(Photo credit: Jay Mather.)

account' that develops and is constantly adjusted throughout the life of the captive animal.

As I have stated, motivation is the real challenge of behavior modification. *Thus, I strongly suggest that guarding the motivation provided by an excellent relationship 'bank account' should be factored highly in all choices about how an animal is handled and trained.* I use this logic on a daily basis to weigh-out and decide between the choices of available techniques and options for all handling. I hope this logic, along with a benefits and drawbacks evaluation of all techniques, will help the reader to make informed and careful decisions for all animal handling and behavior modification problems, without being restricted to particular techniques. If I have one overarching bias, it is this focus on the relationship value between animal and human. I hope to have now explained this bias so that the reader will understand my reasoning in this regard. (There is a full discussion on why and how relationships are developed through the process of classical conditioning in Chapter 4.)

Now let us begin the journey of learning to connect with others in a mutually advantageous, productive and satisfying way....

CHAPTER 2

INTRODUCTION

*Figure 4: Trainer Raquel Bahrami-Baalbaki demonstrating basic
bridge and target training with a dog.*
(Photo credit: Shrein Bahrami.)

B efore embarking on the subject of animal training, we should first agree as to what this term means. Indeed, this is a funny grey area as there has long been an unnecessary distinction between working with animals (termed 'conditioning') and working with humans (termed 'teaching') where, in fact, there is no reason to believe these processes are different in any way.

The definition of training

Behavior modification in any form could be described as learning. Behavior modification brought about by direct interactions (usually

intended) with people is what I would define for the purposes of
this book as **training**. Put more simply: training is learning through
human interaction.

Note that this does not distinguish much between human
education and animal education and leaves open the fact that individuals may 'learn' many things from their interactions, including
things that are not all intended by the teacher. I have chosen to include
both the intentional and unintentional learning together as training since many of the best trainers are in fact successful because
they take great pains to recognize and account for the unintentional
learning that inevitably occurs. Pat Parelli, a notable horse trainer,
posits this idea: "Nothing means nothing. Everything means something." Indeed, many of the most prudent animal training practices
must account for this active and perceptive learning on the part of
the pupil, in order to prevent inadvertent and undesirable behaviors
and conclusions from being made by the carefully observant subject.

It is important to recognize that this active process of learning is happening in all your interactions with your animal, and that
they are not only focusing on your intentional 'training' sessions to
develop their ideas about you or the rules that govern their lives. This
idea is very challenging for most people to pick up since they seem
to think only their intentions matter. This very self-centered viewpoint must be abandoned in order to truly reach out and understand
the perspective of your animal counterparts. In reality, trips to the
veterinarian or the daily feeding routine are all very powerful and
meaningful learning experiences for a captive animal. It is in their
best interest to attempt to predict and, where possible, alter these
outcomes to their best advantage. It is terribly naïve for the human
caregiver to ignore these vital 'training' sessions and believe that
training is only happening when they dictate it is the appropriate
time. *All interactions between the animal and the trainer have an impact
on the animal's learning and viewpoint.*

Nevertheless, we can further expand our definition of training to include that healthy training programs are ones in which the
animal becomes quickly, deliberately and smoothly cooperative and

willing and eager to perform such that they evolve from the current state of behavior to the desired state of behavior. Operationally this helps to guide our actions to produce the most mutually beneficial training system regardless of the methods we use to obtain this result. What we do understand about the mechanisms of learning applies quite liberally between species, and in fact most of the mechanisms of understanding human behavior can be linked back to a basic understanding of animal behavior. While it is certainly true that human beings are far more complicated in their neurological systems and behavioral range, especially in their motivational complexities, research has repeatedly demonstrated that the bedrock driving principles are common among all the Animalia taxa. For this reason, this text will have broad applicability to both human and animal teaching, and many of these principles are of keen value especially to working with certain special needs people or those for whom language is not the most effective method of teaching. Nevertheless, it is my intention to focus this text on the goal of primarily animal behavior modification, while acknowledging that there is a great deal of valuable overlap.

The tools we use to mold behavior are based on the inherent ways animals learn. Learning is a natural and basic biological process determined by fundamental neurological mechanisms common to all animals. Training or behavior modification occurs when a person arranges the environment in such a way as to promote a particular outcome of behavior and understanding. The resultant process of learning would be the same regardless of the manner in which the environment came to promote this behavior.

For example, a sea lion learns that by touching a plaque, he may receive a reward from the trainer. This is accomplished in small steps by the use of any of a variety of shaping tools aimed at drawing the attention of the animal to the plaque and then rewarding the animal when the appropriate contact is made. This process occurs through the learning mechanism of operant conditioning whereby the animal acts out on its environment and the resultant consequences guide his future selection of behavior. In a similar situation, the wild sea lion learns that by nosing the rocky sea floor he may disturb resting benthic fishes and find his next meal. In both cases, the animal has engaged the world in search of things he would like (in this case food), and through these 'operant' actions has learned how to get what he wants by touching his nose to a particular area. In the one case, this reality has been constructed by his human caregivers, and in the other it is a result of the organized nature of the environment. Nevertheless, in both cases the outcome and the underlying learning process are exactly the same (although we would only describe the former as *training*).

This truth is very frequently overlooked by the general public who routinely cringe at the thought of the 'unnatural' or 'manipulative' nature of reinforcement based learning, dubbing it such unflattering terms as bribery or coercion. This mischaracterization ignores the truth that anyone doing anything repeatedly is doing so for some form of pay-off. In fact the individual involved will, given the option, invariably choose a predictable and deliberate environmental outcome (such as can be provided by a conscientious trainer) over a much less reliable natural environmental consequence. Indeed, given the chance to ponder this a little further, I often lament that my environment does not offer to me the more clear outcomes that I would crave to best judge my ideal decisions. Wouldn't it be wonderful if the universe would clearly tell you when you are making a good decision on a career, mate, or a personal investment? How nice it would be to get reliable minute-to-minute feedback on how to achieve what you seek! Predictable guidance is generally not lamented by animals in captivity, quite the opposite. The animals who suffer in captivity most often do so as a result of the random unpredictability of their careless human providers.

This discussion brings up an important point to consider before delving further into the nitty-gritty techniques of animal training. It is relevant to ask what, if any, value animal training holds for both the humans and the animals involved. In many places, especially in some European zoos for example, training is thought to be unnatural and therefore undesirable. In most American zoos, however, training programs are rapidly becoming the modern and humane way to care for their collections. With these greatly disparate viewpoints, it is fair to ask then, "Why train at all?"

CHAPTER 3
WHY TRAIN?

Wild animals

First, I should point out, that while it is possible to train both wild and captive animals, history has proven it is usually disadvantageous to wild animals for humans to alter their natural behavior significantly. While this invariably occurs to a certain extent, generally animals in the wild (and often their human counterparts) are not well served by these changes. One has only to think of the dangers of feeding bears in Yosemite or, in fact, any predatory animal's plight once they have the misfortune to associate humans with food. Even a well-intentioned migrating mountain lion will likely be shot for trespassing if he comes too near a human establishment, let alone looks to humans for food.

These (usually food-related) behavioral changes in wild animals have been known to alter seasonal migrations for everything from small birds to dolphins. This can lead to disaster when the human food source is contaminated, nutritionally poor, or interrupted by economic forces unpredictable to the animals now dependent on this nourishment. *While there may be some cases where applying behavior modification techniques can be helpful to wild animals, these cases are very rare and tricky to manage properly. So for most purposes, it will be best to reserve the art of animal training primarily to captive animals.*

Captivity is an ethical question

Following this logic then, one must be ethically reconciled to holding animals in captivity before finding the subject of this text at all of interest. This question is fundamentally a personal choice and like any ethical belief must be satisfied internally for each individual.

It is beyond the scope of this text to argue this point too substantially, since I believe these issues must have already been considered by the reader prior to obtaining an interest in animal training as a subject. However, being a lover of animals, I have obviously, long ago, troubled over this issue and I will offer some of my insights for the consideration of the reader. This is largely because I have come to the conclusion that most of the defensible reasons for holding animals in captivity are greatly enhanced by a thoughtful training program. Furthermore, and even more importantly, most of the significant areas of concern about holding animals in captivity are best overcome by a careful and well-planned training regime.

It is worth pointing out that since the captive animal will undoubtedly routinely interact with humans as a part of its life, training of some sort is, by definition, inevitable. Anyone who argues differently has a misguided view of their effects on behavior and an insufficient understanding of the principles of behavior modification in general. Indeed for any animal held in captivity and regularly interacting with humans, the only real training question is what type and how deliberate that training will be. How this question is answered will determine how much potential benefit the system will offer to both the humans and the animals involved.

How humans are benefited through animal training programs

Some of the main reasons that animals are held in captivity include companionship, education, conservation, entertainment, research, to perform work, and for human consumption. If we take each of these categories separately it will be easy to point out that a well-trained, cooperative and adjusted animal can only benefit these objectives.

A better companion

Human companionship is the primary responsibility of millions of pets around the world. To the extent that the pet is well behaved, cooperative and comfortable in this environment, both the owner and the pet may be happier. This includes the animal performing his duties admirably, generally by being unaggressive, friendly and available to the owner on demand. Of even more importance is the pet abstaining from disruptive behaviors like damaging property or using the wrong toilet area. All of these goals are outcomes molded by a proper animal training program and well-trained pets are generally the most desirable ones to have. Most recently, this truth is driving an ongoing trend in animal shelters that are increasingly seeking to implement rudimentary training programs to help make their pets more 'adoptable.'

Figure 5: The author performing at a public outreach event.
(Photo credit: ATR International.)

'Edutainment'

Public display or *public education* is a primary mission of most zoos and aquariums throughout the world. This is based, in part, on the principle that we will conserve only what we love and we will love only what we are exposed to. Many people recognize the need to combine this educational goal with something more stimulating in order to reach the most people. This concept is called 'edutainment.' Zoos accomplish this conservation and educational goal through numerous avenues ranging from simply making the animals available to be appreciated 'naturally,' providing vital breeding stock for endangered species, or demonstrating extraordinary attributes in shows and performances. The latter type of presentation may range from heavily educational to mostly entertainment, but obviously, in either case, extensive animal training will be involved. The advantages of training for animals held for a purely observational or breeding purpose involve enhanced survival through the ease of husbandry, veterinary care, and even mental and physical stimulation - all subjects which I will discuss further (see Benefits to captive animals in this chapter).

Human-animal partnerships

Animals held in captivity for the purpose of *doing some form of work* for their human counterparts are sometimes called by the term 'human-animal partnerships.' This perhaps suggests upfront the obvious necessity of a cooperative (trained) relationship. For millennia, humans have been training animals for everything from plowing fields and herding sheep to a more modern purpose such as drug or bomb detecting. These relationships are often governed by historical animal training techniques that will be thoroughly discussed in this text. Since domestication of animals is one of the defining moments of modern civilization, it amuses many in my field to consider themselves as practitioners of the "world's oldest profession."

*Figure 6: Trainer Beau Richter training an endangered
Hawaiian monk seal to cooperate in voluntary
energetics research (NMFS Permit #: 13602-1).*

(Photo credit: Traci L. Kendall.)

Reduced stress

It may be more difficult to imagine how animal training might be of
benefit in either the *research* setting or the *agricultural* field where the
animal is ultimately sacrificed. To start with, for the scientific disciplines, it can be tremendously helpful or even an absolute necessity
to have the willing cooperation of the animal subject. Even in those
cases where cooperation is not a requirement, studies indicate that
many factors are adversely affected by the stress of an involuntary
procedure. Stress artifacts are most serious in the study of physiology
and can create misleadingly extreme ranges of physiological data. For
example, early work investigating marine mammal diving physiology
used a forced-dive paradigm where the seals were strapped to a board
and submerged in water while, among other things, their heart rate
was monitored and recorded. This methodology led to the misimpression that pinnipeds used extreme bradycardia and anaerobic
metabolism to manage their diving abilities, where in fact as we now

know these "pulling out all the stops" reflexes are only used in a small percentage of normal dives where the animal is pushing its maximal capabilities. Under normal circumstances the animal, being in control of the duration of the dive, will choose to use less costly aerobic metabolism most of the time. Bob Elsner in 1965 used trained animals to demonstrate these organisms' abilities to voluntarily control their heart rates at will and to further elucidate many other interesting aspects of their diving physiology.

But even without the need to reduce stress artifacts, perform in shows or do work, keeping animals alive longer and healthier is an indirect but crucial benefit to the training of captive creatures. Captive animals derive tremendous physical and psychological benefit from a thoughtful training program. These benefits will help all captive animals live better lives including those whose destiny may be ultimately for human consumption.

Figure 7: A harbor seal at the Aquarium of the Pacific receives a routine tooth brushing as part of a program of voluntary husbandry care.

(Photo credit: Michelle Sousa.)

Benefits to captive animals from a conscientious and thoughtful program of training

The simplest and perhaps most profound benefit to captive animals who are trained properly to cooperate is the tremendous enhancement this affords their regular care, also called *husbandry*. Husbandry issues such as cleaning enclosures or veterinary exams and treatment are often chaotic, forceful and neglected in poorly trained animals, especially dangerous ones.

Improved husbandry

In many zoos all over the world, the inability to easily and predictably move an animal from one environment to another to clean the enclosure or to separate animals, results in suboptimal health and living conditions for these creatures. To move animals around, zoos often will have poorly implemented a rendition of one of two basic training techniques: baiting or negative reinforcement. In the case of baiting, the animals are encouraged to move into alternate enclosures by placing food into those areas, leaving the primary enclosure available for cleaning. In the case of negative reinforcement, the creatures are often driven off exhibit by the use of a fire hose or other aversive stimulus. These are certainly defensible (if not optimal) solutions, but they are generally employed with such little skill and understanding as to be of only rudimentary and limited usefulness. For example, the animals may only shift at a certain stereotypical time of day or may occasionally fail to shift successfully by outsmarting or avoiding the keeper. It is worth noting that, in most cases, the zoo keepers and zoo management do not seem to understand or admit that the use of these techniques constitutes training. If they were only willing to accept and invest in that truth, they could develop much more functional and sophisticated communications with their charges. This would enable not only quick and easy shifting at will, but also lead to many of the other important benefits of training listed in this book.

Far more dramatic procedures to improve health and well-being can be found in the increasingly numerous examples of animals participating in trained complex *veterinary* procedures. Animals of all types have now been demonstrated to cooperate in every aspect of their care, such as voluntary blood samples, x-rays, inoculations, ultrasound, wound suturing, tooth removal, biopsy and anesthesia delivery, to name just a few. In order to perform any of these procedures, there are only two viable alternatives to training the animal: restraint or anesthesia. Both of these options have substantial downsides.

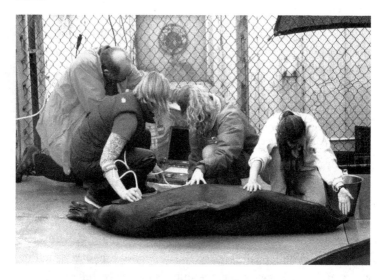

Figure 8: Chief veterinarian David Casper and ultrasonographer Sophie Dennison perform a voluntary ultrasound examination on a trained sea lion at Moss Landing Marine Laboratories.

(Photo credit: ATR International.)

Reduced injury and risk

The risk of injury to both humans and animals from restraint-based procedures is well documented and has resulted in the creation of many clever restraint devices called squeezes or crushes. However, even when using such a device, there is a high degree of risk to the hysterical, struggling animal. This is due to the fact that by observation alone, it is very difficult to tell the difference between legitimate pain from injury or simple fear and struggle. For this reason, most professional animal keepers know of several animals that carry permanent restraint-based injuries for the rest of their lives, to say nothing of the mental trauma that this form of random physical punishment may instill on the hapless recipient.

Anesthesia is dangerous, expensive and generally should be avoided wherever possible. In marine mammals, anesthesia carries with it increased risks of mortality due to an unfortunate interaction between the dive reflex and many anesthetic agents. With some species, the risk can be as much as a 50% mortality rate. Training for cooperation in medical procedures is clearly the cutting edge of optimal animal care, and I hope it will be increasingly embraced by all the captive animal industries.

Improved mental and physical stimulation

Training captive animals can also provide a much-needed source of *mental and physical stimulation*. Some of the best arguments against animals in captivity rightly revolve around a concern for these welfare issues. It is true that a captive environment will inherently be limited in size and space, and this may consequently result in the animal lacking either adequate exercise or occupation. These issues are both well addressed through a training regime.

It is often believed that captive animals lack the physical stamina and performance of their wild counterparts. Certainly the lack of necessity to locate food or mates and avoid predators *could* result in a substantial reduction of physical exercise unless this behavior was influenced to occur for other reasons. In fact, just like trained athletes, performing animals often develop highly athletic capabilities that, in some cases, even exceed their wild counterparts. It has been demonstrated empirically, for example, that trained performing dolphins are capable of higher or equivalent speeds and jumps than those managed by their wild conspecifics. This outcome may seem surprising unless

Figure 9: Nicolette Canzoneri uses training to enrich and stimulate a mountain lion at Moorpark College's Exotic Animal Training and Management program.

(Photo credit: Chuck Brinkman.)

one considers the different nutritional restrictions that wild animals must face. Since wild animals will not know when or if their next meal is coming, they cannot afford to expend more than the minimum needed on any energetic pursuit. As a result, they will likely fail to develop the extreme capabilities that might be possible in an environment of infinite plentitude such as can be provided in a captive situation. Trained animals (like humans) are benefited by regular programs of exercise behaviors which offset the lesser incentive to exercise when food is provided and predators are unlikely.

Similarly, the lack of daily occupation found when food is plentiful and predators are non-existent can create boredom or, in the worst cases, stereotypical behavior[1]. The lost concerns of a wild

---

1   A stereotypical behavior is an unhealthy behavior pattern characterized by a repetitive response that is without variation for extended periods of time. Stereotypic behavior is usually brought about through lack of stimulation.

life can be and should be replaced with other challenges and things to think about and control. The need to control one's own life, make choices and alter the environment is well understood to be a basic life need. In a training program, the animal faces challenges, accomplishes deliberate goals, learns and grows, masters new skills, and most importantly can interact to make clear choices about how to get what he/she wants or does not want. This empowering option of interacting within an otherwise unchosen environment provides animals mental stimulation and satisfaction, as is easily demonstrated by their eager participation, increased activity and the elimination of destructive and stereotypical behaviors.

About 'unnatural behaviors'

Contrary to popular belief, there is not good evidence that the preponderance of 'unnatural' behaviors is increased in trained animals. Many people in the zoo environment focus overly much on this concern and use it as a reason to limit their training programs. Others worry needlessly that something that wild animals do not do is somehow inherently unhealthy for captive animals, such as temporarily hitching a horse to a post for example.

This argument has always struck me as a very shallow one anyhow; untrained (or more properly, unintentionally trained) animals are just as likely to exhibit 'unnatural' behaviors resulting from their limited and synthetic environment. Is it natural for a cheetah to eat from a metal dish? No. But more importantly, once we have brought them into captivity we have created this contrived environment and so we should make the best of it for the animals and not become snobs over what limited range of behaviors we deem appropriate for our captive creatures to perform. Is the environment not already limiting enough? Why choose to arbitrarily restrict healthy, responsive and active behavior just because it reminds us that these animals are no longer living in the wild (a fact which seems painfully obvious)? A captive animal cannot be a wild animal, as we have removed their predators and the complexity of their wild ecosystem and they are forced to see and interact with people each and every day. Even in wild animal parks where a great attempt is made at replicating the wild environment, they cannot hope to truly replicate nature and should not be made to seem inferior for that inevitability.

A great welfare benefit can be afforded by 'environmental enrichment,' in which environmental manipulations are made with the goal of increasing the animal's behavioral choices and drawing out their species-appropriate behaviors. These manipulations, such as hiding food around the enclosure, prompt the animal to engage in some foraging activity prior to eating its meal, for example. There is no reason that environmental and behavioral enrichment (another synonym for training) cannot and should not be attempted in parallel to ultimately provide optimal improvement in animal welfare.

Having the time to train

Another common argument against training animals in captivity is the time and therefore the expense that may be involved. People argue against training by saying it takes too much effort, but every human interaction is training, by definition. If an animal is in captivity someone must be taking the time to care for the animal, feed it and clean its environment. Instead, the choice can be made to productively train them using essentially this same time and opportunity. Just 10 to 15 minutes a day can accomplish useful training and the benefits well outweigh the disadvantages

WHY TRAIN, *IN SUMMARY*

I believe that there is overpowering evidence of the benefits to both humans and animals brought about by a deliberate and thoughtful training program. In a healthy training program both humans and animals receive reduced risk of injury and better control. Humans are better able to accomplish important goals of companionship, education, conservation, entertainment, research, and human-animal partnership work, and they can do so ultimately with less manpower, time invested and cost. Animals are benefited by better care, health and physical and mental well-being regardless of the purpose of their captivity. These mutual benefits make not just the case for training, but I believe they make the moral obligation for it as well. *We are choosing to hold these animals in captivity. We owe it to them to provide the best possible life and well-being while they are in our care.* This is clearly accomplished by learning and judiciously employing thoughtful animal behavior modification techniques and decisions. I hope this text will help to outline the paths to a fruitful training system and that this will help many who were previously unable to aspire for and reach this ethical goal.

CHAPTER 4

COMMUNICATION: CLASSICAL CONDITIONING

INTRODUCTION AND OVERVIEW OF COMMUNICATION THEORY

As I have previously stated, this book is divided into four basic categories of behavior modification technique and theory: Communication, Motivation, Desensitization, and Aggression. I will be describing them in this order, which is the opposite of their importance and priority in the training system. That is, if you have a problem with an animal in each of the four categories, it would be my recommendation that you prioritize first for the aggression problem, second for the desensitization problem, thirdly for the basic motivational issue and finally worry about clearing up your communication confusions. Now certainly it will be possible to accomplish many of these goals simultaneously, but there is no point in focusing on explaining something more clearly to someone whose major focus is eating you, for example.

Nevertheless, communication is the central foundation of the interaction between human and animal (or teacher and pupil). It is also the easiest subject to master, so we shall focus first on all the ways to explain to someone what we mean and what we want and – for the clarity of this discussion – temporarily put aside any concerns over the animal's enthusiasm for cooperation or alternative desires (*i.e.* its motivations).

Training involves two types of learning processes or conditioning[1]: classical and operant.

Learning by association - classical conditioning

Classical conditioning (also called associative learning and respondent, Pavlovian or reflexive conditioning) is the process by which something that previously had one value changes by repeated predicable association with something that has a different value. In its simplest form, classical conditioning is the process of learning that two reliably concurrent events are related. From there it is the process by which we come to realize that "this symbolizes that." Classical conditioning is a type of passive learning. It involves making mental associations and values, not necessarily 'doing' behaviors, however - and this is the tricky part - behaviors can and often are associated with the newly generated meanings. Wherever classical conditioning does reproducibly create behavior, that behavior is always an involuntary reflex.

My description of classical conditioning will vary somewhat from what is traditional. Since involuntary behavior is rarely a desirable goal, functionally in behavior modification, we use classical conditioning to create communication symbols and also to promote feelings or values in the animal. These symbols are most commonly commands or signals used to request or inform the animal, but classical conditioning can also be utilized to help create and manage things that the animal likes or dislikes.

---

1   Note: conditioning and training are often used as synonyms for animal learning but in fairness, as we have already discussed, there is no defensible evidence that there is any difference in mechanism between human and animal learning. Therefore, conditioning, training and learning should all be considered synonyms from a functional, if not a popular, perspective.

Learning by consequence - operant conditioning

Operant conditioning (also called Instrumental learning), on the other hand, describes cause and effect learning; that is, "when I do this, this happens." Operant conditioning is an active learning process involving voluntary behavior. It occurs through the active physical involvement of the animal; the animal emits a behavior - it is punished or rewarded - and as a result the behavior happens more or less frequently in the future. Functionally, we use operant conditioning to create behaviors. There are many ways of employing operant conditioning, and this is what most of the subject of communication is all about.

CLASSICAL CONDITIONING

Figure 10: Michelle Sousa using a (classically conditioned) whistle bridge stimulus to train an otter at the Aquarium of the Pacific.

(Photo credit: Aquarium of the Pacific.)

Classical conditioning was first described by the physiologist Ivan Pavlov while studying dog salivation responses. It is most easily remembered as 'associative learning' since it is the process whereby the temporal association of a meaningless cue (in Pavlov's case: a bell) with a meaningful event (in this case: the delivery of food) has the demonstrable effect of representatively transferring the 'value' of the meaningful event to the meaningless stimulus. In Pavlov's case, this meant that the salivation that was reflexively caused by the presentation of food came to also be caused by the ringing of the bell that had repeatedly and reliably predicted the presentation of the food. On its own now, the bell would reliably cause salivation - a demonstration of the animal's understanding and prediction that food was coming. To identify these components, psychologists like to add in lots of terms like CS (conditioned stimulus- the bell), US (unconditioned stimulus- the food), and CR (conditioned response-salivation) and UR (unconditioned response-salivation)[2].

Here is my favorite way to think of this process conceptually: it is as if the two stimuli have been 'rubbed' together over time and the essence of one has 'rubbed off' on the other. In this case that would mean that the essence of the food has rubbed off on the bell.

Another way of thinking about the process of classical conditioning is to use an arithmetic analogy. Consider the meaningless stimulus has a value of zero, then when added with either a positive number (a reinforcer) or a negative number (a punisher), the result will carry the same numeric value and connotation (plus or minus). This view will become more useful in a minute when it will help more easily explain a related concept called counter-conditioning (more on this later in this chapter; also see Chapter 7).

---

2   This can be confusing since the CR and UR are the same but elicited by different stimuli through the conditioning process. I have learned that this is often more confusing than valuable to many students, so I will not go further with this method of presentation. Please do seek a psychology text for more on that method of evaluating and discussing the process, if you find it of interest.

Motivation continuum

Since classical conditioning is, in part, a subject where we discuss the development of motivations (through transferring value), it may be helpful to introduce the reader to an important concept that we will discuss throughout the course of the text. This concept is a useful tool in the understanding of motivation. I call it the 'Motivation Continuum.'

The Motivation Continuum is a simple pictorial depiction of the perception of any stimulus to any individual. At any given time, the animal thinks of everything somewhere on this line:

Punishing ——————— Neutral ——————— Reinforcing

You can give the stimulus any numeric value you wish, since the continuum is only concerned with *relative values.* The traditional process of classical conditioning takes a neutral stimulus and by repeatedly, predictably pairing it with a valuable stimulus (either punishing or reinforcing) drives the previously neutral stimulus to become either punishing or reinforcing, based on what it is paired with. Therefore classical conditioning of a neutral stimulus can be depicted along this continuum as follows:

Punishing ——————— Neutral ——————— Reinforcing

Classical Conditioning

You must have a mental connection in order for this process to occur. This is why it is a type of learning. Associations that are not noticed will not be transferred. *Classical conditioning does not involve* **any** *voluntary response or choices, however, which is one reason why it is called reflexive or respondent- it evolves as a direct consequence to occurrences in the environment, not as a result of any choice that the animal has made.*

However you most easily conceptualize the mechanism of classical conditioning, what has happened is that the bell now elicits the same response (salivation) as the food does. And therefore, to the extent that these two stimuli continue to be associated, the bell and the food have similar meanings to the dog, as can be verified by his involuntary reflexive salvation response. In my opinion, *it is not necessary to have a reflexive (involuntary) response associated with this fundamental learning mechanism*. However, since in Pavlov's case the result *was* a reflexive (unconscious) response, it proved, without a shadow of a doubt, the mechanism of the learning process that had occurred. The value had transferred from the meaningful to the meaningless stimulus.

It is true however, that where classical conditioning involves the precise, direct production of behavior, that behavior is always involuntary. Further, *classical conditioning is the only practical way to train involuntary behavior since, by definition, this type of behavior is not under the conscious control of the individual.* That would include behaviors like salivation on sight of food, but it could also be blinking in response to air blown on the eye. Some of these behaviors can also be voluntarily controlled, some cannot. If they can be voluntarily controlled they can be trained by either method (classical or operant). However, if they are entirely involuntary, these behaviors must be conditioned classically.

Unfortunately, the fact that this process was first and is most easily demonstrated with reflexive and involuntary behaviors has left many confused about its mechanism. Advanced practitioners will undoubtedly recognize this concept has been described by others as *restricted to creating involuntary behavior through association.* My view is different, although the two perspectives are not incongruous.

This same type of associative learning occurs whether or not the meaningful stimulus in question happens to involuntarily drive a particular reflexive behavior or not. In other words, this learning process (occurring in the brain) is not restricted to stimuli that cause reflexive behavior, as many people and psychological texts claim. If one considers precisely what learning has occurred in the classic Pavlovian case of the bell eliciting salvation, it is simply that the dog has realized that the bell warns of the fact that food is coming. There is no reason to suspect that perceptive learning of this type should be particularly associated with reflexes at all. It is merely the best way to demonstrate that this learning has taken place. Unfortunately this type of confusion is what typically weighs down psychology in general in attempting to transfer understanding from the laboratory to real life, and the associated unfortunate marriage to limited doctrinal definitions from laboratory research.

Practically speaking, we see identical classical conditioning processes with associated events subject to more complex voluntary behavior all the time. It is just that this meaning transfer is less absolutely *provable* in those cases where the resultant behavior can include a wider variety of responses. For example, in the classic Pavlovian example, the bell might also elicit the behavior of leaning forward or moving to the food dish in addition to the salivation. These behaviors would have been technically formed by operant conditioning since they are under the voluntary and arbitrary control of the dog. Nevertheless they demonstrate that the classical conditioning that conferred meaning to the bell has occurred.

What classical conditioning does is provide a mechanism by which we can learn how to predict and understand important events and, therefore, better survive and navigate the world. The result is that the lines between classical and operant conditioning are somewhat blurred since they can easily, and routinely do, co-occur. We will discuss common scenarios of this type in the following discussion on the uses of classical conditioning in the training process, but first let's continue our basic discussion of the mechanism of associative learning.

Predictable association

An important aspect of classical conditioning is that it is vital to maintain the association between the conditioned (CS) and unconditioned stimulus (US) in order for the associated and transferred value to continue to exist in the conditioned stimulus. If the association breaks down over time and the two stimuli are not reliably co-occurring, the value of the conditioned stimulus will degrade.

Some people mistakenly take this to its extreme conclusion and fear that conditioned stimuli must be perfectly associated with the meaningful drive 100% of the time in order for the learned stimulus to hold its value. This is flatly untrue, for obvious adaptive reasons. Associations in nature do not have to be 100% predictive in order for us to see and believe in a meaningful pattern. The foraging bird does not find a couple of empty snail shells and swear off snail foraging in the future. In fact, our brains have quite the opposite tendency, and may be counted on to superstitiously place meaning on unrelated events based on limited but significant associative occurrences (among other causes). These 'illusory correlations' are forms of cognitive bias that are well documented in human beings, especially, as anyone with a 'lucky' shirt can attest. Whatever the mechanism, it is the case that making associations comes naturally and easily to all organisms and certainly does not require a perfect and continuous track record.

However, initially there is a strong importance to the precision and timing of the consistent and predicable association of the two stimuli. So in the early conditioning phase where the animal is learning to draw new perceptions about the stimulus being conditioned, it is ideal and very useful to have these events maintained at a 100% association between the presentation of the meaningless (CS) and meaningful stimuli (US). Over time, this association will need to be maintained, but can certainly be lessened.

How to create classically conditioned stimuli deliberately

Intentional classical conditioning is generally performed by presenting the meaningless stimulus-to-be-conditioned (CS) and then immediately presenting the meaningful stimulus (US). For example, the bell is sounded and then immediately the food is presented. This

process is then repeated over and over again, continuing to tempo-
rally correlate the presentation of the bell with the food. It is helpful to the conditioning process for the CS to be presented initially
preceding the US, in order for the stimulus to be recognized and not
ignored by the animal. However, so long as the two events are co-
occurring, even simultaneous, this learning will take place if the animal notices this correlation.

After the initial learning has taken place and a solid foundation of understanding and belief has been developed, this meaning
will hold up as long as the association remains reasonably reliable.
The minimum needed frequency of maintained pairing between
the CS and the US will depend on the species, the individual and
certainly on the conditioning history between the two stimuli. The
association must be well above random chance. I generally attempt
a minimum of a 75% association in general, with some variation
depending on the circumstances. This should only be considered a
guideline, not a hard and fast rule. Ultimately, the behavior of the
animal in response to the CS will determine if the maintenance frequency is sufficient.

Creating new perceptions

Recognizing predicable associations of meaningful events is critical to navigating our world, but it is also a way that we come to
expand our drives and feelings, more than merely our basic survival needs. *This is one of the critical elements that classical conditioning serves in each of our lives - it is a big part of how and why
we like and hate certain things.* To a certain extent, things that are
not necessary to our survival can develop meaning and value to
us, in part by what (or whom) we associate them with initially.
Very complex motivations can result from these ongoing associative perceptions throughout our lifetimes. Humans are especially
unique in how complicated, dramatic and elaborate these associations can become.

To understand this better, consider a cultural phenomenon that many of us are personally familiar with: 'our song.' The
idea of a couple's song is a great tradition in our culture. This song
will usually be played for the ceremonial first dance at a wedding,
for example. The origins of this song typically emanate from a
classical conditioning experience often early in the intense and
emotional period of the relationship's development. This song's
concurrent association with a particularly powerful moment in
the couple's history is what starts the conditioning process that is
then often reinforced by repeatedly playing the song while thinking
about or being with the other person.

For your amusement, here's an example from my own personal experience. I was once traveling on holiday in Hawaii and,
while en route, I met a lovely, devastatingly handsome man with
whom I proceeded to engage in an exciting island romance over the
course of the following couple of weeks. I still have fond memories,
as I remember all the romantic things we did in this beautiful place.
He had rented a car and we drove all around the island having all
sorts of adventures. As it happens, a new 'hit' song was out at that
time called "More Than Words" and, as does so often happen with
popular new songs, it was played over and over again on the radio
during this time. Now, I can recall my feeling about this song prior to
arriving at the island was that it was somewhat boring, so it would be
fair to characterize my inherent predisposition as neutral to vaguely
negative. However, once this romantic song (the CS) was heard over
and over again associated with my new love (the US), it is safe to say
that for a time, this was my most favorite song in the world. The value
of this song to me was directly associated with this time and this man
and, as such, it carried with it one of the strongest human reinforcers
known: love. In fact, once I got home, I immediately purchased the
album and played the song over and over again, all the while remembering the sweet times my boyfriend and I had shared.

What happened next demonstrates the importance of maintenance in classical conditioning. As time went by and we drifted
apart, there was eventually a rift between us that hurt me deeply and

for which I blamed him. My feelings toward this man then became very negative, and the resultant effect on 'our song' was equally dramatic. I came to desperately hate this song for it now represented a person I did not want to be reminded of. Although the strength of my feelings in this regard have faded with time, still to this day when this song is played on the radio, it is for me like nails on a chalkboard. I can't turn it off fast enough! Thus it is with conditioned stimuli, their primary value is linked to what they have been associated with, and this can change over time as the associations change.

Relationship formation

Here I would like to propose that it is by this mechanism that relationships are formed. *The process of relationship development is a very complex one since it is not usually just the result of a single associative event, but the cumulative result of all of the meaningful associations between any two individuals.* In this sense, it is similar to a bank account as I mentioned earlier in the text. Using an arithmetic model of classical conditioning, one can see how associating with high value desirable events makes the relationship bank account very large and positive, where conversely, being associated with strongly aversive events can be seen as a withdrawal. It is important to note that the exact value of these meaningful events is determined only by the individuals involved and cannot be considered universal in any capacity. Indeed, many of us often fail to understand the attraction between any two individuals, and that is precisely because what drives us and what we value is unique to us and does not necessarily have value to others, although it often does (more on this in Chapter 6).

As I have already stated, the motivational value of the relationship as it is perceived by the animal is of great importance and potential value to the accomplished trainer. In my long career I have many times recognized that my positive relationship provided the marginally needed extra motivation to accomplish especially difficult and challenging goals. This has been especially true at the end of a long day of work, when the food motivation has run out, or when the animal was inherently afraid or overwhelmed by the situation. Thus, studying and understanding the mechanism of the daily ongoing functioning of classical conditioning is critical to many higher level training accomplishments.

Always come bearing gifts

Everything described from here forward acts to increase your significance to the animal and thus establishes a relationship with the animal. If you choose to associate with reinforcing experiences then your relationship gets more reinforcing, and the opposite is true if you associate yourself with punishing experiences. In this sense the relationship is the sum total 'bank account' of what you have associated with. This significance and relationship builds continuously, so that the longer you work with an animal, the greater your significance and also (if you make good choices) the better your relationship.

One of the simple strategies to help maintain your best relationship value is my personal philosophy to always *come bearing gifts*! This technique attempts to, where possible, start off all encounters with the animal by offering them reinforcement. Ideally, it is best to deliver this reinforcement by hand or as personally as possible, so as to strongly link the reinforcement delivery to your deliberate intent. Otherwise it is possible for the animal to believe that you are the person who stupidly spills food in their enclosure each day, and in this case your value will still increase, but it will carry with it a different, less useful flavor.

In the beginning of the relationship, offering reinforcement prior to any expectation will help you build up your positive associations and increase your significance to the animal. This will, in turn, help you engage their attention for further behavioral conditioning. As time goes by, you will become a person who is very positively anticipated by your animal, and this eagerness of attitude is one of the more useful and desirable qualities in any healthy training program. One cautionary note here: *be careful to avoid delivering reinforcement following any undesirable behavior the animal may be involved in at the time.* Whatever you reinforce, you will see more of in the future. So aim for a neutral or positive behavior to reward with your preemptive gift giving!

One of the reasons to have a constant awareness of the phenomena of classical conditioning is that it is occurring at all times regardless of our deliberate intent. Expect animals to draw associations between things that have meaning to them. For example, for many animals, people in long white coats (*i.e.*: veterinarians) are bad, since they are generally associated with frightening or illness-related experiences. As a result, in many zoos, the mere arrival of the veterinarian can often provoke panic and chaos unless this has been properly anticipated and counter-conditioned (see below). To maintain a healthy relationship, it is necessary to minimize association with aversive events and actively pursue neutralizing them whenever they may occur.

Counter-conditioning

The unfortunate attitude that many animals feel towards their medical caregiver is quite natural and to be expected; many humans similarly dislike hospitals and the doctor's office. If one does not want such a conclusion drawn, one useful tactic is to provide the appropriate conditioning in the reverse. This describes the process of *counter-conditioning*: a desensitization technique which uses the principles of classical conditioning but pairs two stimuli of opposite values in an attempt to neutralize the value of one of them. Thus, if you want your animal not to fear the vet, it behooves you to proactively engage the vet in reinforcing experiences with your animal. For example, arranging to have your vet periodically deliver a favorite and rare treat to your animal will associate him or her with a high value reinforcer that will later help to reduce the disadvantageous association with painful inoculations. The goal in counter-conditioning is to alter the value of a particular stimulus by bringing it toward neutral. If the conditioning continues thereafter, it would technically be described as standard classical conditioning, where a neutral stimulus is given value by continuous association with one that has value already. We will discuss counter-conditioning further in the Desensitization section but I feel it is relevant to include here, since it is, in my opinion, the identical learning process, but involving the pairing of two meaningful stimuli instead of one meaningless and one meaningful.

Now that we have covered a basic understanding of the classical conditioning process, let us explore specifically how it is best utilized in the training process (benefits) and what some of its inherent limitations might be (drawbacks).

THE BENEFITS AND DRAWBACKS OF CLASSICAL CONDITIONING

➤ *The benefits of classical conditioning*

Conditioning a cue

One of the major places classical conditioning is used in almost all training programs is *to condition cues or commands which are professionally referred to as* S^{D}s (pronounced ess-dees). A discriminative stimulus (S^D) is the psychologist's way of saying a stimulus in whose presence the opportunity to receive reinforcement for a particular behavior will occur. In the training application, this is a cue or command that elicits a behavior which will be reinforced.

In practical application, it is necessary to establish cues that control the onset of the behavior we have developed. The way this is done is by preceding the behavior predictably by the cue over and over again, until the animal understands the association of the two and comes to recognize the cue signals the onset of the learned behavior (and then the reward). This associative learning is the process of classical conditioning.

For example, the trainer has trained a dog to sit by baiting him with a small treat over his head. Now, prior to holding up the treat, the trainer says, 'sit,' and then holds up the treat. When the dog sits in response, it is rewarded. Over time, the dog will begin to recognize the connection between the 'sit' command and the sitting process which leads to the treat.

It should be pointed out that classical conditioning is the process by which the dog learns to understand the meaning of the word 'sit' - as an opportunity for reinforcement for the act of sitting. However, the use of the cue or the treat to drive behavior, the act of sitting and the process of learning to sit, would be considered operant conditioning. These two learning processes (classical and operant) are very frequently co-occurring since the maintained classical conditioning of the cue is assured by its persistent association with the behavior it describes. *This is one of many places in which the lines between classical and operant conditioning are blurry.*

Conditioning a bridge stimulus

In more advanced and modern training programs a special stimulus is often used to signal that good things (typically food) are coming as a result of the animal's behavior. This special signal is called a 'bridge stimulus' (see more in the Bridge Stimulus section in this chapter). *The bridge stimulus is trained and maintained by the process of classical conditioning.* This process works identically to Pavlov's initial experiment with the bell. In that scenario - the bell was the bridge. Bells are not generally that practical to use in a standard training system, however.

One of the most common types of bridges regularly used today is a clicker. It is conditioned just as the bell was, by pairing the delivery of food and the click, with the click preceding the food just a little bit. With repetition over time, the click is an indicator of food coming. Later, you can vary the expectation of food somewhat and how quickly it follows.

As with any signal, you need to be able to verify that the animal understands the meaning. You can test the bridge concept by bridging, preferably when the animal is not misbehaving or looking in your direction. An animal who understands the bridge should turn immediately and come to you expecting food to be delivered. It is very important to do this test without looking like you are going to deliver food, since that might inadvertently cue the animal to respond in a similar manner. In animals with advanced behavioral understanding, you can also test the understanding of the bridge stimulus by placing the animal on an extended behavior, then when the bridge stimulus is given the animal should break station and turn to the trainer to receive its reward.

Just like with S^Ds, the *use* of the bridge stimulus to communicate to the animal the correct behavior and shape and condition new behavior is technically operant conditioning. However, the continued association between this stimulus and reinforcement maintains and develops its meaning through classical conditioning.

Conditioning advanced communication stimuli

Similar to the training of an S^D or a bridge stimulus, there are other forms of *even more advanced and rare communication symbols that are conditioned using classical conditioning.* In fact, it would be safe to say that any representational or symbolic communication is conditioned or taught to have meaning using classical conditioning based learning (although in human beings language may have additional parallel mechanisms of learning). There are many types of unique and specific conditioned stimuli that have a variety of symbolic meanings according to the needs of the trainer and the training system. Some of these communication symbols include: the differential reinforcement stimulus, the delta, the keep going stimulus, the redirection stimulus, and the end of session stimulus. These communication symbols will be discussed further below, but are generally thought to be advanced training concepts that most behavior modification texts will not include. This is, in part, because of the difficulty in training them properly. In any case of symbolic meaning development, it is necessary to create the right scenario in order for the animal to see the association between the symbol and its implication. This can be tricky, and the predictability is critical to the meaning formation and learning process.

Conditioning secondary drives

In addition to creating symbolic meaning, classical conditioning also creates drives, perceptions or values. The *two types of drives that can be created through classical conditioning are called secondary reinforcers and secondary punishers.* The term secondary distinguishes that these are learned values not intrinsic ones which would be called primary. Secondary drives are useful in the savvy trainer's tool bag because they allow the trainer to expand the list of available motivators that can be used to drive an animal's behavior, a subject I will discuss throughout the topic of Motivation.

Secondary reinforcers are things that the animal doesn't care about at first but become desirable through learning. One of the most basic mechanisms to create secondary drives is through the process of classical conditioning. In fact, it could be argued that classical conditioning is the fundamental mechanism underlying all development of secondary drives, but this is not a certainty. Examples of common secondary reinforcers include clapping, petting - or in the case of humans- money! Examples of secondary punishers, or things that the animal didn't care about at first but learns to dislike, are items used by veterinarians such as needles or lab coats or training props such as whips or bull hooks. Conditioning secondary motivators involves only repeated association, since these stimuli do not cue anything to occur or explain anything. Therefore, they do not need to precede the meaningful stimulus with which they are associated; they need to merely co-occur with it reliably.

It is true, however, that all stimuli that are classically conditioned become, by definition, either a secondary reinforcer or a secondary punisher. This means that the communication symbols already discussed all carry a value to the animal once they are conditioned. For example, the bridge stimulus is also a secondary reinforcer. While it is true that all stimuli that undergo classical conditioning become either secondary punishers or secondary reinforcers, it is not true that all classically conditioned stimuli become meaningful communication symbols. If something conditioned has symbolic meaning beyond its reinforcing or punishing value, this will depend entirely on the precision of the predictive association it has to other important events and whether this association has been perceived by the animal.

Forming the relationship

As we have already discussed, *the relationship formed between the animal and the trainer (or the animal and the training system) is created through the process of classical conditioning.* This on-going process can create a valuable motivational tool if done correctly, or the opposite, if caution is not used in your associations.

Conditioning involuntary behavior

Of course, to most psychologists, classical conditioning is the means by which we can *condition involuntary or reflexive behavior.* With certain more primitive species, like insects or fish, this may come up more frequently. But with most organisms the behaviors we seek are voluntary in nature or can be duplicated, albeit less reliably, by voluntary behavior. In the rare case where the desired behavior is reflexive, however, classical conditioning will result in its highly reliable presentation.

Counter-conditioning

Finally, *the classical conditioning-based learning process called counter-conditioning can be used in desensitization training* to drive the value of a target stimulus to neutral. Usually this is done to eliminate fears by pairing an aversive stimulus with a reinforcer where the reinforcer can help counteract the aversive value. We will discuss the use of this technique further in Chapter 7.

➤ The drawbacks of classical conditioning

Not useful to form voluntary behavior

The biggest problem with classical conditioning as a tool is that it is *not very good for training behaviors,* which is usually the primary goal of any training system. Behaviors that are reflexes can be trained this way, just as Pavlov demonstrated with his initial experiments, but very few behaviors that we are interested in would fall into this category. Therefore, most of behavioral conditioning falls into the realm of operant conditioning work, so much so, that many people think of operant conditioning as synonymous with creating behavior.

A constant process

One of the important things to keep in mind about classical conditioning is that it is happening constantly whether or not you intend, or are even aware, that associations are being made by the animal. *Superstitious behaviors and beliefs are being created all the time by the animal picking up on associations that are accidental or unintended.* Superstitious behaviors result from misunderstanding. They are produced where there is no intended relationship between response and reinforcement. This can create artifacts in trained behaviors that you do not desire or it can condition new cues that cause the animal to perform a behavior prematurely. It can also ruin the value of your relationship or color the value of the relationship between the animal and the veterinarian. These important consequences must be foreseen and taken into account at all times when interacting with your animals. One of the distinguishing characteristics of excellent trainers is their ability to predict and stave off problems or confusions before they occur, and part of that is understanding the unintended implications of on-going associative learning.

Reliable maintenance is necessary

Another important issue with classical conditioning is that it *requires lots of continuing repetition and maintenance.* This can take time or often be less practical than is desirable. For example, I helped to develop a product that would reduce conflicts between wild sea lions and harbor masters. The sea lions would invariably inhabit (and often destroy) valuable harbor docking causing financial and personal safety issues. We designed a very mild electric irritant coating that could be placed on the docks to keep the sea lions from wanting to sleep on them. The field was so mild that it was safe for humans or animals to walk on, but it caused enough discomfort that the animals didn't want to sleep on it. The system worked perfectly, but as soon as it was up and running, I was forced repeatedly to insist it stay on. My colleagues wanted to believe that the visual stimulus of the appearance alone would sustain the deterrence once the animals had learned about the association with the irritating electric field. This idea was tested many times by leaving the electric field off and watching the animals return before my reluctant colleagues gave in to the truth of classical conditioning. It needs to be maintained in order for it to be effective. Without the electric field, the dock was just another dock and the animals were happy to return. After it was turned on, the animals only tested it occasionally to determine that it was indeed still associated with the unpleasant electric field.

One note of interest on this subject is *that it is possible to create more lasting conditioning if the meaningful stimulus is extremely powerful or valuable to the animal.* This can be exquisite pain or pleasure on first presentation, such as with electric fences used for livestock. But even in those cases, the odds that the conditioning won't need to be maintained with repeated exposures are small.

Classical conditioning, in summary

Classical conditioning is learning by association. It plays an important role in both how we predict events in our world, as well as how we form new values, preferences and feelings. We deliberately utilize classical conditioning in the training process to give meaning to cues and symbolic language, as well as to change the value of events or stimuli in general. Classical conditioning cannot be used to directly form voluntary behavior, however, only involuntary behavior. It should be understood that this form of learning is occurring at all times regardless of the trainer's intent. Therefore, guarding against unwanted or incorrect associations is a sign of an advanced trainer.

CONDITIONED COMMUNICATION STIMULI

Now that we have covered the topic and process of classical conditioning, it would be reasonable to discuss some of the important communication training tools it makes possible. These tools are useful in the process of operant conditioning but are trained to achieve and hold their meaning through the process of classical conditioning. Listed here are just some of the more common categories of conditioned communication stimuli, but creating symbols for important concepts is potentially limitless.

THE BRIDGE STIMULUS

Bias disclosure: of all the tools in my training tool box, I value the *bridge* above them all! If I were forced to choose only one magic tool, this would be the one. Although I will easily admit that it is certainly possible to train without one, I would prefer not to have to. I have promised not to attempt to sell you any particular training system, so I feel it is necessary to admit this important personal bias.

As we have discussed, the bridge stimulus is trained through classical conditioning. What it does is define and **pinpoint in time when exactly the behavior that the animal is performing is correct and desirable**. It usually begins as a signal that food is coming (although any strong reinforcer can be used to condition a bridge). The predictive value and importance of this information to the animal draws the animal's attention to the instant the bridge happens. It focuses the mind at that instant. In this way, the bridge evolves from more than just a secondary reinforcer to pinpointing in time when the individual is doing something that will produce reinforcement.

The use of the bridge stimulus in animal training became widely popular starting in the 1940s, thanks largely to students and colleagues of B.F. Skinner (the founder of modern neo-behaviorism), most notably Marion and Keller Breland, Bob Bailey and

Karen Pryor, who have each written notable texts about their animal training systems and philosophies.

A secondary reinforcer

As we know, the bridge is a *secondary reinforcer*: a conditioned stimulus that has become a learned reinforcer. Even though the bridge starts out as a meaningless stimulus, it evolves to become one of the strongest reinforcers available to the trainer as a result of its long history of association with food and many other reinforcers, as well as its association with enriching training experiences. Many behaviors with which the bridge is routinely associated are, themselves, reinforcers. Other powerful reinforcing events can be associated with the bridge as well. Some examples include the opportunity to have an occupation, to accomplish goals and learn something new, and through these means to have increased control and understanding of the world. As a result of all of this inherent desirable association, the bridge stimulus is typically a highly valued secondary reinforcer.

The beginning of a reliable system of communication

Many powerful and often very self-affirming opportunities are generally connected to the introduction of the bridge stimulus; therefore, in many cases the introduction of the bridge functionally begins the training relationship with the animal. The introduction of the bridge can be easily accomplished whenever feeding the animal, or whenever you "come bearing gifts."

In many systems, before there is a predictable, reliable stimulus to point the way, the animal is forced to make do with other ad-hoc associations it is able to pick up from its environment to determine when important events are occurring. Unfortunately, since those environmental cues are neither deliberate nor intentional, they may be inconsistent or unreliable.

The security and confidence provided by a bridge stimulus cannot be overstated as a form of clear communication to an otherwise guessing animal. Imagine somehow that you came to be on an alien planet. Day in and day out, you struggled to understand what was happening and what they wanted from you. And then one day, they started to create a system of noises that told you when you were on the right track and would receive the comforts that you sought. How valuable would that reassuring knowledge be to you? I have witnessed many times the almost cathartic effect this important, consistent and predictable communication tool can provide. Merely by being the bringer of this information, you greatly increase your significance, and as a result, help to further build your relationship with the animal.

It is worth noting that the bridge stimulus is such an important tool for creating desirable behavior in animals, that many advanced trainers, who have not been formally trained in the concept, are using a form of bridge stimulus nevertheless. Some of these trainers are doing this deliberately, in which case they are often praising their animals in a distinct and instinctively time-specific manner exactly when they have done the right thing. Just as common, however, are the 'Clever Hans'-type trainers who have some personal habit that their animals have learned to use as an appropriate 'tell' of when the behavior is correct, even though the trainers themselves have no conscious intent to impart this information.

The famous Clever Hans was a horse owned by a man named Wilhelm von Osten in Germany at the turn of the 20th century. The horse could apparently perform great feats of mathematical prowess, time telling, and other wonders by tapping out the correct answer with his hoof. People came from far and wide to witness the horse-genius' mathematical wizardry. The *New York Times* featured the marvel in a front page article and a "Hans Commission" was convened to investigate. This included a variety of experts: zoologists, psychologists, horse trainers, school teachers, and even a circus manager. Though today very few of these people would have been confused by this phenomenon, at the time, the Commission concluded that there was no trickery, and that the horse apparently possessed these wondrous talents.

This attracted the attention of a psychologist named Oskar Pfungst. Pfungst eventually determined that Clever Hans could only answer correctly if he could see his owner and if the owner, himself, also knew the answer to the question. Needless to say, some form of very subtle cue was being offered by von Osten that escaped normal detection and about which, as it turns out, von Osten himself was apparently unaware. The cue in question was in fact a bridge stimulus, and it was the relaxation of apparently subconsciously tensed muscles in his body and face. As Hans got nearer to the correct answer, the owner tensed and then finally relaxed as the correct answer was achieved, thereby bridging Hans for a prolonged tapping behavior.

The story of Hans demonstrates how powerful classical conditioning can be and how it is possible to have a bridge stimulus even if you have not intentionally conditioned one. This suggests that bridges have been around as long as training itself, even though they were not recognized as such until recently. The story of Clever Hans is also an incredible testimony to how powerful it is to have an animal who is trying to figure out what you want, pointing again to the value of motivation as a training tool.

A temporal cue

Functionally, the *bridge pinpoints in time a precise moment when the individual has done something correctly*. Therefore, it is very useful for this to be a sharp, short signal that is easily distinguished from the environment. We will further discuss the selection of bridges in a moment, but for now let us concentrate on this as a distinct temporal cue. Without such a cue, the animal would simply receive reinforcement and be forced to back-calculate which of the many things it had been doing was the behavior that earned the reinforcement. This can be especially difficult when you stop and realize just how many things a typical individual is doing at any one time. As I sit here now I am typing, crossing my legs, chewing gum, blinking, smiling, occasionally looking off into space and a host of other possible 'behaviors'. If I was reinforced at this moment I am most likely to guess that it was for my typing behavior, since I am personally most focused on that. However, a bridge stimulus would certainly help me to clarify the issue a great deal. If the goal behavior was staring off into space, that would be easy to separate from the typing behavior by pointing it out with a well-timed bridge. Even with this critical temporal information, there is still more that can be done to clarify the exact behavior for the animal as we will discuss shortly in the operant conditioning section.

Reducing reinforcement latency by bridging the gap

This stimulus is called a bridge because it *bridges the gap in time between when an animal has done something correctly and when they will receive reinforcement.* It is therefore a kind of place-holder to mark the correct behavior without having to immediately deliver primary reinforcement to make the same point. This effect is important to the practicalities of most real-life training situations. Generally, in order for an animal to easily connect its behavior to a reinforcing consequence, it is critical that that consequence is timely, avoiding latent reinforcement. Therefore, in an optimal situation without a bridge stimulus, the trainer needs to aim the reinforcement at the animal at the very instant the behavior is performed. This can pose many practical challenges in all sorts of working situations.

Imagine trying to time the reinforcement delivery perfectly for a back-flip behavior. If it arrives too late, the animal has finished the behavior and is now sitting calmly when the reward is given. As a result, we could expect to see more sitting in the future and less flipping since this is the behavior most closely associated with the reinforcement. If the reinforcement arrives too early, the animal may abort the flip and instead grab the flying reward. Having the bridge symbolize the precise moment when the animal has earned a reward without actually interfering with the on-going process is a vital tool of communication and reinforcement timing. It is possible to live with a certain amount of reinforcement latency, since over time the animal can be expected to generalize enough to extrapolate the aspects of the correct scenario of reinforcement. However, there is still no substitute for precise and clear communication.

This aspect of the bridge also allows a greater flexibility of reinforcement type and schedule. Since the bridge itself is a secondary reinforcer, further reinforcement is not necessarily required. We will discuss reinforcement schedules further in the Motivation chapter, but suffice it to say that there is a lot of opportunity provided from the freedom to not deliver a primary reinforcer for every correct behavior, while still reassuring the animal that they are performing well.

Terminates the behavior

The bridge stimulus signals to the animal that reinforcement is coming, so an animal who understands this meaning should stop what they are doing and turn to the trainer to receive reinforcement. This, therefore, will *terminate the behavior* that the animal is performing at the time the bridge is delivered. Many trainers also consider it necessary for the animal to return to them to receive their reward. As this generally happens naturally since the animal is eager for its reward, it does not require much to place this condition on the situation. It entirely depends on the nature of your training system and its goals whether or not it is desirable for your animal to return to you following the bridge. Many people like it as a reset in preparation for the next behavior, while other situations make it more preferable to keep the animal in place in order to move smoothly into the next behavior occurring in that location. Some trainers take the return of the animal as a clear indication that they understand the bridge correctly. Strictly speaking, I do not believe that it is necessary to have the animal return in order to reasonably demonstrate that they understood the bridge. Abrupt termination of behavior has always been a satisfactory criterion for me; however there are certain species and situations where I prefer that the animal return. This choice really depends on the needs of the trainer.

The tendency for an animal to return to the trainer once they have been bridged, can lead naïve trainers to incorrectly use the bridge stimulus as a 'recall stimulus' or a cue that tells the animal *to* return to the trainer. This is a big mistake since any behavior that was occurring at the time of the bridge will be inadvertently reinforced. Often a recall is used when things are confused or disorderly in order to reset and start again. This makes it likely that the animal may be performing behavior that the trainer does not wish to encourage, but by using a bridge stimulus (instead of a conditioned recall S^D), you tell the animal that this behavior was correct and that they can expect to receive reinforcement for this in the future[3].

Selecting bridges

Any brief, discernable, distinct stimulus can be conditioned as a bridge. This can be a sound, a sight or a tactile sensation, but generally precludes smells and tastes. Smells and tastes cannot be used easily to pin-point a moment in time. Some examples of commonly used bridges include whistles, flashing lights, the word 'good', a double tap, or a clicker.

So then how do you choose what stimulus to condition as your bridge? First, let me state again that you can choose to condition *any* short-duration, discernable stimulus as a bridge signal!

---

3   Side note: there is some argument that using a recall in a situation where the animal is behaving badly may also risk increasing this behavior in the future. That is because all S^Ds are also secondary reinforcers; therefore, their delivery can be reinforcing to what precedes them. While that certainly may be true, the recall stimulus trained properly will have been conditioned to occur in a wide variety of deliberately randomized circumstances. It is the nature of a recall to be disassociated from context deliberately. Thus, it is much less likely to be connected to the temporal context of its delivery than a bridge stimulus whose very nature implies that important connection.

Anyone who tells you differently is selling you something. There certainly are a lot of people with an allegiance to their particular bridge stimulus, and bridging stimuli do tend to be inherited from mentor to pupil in this field where apprenticeship is commonplace. What I recommend is to consider what makes the most sense for you personally, as well as the species and system you will be working with. To help with this evaluation, let's compare and contrast some of the advantages and disadvantages of the three most common types of bridging stimuli: *the verbal bridge, the clicker, and the whistle.*

➤ The benefits and drawbacks of the VERBAL bridge

Benefits of the verbal bridge. A verbal bridge is simply a word from any language (or any uttered sound) that is short enough to pinpoint a moment in time, and this word is then classically conditioned as a bridging stimulus as described previously. All other things being equal, the verbal bridge is the default choice of bridging stimuli owing to its many simple yet elegant advantages.

The most obvious advantages of the verbal bridge are that you already own it, and it will more or less always be ready to use at a moment's notice, with no preparation, inconvenience or sanitation risk. Contrast this with something that uses up one of your hands (or mouth or both), must be bought, worn, picked up to use, and potentially soiled by saliva or whatever reinforcers you are delivering. The verbal bridge does not have to be held in the hand or mouth, remembered, sanitized, or purchased. It cannot be stolen from you and ingested by your animal, nor used to strangle or drag you anywhere (true stories).

In some situations, the ability to mask the bridge within conversation can be a desirable quality. Performers often use the word 'ok' to surreptitiously bridge their animals within the context of the show without drawing the audience's attention by using a strange noise. Of course in those situations, training must happen in a limited context to avoid accidental environmental bridging from a commonly spoken word.

Owing to the real life practical inconveniences of physical bridging stimuli, many trainers whose primary bridge is a whistle or a clicker actually rely on verbal bridges in moments where life catches them without easy access to their preferred bridge. Let me give you a couple of examples from my own experience. A dolphin trainer who has been having a brief conversation and so has removed his whistle from his mouth, finds his young calf mimicking an elder dolphin in a complex aerial maneuver. Wanting to capture and reward this excellent behavior, he wastes no time returning the whistle to his mouth and instead loudly whistles through his teeth. This sound generalizes closely enough to the conditioned whistle tone and enables him to communicate with the calf to capture the surprise behavior.

It is often in these surprise situations that the physical bridging stimuli can become cumbersome. In the second example, a young woman and her service dog are making a public presentation about the advantages of bridge training and what a difference it has made in her work. The woman stands at a podium. She has her dog on a leash, her clicker, and her presentation notes. At one point the sound system makes an unexpected piercing shriek, painful to us all, but especially to her dog, presumably, who has the most sensitive hearing in the room. This woman, as an excellent trainer, understands the importance of rewarding the animal for its calm behavior before it gets upset. Unfortunately, she has let go of the clicker in favor of holding the notes and the leash. With no time to waste or hands to retrieve her bridge stimulus, she does what comes naturally and says to her dog reassuringly, "Good," while reaching into her feed pouch for a treat which she then delivers.

Having multiple bridges can be a good solution to some of the pitfalls of any given choice and will be discussed further in the section to follow on multiple bridges. In order for these back-up bridges to be fully effective, it is best to deliberately condition them. Like Clever Hans, however, I suspect many willing animals help us to condition these back-up bridges through generalization and situations like those described above (although it is worth noting that just as many do not).

Additional advantages to the verbal bridge will depend greatly on the nuances and organization of your training system. In my work I tend to train a number of animals close together, each with a separate trainer. Using a verbal bridge which sounds a little different from one trainer to another and is clearly delivered from a particular individual can help the animals distinguish who is delivering the bridge and thus whether or not it applies to them. (Of course, in any system like this one, it is reasonable to expect animals to be overly 'optimistic' in their interpretation of who is being bridged regardless of the stimulus used.) As I will discuss, whistles offer a similar solution in that each whistle can have its own special tone for a given animal, keeping all the bridges distinct. There are many ways to get around these issues, however, and using a name or pointing to an animal can also help distinguish to whom you are talking if you have a group of animals working in close proximity.

I primarily work with complex, intelligent animals who are readily capable of grasping very sophisticated and nuanced communication signals. For that reason, I enjoy using my voice which allows a greater range of intonations to carry with it a range of meanings in my bridge stimulus. These include using an Intermediate bridge, a Keep Going Stimulus and Differential bridges which indicate a range of correctness (see Advanced Communication Stimuli in this chapter for more on these techniques). Informing the animal about the quality of their behavior is one of my most valuable tools. It follows then that expanding the ways in which I can describe their behavioral status is of great use in clarifying my communication and thus increasing my animals' ability to understand my wishes[4].

---

4   The very thought of such a system seems to greatly disturb many other 'professional animal training instructors.' Generally, these forms of specialized conditioned stimuli will be considered, at best, very advanced material and, at worst, complete malarkey, so please take that into consideration for your own safety and best informed position. What I would suggest in response to critics is that hundreds of my students and animals have very successfully managed to master these concepts, and while I'm sure many have occasionally failed, that must be true of all pupils. Again we will further discuss the pros and cons of these advanced stimuli in the following section.

Drawbacks of the verbal bridge. One of the main criticisms of the verbal bridge stimulus is that it may not be adequately distinct from the environment and so cause confusion or difficulty conditioning it. This could be a particular problem if your choice of stimulus is a commonly uttered word that the animal may easily hear in casual conversation in its environment. While this may pose a problem with any bridge stimulus (I once witnessed a child with a plastic gum container wreak havoc on a clicker trained dog performance), it is certainly much more likely with a commonly spoken word. For example, either the trainer or others in the environment could easily accidently say the word 'good' not intending it to bridge the animal.

For this reason, most people who use verbal bridges attempt to make them unusual words, such as words from a foreign language. My mentor, Kayce Cover, is very fond of the bridge 'x' for example, as in "x marks the spot". It is also possible to use words or sounds said in such a way as to make them deliberately different than the version typically spoken. My bridge, for example, could be described as a loudly barked, high pitch form of the word 'good.' Many people listening to this bridge don't even recognize it as a word, so much as a sudden, piercing sound emanating, paradoxically, from a human being.

Of course, while that does solve the problem of making the bridge distinct and easily recognizable, for many people this noise is simply difficult and awkward to produce and doesn't fit well into their training environment. Similarly, many people are a bit uncomfortable or shy about making so much noise themselves and feel more confident using a device to communicate with their animals.

Another disadvantage of the verbal bridge is the fact that everyone's voice sounds different. This could make working with multiple trainers more difficult for the animal since the bridge stimulus will not be identical. However, while theoretically true, I have never actually seen this problem occur. Fortunately, animals generalize naturally as a part of adaptive learning and, in my experience, the verbal bridge transfer is a seamless event (although it is prudent not to attempt this too early into the initial bridge conditioning phase).

Even if there is a slightly depressed clarity that comes from various intonations of the same sound, animals, just like humans, can generally manage the 'accent' without difficulty. Obviously the more difference there is between any new voice and that originally conditioned, the more potential there is for this problem to arise.

There are numerous training situations where making a noise or talking to your animal would be prohibited. Certain horse training disciplines for example forbid any verbal communication with your animal (of course a whistle or clicker would be in that case similarly inappropriate). Working with fish, I often prefer a flashing light bridge since it is more directional and easily noticed in the aquarium than a verbal bridge would be. Similarly, if you lose your voice or find it difficult to make noise (like when you have a cold for example), a verbal bridge would be a handicap.

There is also a belief that certain species of animals respond better to certain types of bridge stimuli. One such example is the belief that dolphins do not respond well to verbal bridges. I have seen only a little credible evidence that this is so. In many cases, attempts to condition a second bridge stimulus may fail due to what is called the 'blocking' effect that I will shortly describe further in the section on Blocking. This can lead to the erroneous conclusion that the second bridge was unsuited to that species, for example. Logically speaking, I see only one reason to anticipate that an animal should be predisposed to a particular stimulus association, and that is if it falls within their sensory abilities or, in this case, their optimal hearing threshold. As long as the stimulus you choose can be easily discerned by the animal, there is no logical reason one would ultimately be better than another.

➢ The benefits and drawbacks of the CLICKER bridge

A clicker bridge is a small device held in the hand that has a depressible metal bar within it (see Figure 11). When pressed, the clicker makes a distinct popping click noise. Clicker bridges are now widely used with both domestic and exotic animals largely due to a very successful 'Clicker Training System' offered primarily by a famous

*Figure 11: Dog trainer, Nancy Wenkel using a
clicker bridge and positive reinforcement.*

(Photo credit: KJ Nelson.)

and eloquent animal training professional, Karen Pryor. Ms. Pryor
has been around long enough to see the development of many of
these techniques and, as such, got in at the ground level with many
successful books describing her experiences and preferred training
strategies. She now has a world-wide system that provides a simple
way of utilizing some of the most effective and safe training strategies, provided in a user friendly way to a beginning practitioner.

The centerpiece of Ms. Pryor's system is her choice of the
clicker as a bridge. However, the reason her system is so successful is
not because of her choice of the clicker; it is the because of the *use* of a
bridge stimulus. The contrast between using a bridge of any kind and
not using one is night and day to the animal and the trainer. Anyone
attempting to train previously without a bridge cannot help but be
impressed by the tremendous advantages this form of clear communication provides. This dramatic effect is so profound, it can inspire an
almost religious enthusiasm in the converted. Thus, the many advan-

tages of bridges in general have been erroneously conferred on one in particular - the clicker - to such an extent that some people use the term 'click' instead of 'bridge.' I find this level of bias and fervor unfortunate; it is like saying 'English' when you mean 'language.'

Benefits of the clicker bridge. Unsurprisingly, many claims have been made as to why the clicker is "the superior bridge to rule them all," as it were. I will outline them here although I myself have seen little evidence to support many of these claims.

The primary and real defensible advantage of the clicker is that it is identically reproducible and distinct in the environment. Both are very desirable qualities for conditioning a bridge stimulus. Everyone who can hold something in their hands can perform a click bridge. The sound is definitely unique enough to stand out but not piercing or terribly loud. Many people feel the tonal quality provides a nice happy medium of distinct but not abrupt. The fact that it is identically reproducible makes its predictability and meaning more assured and precise.

There have been claims that the sound of a clicker intrinsically makes it easier to learn than other sounds. Weak supportive evidence of this claim comes in the form of EEG readings that spike when the click is heard for the first time.

I admit to not knowing enough of the details of these findings to have a strong opinion; however, it is easy to state that even *if* clicking produced a unique brain wave pattern in some animal, it does not necessarily follow what that would infer about its implication as a learned stimulus. Nor could it be understood what those brain waves actually represent to the animal. I am not aware that there is any credible evidence that a click stimulus registers substantially differently than many other distinct stimuli that could be tested. Furthermore, it would be reasonable to predict that these reactions would be very different between species depending on their inherent auditory adaptations and natural history. Thus, I find it somewhat outrageous to claim that this single tone is somehow the universal primary noise to unite all of the animal kingdom.

Another advantage for certain trainers to the clicker bridge is in its physical nature. Some people find it easier to time their bridges correctly by hand than by mouth. I can certainly understand someone having a greater facility with one versus the other strategy, which may be intrinsic to the individual or based on personal habits like sports or video game playing. Certainly, proper bridge timing is a critical skill and anyone having trouble should try multiple options to see which works best for them in the beginning. Teaching novice trainers to work with the clicker may make the concept and timing easier to pick up and many systems (including my own) may use this as a helpful aid. People who are somewhat introverted or reserved may find the clicker more comfortable than speaking aloud. Practice makes perfect though, and eventually any professional trainer should be able to use a variety of bridging stimuli correctly.

I am aware of some claims that training using a clicker is actually faster (for reasons of clarity and timing) than with other bridging stimuli. Again, I cannot support these claims either with logic nor evidence. I have seen an ad-hoc 'experiment' conducted by an avid clicker trainer who claims that her clicker dogs learned faster than those with whom she used the verbal bridge. There are so many holes in this experimental design as to make it completely pointless, including: the effects of experimenter expectancy, experimenter capabilities with both types of stimuli, past experience of the subjects, sample size and subjective criteria, to name a few. I would be very interested in a credible experiment on the subject and would one day love to conduct such a thing myself, although I doubt the results will determine much more than we already know, and at best they would only apply to any species we tested them with. Even if it is true (which I highly doubt), that some animals may learn slightly faster with a clicker bridge, those effects are, at best, marginal, and the preponderance of evidence suggests that this misimpression is merely the bias of overly enthusiastic practitioners who have with the (clicker) bridge been given a new lease on training. Ironically they are themselves victims of classical conditioning, and their belief in the power of the clicker is as real for them as it is for their animals. This misimpression in the end does little harm. If anyone reading this text holds this sentiment, please take no offense at my candor. I, too, rejoice in the bridge, whatever its type!

Drawbacks of the clicker bridge. I have already listed the main reasons that I only rarely use clickers; these objections are small but they center around practical issues. For me, the inconvenience of having to hold something in my hand, thus leaving me with only one, outweighs any advantage the clicker could be seen to have. Hands are useful for props, cues, reinforcers, safety, balance, swimming and the list goes on and on. Choosing to be without one of my hands all the time I am working with my animals is a big disadvantage to me, but that is not to say that lots of people who work in different programs are not very successful with this tool, and do not consider this too much of an encumbrance.

Although the cost is minimal, the clicker must be purchased (and you need spares since they are easy to lose). In my environment, around salt water, they tend to break easily.

If you need to bridge your animal and happen to have put it down or lost your clicker, you are out of luck. That problem would only come up occasionally but it could be very disappointing when it did.

Additionally, working with predators often means your hands are dirty with meat products of some kind, and this quickly soils the clicker and makes the situation rather unsanitary. Regular clicker maintenance is therefore a necessity.

Lots of animals (especially those with hands) will try to steal your clicker from you, making it a danger to both you and them. While this is easy to train out, there are some animals, like otters, with whom object obsession can be a real problem. Additionally, since animals are expecting food to come from your hand, larger animals are in danger of swallowing an accidently dropped clicker. I have watched this happen personally. Lanyards or bracelets can reduce the risk of losing your clicker, but they also pose an increased risk to you if your animal should get a hold of the item while it is still attached to you.

The inadvertent or over-clicker is another problem I have witnessed with the clicker bridge stimulus. This seems to result from the satisfaction of clicking to the person doing it. There is a kind of manual satisfaction derived from clicking a clicker that can lead a distracted person to clicking for their own satisfaction instead of to reinforce the animal. Obviously this tendency will vary between individuals, but it can be easily demonstrated if you hand a room full of people a clicker each and ask them to hold them in their hands for the duration of a lecture. I have never made it through without an incidental click.

Finally, the simple and single tone that the clicker produces does not offer a wide enough range for some advanced applications. One problem is that in many situations the noise simply doesn't project well enough to travel to the animal's location if you are separated by distance, water, activity or ambient noise. In those cases, a whistle can be blown louder or a word can be shouted, but a click will stay the same (perhaps its greatest strength and its greatest weakness). Additionally, the lack of tonal variability precludes the use of more elaborate communication stimuli as will be discussed further in the following section.

➤ The benefits and drawbacks of the WHISTLE bridge

Benefits of the whistle bridge. The most obvious advantage of the whistle bridge is that, like the clicker, it provides a pure, distinct, predictable tone. Furthermore, unlike the clicker, this tone can be produced loudly or softly and it is possible to vary the tone of the whistle for different animals or purposes. Whistle tones are generally high pitched in nature and so stand out well from the environment. They also offer a range of tones generally challenging to produce easily by one's voice. This can be a distinct advantage with certain animals, like dolphins for example, who apparently hear better in these ranges. In fact, it is even possible to have whistle tones that exceed human hearing capacities, should a silent whistle be desirable for your circumstances (provided of course, that your animal is in fact capable of hearing the tone).

Unlike a clicker, the whistle leaves your hands generally free and although your mouth is then encumbered, experienced trainers can learn to speak reasonably well with a whistle hanging out of their mouths. It helps to use an extension piece of flexible aquarium tubing to make the bite down more palatable (see Figure 10 page 35).

Drawbacks of the whistle bridge. The whistle bridge, being an object, generally has some of the same drawbacks as the clicker. It must be purchased, can be swallowed or stolen by your animal, and it has an even larger sanitation dilemma than the clicker. Saliva is inevitable on your whistle, making them personal items that would, for health reasons, ideally not be shared (except among close friends). Generally, whistles are worn on a lanyard around your neck, making it easy for certain types of animals to grab ahold and pull you by the collar.

Although it can be mastered, speaking with a whistle in your mouth is definitely awkward. Talking with a whistle in your mouth often leads to inadvertent bridging when breath is accidently allowed through the apparatus. As I have stated previously, inadvertent bridging (possible with any of the stimuli discussed) is to be avoided to prevent reinforcing the wrong behavior.

Holding a whistle in your mouth also tends to cause slurred words and would have to be considered undesirable for a professional presentation or demonstration. This makes it optimal to either separate the presenter from the trainer (as you see in many aquaria shows) or take your whistle in and out of your mouth. And of course, if you don't have it in your mouth when you want to bridge your animal, you will be unable to communicate effectively. Unless, that is, you have another form of back-up bridge, which brings us to the final point in our discussion on the subject of bridging stimuli: multiple bridges.

Multiple bridges

One solution to the drawbacks of any particular bridge stimulus is to have conditioned more than one and use each to their best advantage. You can have more than one bridge as long as they are always consistent in their meaning. In this sense, conditioned stimuli are just like words. A lot of words basically have the same meaning (for example: red, maroon, blush, auburn, mahogany, vermilion, rose, rouge, scarlet) but confusion would arise if any given word means more than one thing (red cannot sometimes mean red and other times mean blue for example) - just as there is occasional confusion in the spoken word over similarly sounding words that are spelled differently, such as red and read.

Very few people intentionally condition more than one bridge stimulus, although their animals may have picked up on relevant postures or words which, like Clever Hans before them, they learn mean reinforcement is coming. For example, one bridge stimulus that almost all systems have inadvertently conditioned is anything associated with reinforcement delivery - such as the act of reaching into the feeding pouch or bucket or the noise of food being placed in a dish. This is somewhat inevitable, but can be avoided with careful desensitization if necessary. I don't usually bother with doing so, since these associations can be as useful as problematic, and an awareness of the phenomena is enough to navigate any pitfalls.

Advanced systems often have bridges across multiple sensory modalities in order to provide greater flexibility for different working conditions or to maximize the benefits that different bridging stimuli offer. For example, I maintain a verbal bridge for general uses, a visual finger point bridge for use when I cannot make a sound (such as on a Hollywood sound stage), and a tactile double tap bridge for close-up physical work where the animal cannot see me but the elegance of a quiet bridge is preferable for performance reasons. (For the record, I have worked with both whistles and clickers but now generally use these as teaching tools for students more than training tools for animals.)

Blocking

It should be noted that there is a phenomena that psychologists call 'blocking' which can make it *much* more difficult to condition additional bridges, particularly if the first bridge is solidly conditioned already. Blocking is a strange phenomenon whereby understanding one signal can interfere with the understanding of another. Blocking theory is typical of what I find cumbersome and overly complicated about much of the laboratory approach to behavior, so I will refrain from much of the confusing and tedious detail. Suffice it to say, that while it can be very much more difficult to condition the second or third bridge stimulus, it definitely can be done. The problem largely stems from the fact that once the animal knows a stimulus that means reinforcement is coming, then that is all they are looking for (the "one true God," as it were). So your primary bridge should be considered carefully since creating additional ones can be challenging. My experience is also that certain species seem to have more trouble with blocking than others.

The solution lies in getting the animal to open up to the possibility of new meaning out there and get its brain searching for the connection again. I find it useful to create circumstances that help the animal recognize the second bridge by more than just its association, but also through actions that they typically perform in response to the bridge. For example, I start by having multiple stations where food can be delivered, each with the new bridge stimulus. The new bridge is delivered and then the food is offered. The animal must move to the location where the new stimulus was performed in order to receive reinforcement. This active searching focuses the animal's mind on the new stimulus and helps them to make the surprising connection that there is the possibility of new bridges. It connects the typical action of moving to receive the reinforcement following the bridge stimulus with the new bridge stimulus, making the analogy easier for the animal to comprehend.

➤ The benefits and drawbacks of the bridge stimulus

Now that we have thoroughly covered all aspects of the bridge stimulus, let us discuss some of the benefits and drawbacks to this important communication training tool.

Benefits of the bridge stimulus

The best testament to the value of a bridge stimulus in a behavior modification system is the nearly euphoric attitude adopted by both animals and trainers who have previously toiled without such a system of *clear, precise communication*. The bridge enables the trainer to pinpoint in time exactly when the behavior is correct. This is the most important piece of information to provide. As I have said before, this is my favorite of all the tools I will be describing for effective and healthy training. Since you are associating yourself with a reinforcer, using a bridge stimulus also helps to *increase your relationship* with the animal, and this will ultimately be to your advantage motivationally.

Another subtle and critical advantage to the bridge over just using reinforcement is that it separates the intentional communication with the animal from a focus on food by *bridging the gap in time between correct behavior and reinforcement delivery*. This promotes better focus and attention from the animal on the task, making it easier to communicate with them effectively. This also results in much better timing and accuracy of information which also tends to reduce frustration-based aggression.

Drawbacks of the bridge stimulus

Honestly, there is not much downside to using a bridge, if used correctly. If it is used incorrectly, you can erroneously communicate to the animal that they are doing something right when they are not. If this is an undesirable behavior, the consequences can be grave in that the undesirable behavior will increase in frequency. As we discussed, this can happen easily if the tendency to return to the trainer in response to the bridge leads a naïve trainer to use the bridge as a recall cue when things are not going well. For this reason, some training systems restrict access to the bridge stimulus for their novice or beginning level trainers, until the trainer can be properly 'trusted' with the bridge.

Bad bridge timing in general can lead to confusion for the animal and confusion can, in the worst case scenario, lead to aggression. In other cases confusion simply gets you nowhere with your animal. I have heard some more traditional trainers use this as a criticism of the bridge; however, a case of bad timing is going to be a problem whether you are using a bridge stimulus or not!

Overuse of the bridge without proper maintenance of conditioning can easily cause the bridge to break down. One of my friends calls this the case of the 'flying clicker' because you see this a lot with naïve clicker trainers getting overly focused on their goals and forgetting to reinforce after the click. Without proper and consistent reinforcement association, bridges will cease to have meaning (although this will be less likely as time goes by and a substantial history of conditioning supports the stimulus). Some trainers feel that the best way to avoid this is to restrict themselves to reinforcing for *every* bridge. While I understand this instinct, that view is too limiting and extreme for me and causes some disadvantages that we will discuss in Chapter 6 regarding schedules of reinforcement. Suffice it to say that the bridge does need regular conditioning; for me this occurs organically as I recognize that to motivate my animals they need to be reinforced for their work. As a result, the bridge is regularly conditioned since I am using both it and reinforcement often and in association. I recommend you find a way to ensure this predictable, reliable association is maintained however you feel best able to be certain about it, and if you are a beginner, that may mean restricting yourself to reinforcing for every bridge until your instincts have had time to develop.

Some trainers find using a bridge a sort of an inconvenience. They would prefer that the animal just figure out what they are getting reinforced for. The belief is that this helps the animal function better when they do receive less information. Certain systems may require this, in particular if the animal is going to be forced to problem solve away from the trainer's ability to provide immediate feedback (like deep underwater or at a great distance from the trainer for example). In those cases it may be optimal to prepare the animal by alternating between using a bridge and not using one, so that they are prepared for situations in which less information may be available to them. Overall, though, this would not preclude using the bridge, where possible, to speed up the animal's learning process and make it more rewarding and clear. As my friend David Lichman puts it, "More information is always better."

OTHER ADVANCED CONDITIONED COMMUNICATION STIMULI

Certain communication techniques involve very advanced levels of information trained into a stimulus representing that concept. All of these stimuli are conditioned using associative learning and are summarized here for that reason. These stimuli are generally used only by advanced practitioners, as they are very difficult to condition and use correctly. However, if used correctly, they offer enhanced communication with the animal and therefore a potentially expanded training relationship. Additionally, these types of communication stimuli may be of more interest to people working with neurologically complex animals, for whom more information may offer more enhanced and nuanced responses.

Many animal training professionals surely will not approve of my inclusion of these unusual communication systems. Some of my colleagues have described them as controversial, ineffective and dangerous. Everyone is entitled to their opinion and certainly *I am not suggesting that every tool be used by every trainer.* As I will point out, many of these tools can be hard to use in systems with lots of trainers or novices, so keeping things simple in those systems may be easiest and best. However, whenever new techniques and ideas are raised, they very often meet with resistance and skepticism at first. That is the way of things: we resist what we don't know and don't understand. I am very interested in working to push forward those boundaries, to open new possibilities for the future of the animal industry, not simply teaching about what is known and practiced. Without that progress, we are bound to recirculate the same ideas and left with the depressing thought that there is no hope to advance what we are doing any further. Therefore, I take it as an honor to be included among the ranks of many people before me who inspired others by trying new things and stimulating ideas through controversial thoughts.

THE DIFFERENTIAL REINFORCEMENT (BRIDGE) STIMULUS

A differential reinforcement bridge stimulus is a term I use for a range of bridging stimuli that indicate different reinforcement (ratios). The differential reinforcement bridge puts more information into the stimulus which correlates to the quality of the behavior and the resultant reinforcement.

The principle of response differentiation and differential reinforcement (which will be discussed further in Chapter 6) is that reinforcement is delivered selectively for one topography of a performance as opposed to another topography (or as originally defined by psychologists, in the presence of an S^D or not). Both of these psychological principles (really functionally the same principle) are further described by something called the 'Matching Law' which states that the relative rate of response matches the relative rate of reinforcement. Or, put more simply, the more highly reinforced the animal is for any given response, the more of that precise behavior in that precise situation you should see in the future.

Refined use of this technique gives qualitative information to the animal about how good its behavioral response is. In other words, if response A earns 10 pellets while response B earns only

1 (assuming nothing other than pellets is also adding into the reinforcement value of B), then response A should be more likely to occur than B in the future. This is a way of explaining to the animal the difference between good and great.

The typical differential reinforcement bridge is a variety of bridging intonations that indicate differing levels of performance and associated reinforcement. For example, the difference between an ok and an excellent performance is indicated in the volume (louder) and enthusiasm (greater) with which the trainer gives the bridge stimulus. This is similar to the difference between getting an A or a C in school. In order to condition this meaning one must reliably associate different ratios (amounts) of reinforcement with these varying intonations (or a higher value reinforcement type could also be used).

➤ The benefits and drawbacks of the differential reinforcement stimulus

Benefits of the differential reinforcement bridge stimulus

This method of communication about the quality of the behavioral response occurs *at the moment of the response*. Thus, it reduces the disadvantageous effects of latency that can occur if the animal must wait to find out about the merits of its behavior when the reward is finally delivered as opposed to when the behavior is actually produced. This offers even more precise and timely feedback for the animal to understand which of their responses is better than others and how to receive more reinforcement. This type of communication is most useful when an animal is in the process of learning a novel behavior and trying to grasp the particulars of the successful execution.

Drawbacks of the differential reinforcement bridge stimulus

The biggest problem with these conditioned stimuli is careful conditioned maintenance. This level of information requires a great deal of consistency to have the meaning properly conveyed to the animal. Therefore, the rigors necessary to accomplish this conditioning and maintain it properly could be difficult in many training systems, especially with a large staff, or for novice and beginning level practitioners. One solution to this problem is to simplify the system and keep it at just two intonations: a normal bridge and a jackpot or high reinforcement tone (such as a slot machine payoff - *ka-ching!*).

Many trainers find this level of communication unnecessary and overly complicated, and that is not an unreasonable position. Certainly you do not need to enhance your stimulus in order for the animal to infer from your reinforcement which is the better topography of the behavior. This tool is one that many people inadvertently use anyway by getting excited and blowing the whistle extra-long and loud, for example, but it will have more use to the animal if it is deliberate and reliable in its application. To the extent that it is used inconsistently, the differential reinforcement stimulus will be effectively meaningless.

TERTIARY REINFORCEMENT (BRIDGE) STIMULI

Conditioned stimuli that indicate to the animal that it is on the right track and to push forward toward a terminal bridge[5] that is on the horizon, have been variously described as either a Keep Going Stimulus (KGS) or an Intermediate Bridge (IB). These are signals that encourage the animal to make more effort continuing along the current response in order to achieve the imminent goal of satisfying reinforcement. These signals acquire their meaning through the association with a bridge stimulus and as such they are called tertiary (as opposed to secondary) reinforcers.

To say the least, these signals are a subject of some considerable controversy both in their application and in how to define them. For example, the term 'Intermediate Bridge' is widely disliked

---

5   Here I use the term 'terminal bridge' to denote the traditional bridge, recognizing its function to end current behavior.

by many rank and file behaviorists. Some psychologists have a very limited view of what any given term means, linked rigorously back to whoever first described the concept. As a result of this view, bridges must terminate behavior, which the Intermediate Bridge does not do, ergo it should not be called a bridge (although in fairness it is not called a 'bridge' but an 'intermediate bridge' and I do think this term aptly describes the function of this stimulus). I do not like to debate terminology as it seems to me to be a question of semantics, not principle. My approach is to be all inclusive, so we will leave that to others and merely focus on the function of these stimuli.

I and many others have struggled to properly categorize these techniques. One of the central debates is whether or not a KGS is, in fact, the same thing as an IB. Whatever you may choose to call them, both these stimuli indicate to the animal that it is on the right track - and given continued performance - on the path to reinforcement. In some sense, these signals bridge the gap between the animal's current performance and the terminal bridge and in this aspect one can see the direct similarity to a bridging concept. These stimuli function to reassure and reinforce behavior *as it is in progress* instead of when it is complete.

However, in practical application the two stimuli are functionally different. A KGS is a rather bland signal given in the middle of a behavior to indicate to the animal that the behavior it is engaged in is correct and should be continued to eventual reinforcement (earlier in my career I erroneously called this a soft secondary bridge). This signal is typically given in the middle of a prolonged behavior, more or less as a reminder that the trainer is still present, attentive and aware, since in many systems the absence of information from the trainer may be an indication that the animal is actually on the wrong track and might be wasting considerable effort.

In contrast, the IB is a series of continuous and instantaneous signals marking a progression of successful instants advancing toward a successfully completed behavior. The IB allows a trainer to give continuous encouraging feedback to an animal as it nears the completion of a requested behavior. Used correctly, this technique dramatically pushes behavior forward at crucial moments especially when the animal is in the beginning and uncertain phase of learning a novel behavior.

The difference between a KGS and an IB is analogous to the difference between a friendly wave and a roaring fight song. The KGS is merely a reminder where the IB is an avid support. Considering these similarities and differences, I think it might be reasonable to suggest that the IB is a special form of KGS but not that they are the same. Ultimately the IB is a very powerful and bold tool while the KGS is merely another form of attention and encouragement, but each has its place in the training tool box.

The Intermediate Bridge (IB)

The intermediate bridge is a nearly continuous signal that encourages, supports and draws out increased effort and confidence in the animal. Through the use of this unfaltering communication, very strong reassurance and stimulation promotes behavior as it unfolds. This signal can make it much easier to promote the first behavioral extensions, increase effort, and to opportunistically accentuate alternative topographies of a behavior in progress.

Methods differ as to how to condition the intermediate bridge, depending on your choice of terminal bridge stimulus and schedules of reinforcement. I use a modified rapid-fire form of the terminal bridge stimulus (good, good, good, good, good in a building crescendo) followed by a large reinforcement. A completely unique stimulus will work as well although it will be initially slower to train and may be more complicated to use. In order to train this concept quickly, the crucial aspect of conditioning this stimulus is to select moments when the astute trainer can see that the animal is on the verge of greatness but lacks the confidence to recognize this. At that moment, pushing forward for initially even a second or two can lead the behavior and the animal ahead to the next level. Thus, continuing through this window can rightly earn increased reinforcement, and this connection helps to give the animal the ability to recognize that this stimulus means continue to great reward. The use of a variable schedule of reinforcement allows that animals do not necessarily expect additional reinforcement after every bridge (see Chapter 6 for more on variable reinforcement). This enables rapid fire bridging to positively encourage the animal through the initial couple of seconds of behavioral continuance without breaking the behavior before reaching the terminal bridge. If the animal discontinues at any point, the IB is stopped, and no terminal bridge or reinforcement is delivered. Alternatively, as the animal increases or alters its effort from the onslaught of encouragement, it quickly arrives at a point where reinforcement is warranted and the concept develops naturally from there. The animal earns the reward by continuing in the presence of this stimulus at first for only a second or two and then for longer periods once they understand the concept and that this stimulus is associated with great rewards to follow.

Additionally, verbal bridging helps enormously in the use of this stimulus, since it allows great tonal variation. It is much harder to manage multiple physical devices for varying tones in most natural situations. For this reason, few people who use a whistle or a clicker also use an intermediate bridge, although in those cases, the use of a verbal IB is the most practical and frequent choice.

➢ The benefits and drawbacks of the IB

Benefits of the IB. New steps (called approximations) in developing novel behavior can often bring about uncertainty and confusion for animals in the learning process. The IB provides the needed *critical push forward* to feel positively *encouraged* during these moments of doubt. This often enables animals to make quicker, more confident, and positive choices in the learning process. The intermediate bridge is also very good for morale and motivation, since less guesswork for the animal means more success and less potential for frustration. As a form of positive reinforcement, the use of the IB is inherently encouraging and thus fosters the relationship and a *positive learning environment* for the animal. Although many people who are unfamiliar or who have not actually attempted this technique tend to doubt its effectiveness, it is quite easy to see the immediate behavioral reaction of an animal surging forward with increased effort and confidence on delivery of the IB. While the IB is still not widely recognized by most animal professionals, I often notice trainers providing various unintentional forms of encouragement to hesitating animals which again may result in a less efficient, if still effective, unconscious form of the IB, depending on the consistency that the trainer employs.

The IB is a highly useful stimulus to initially *extend behavioral duration*. One thing other trainers routinely notice about my animals is that they sit still performing behaviors for long periods of time very confidently. Largely, this is a direct result of my use of the intermediate bridge which allows me to explain to the animal to continue performing even when they have lost confidence. This is much easier than the alternative of silence and hoping that the guessing animal will learn to continue through its mounting frustration. By explaining that if they just continue on a bit more, they will be richly rewarded, you can often provide the needed encouragement just on the critical thresholds of extending behavior. The IB can also be helpful in expanding on the number of repetitions desired in a behavior, for example, to teach a dolphin to jump five times in a row instead of four.

Drawbacks of the IB. The biggest problems with the use of the intermediate bridge are in understanding the nuances of training it and using it properly. To maintain its meaning, it needs to be *reliably paired with a terminal bridge and high reinforcement*. This can be tricky in real life situations where a less experienced trainer can easily choose a wrong moment to employ it, or worse, overuse it - and destroy the meaning by failing to maintain the association with magnitude reinforcement. Overuse of the stimulus will cause it to be desensitized and lose its significance.

Lots of trainers find the use of this tool *overly complicated and noisy* as well. This tool can be hard to manage in a large organization with lots of trainers. My suggestion on this score is to only use the IB at an intermediate or advanced level and in those moments when you feel the animal is on the threshold of the next step in its behavior. This helps limit the use of the tool to its best moments and reduces the chance of overuse. The noisiness of the stimulus generally can't be avoided, though nothing but practicality precludes using a flashing light or some form of touch in the same manner. Unfortunately, each of those stimuli would require a particular limited scenario to work. Once the animal has gained confidence in the behavior, the IB is no longer needed and can be phased out to eliminate the bothersome extra noise.

While the animal is learning the IB or if it is being overused, the IB can be misinterpreted by the animal as a terminal bridge. If this does occur, simply re-issue the S^D and continue where you left off. To avoid these pitfalls the trainer must focus on using unrelenting rapid-fire stimulus and to avoid pushing the IB for too long or overusing it.

The Keep Going Stimulus (KGS)

The KGS is a non-terminal encouragement signal that is typically based on the value of interaction from the trainer as a reinforcer or is somehow derived from the bridge signal (such as a variation of a tone). Any interaction from the trainer (assuming there is a positive relationship) can be seen as a reinforcer to the animal, and it is from this basis that the signal has its foundation.

➤ The benefits and drawbacks of the KGS

Benefits of the KGS. This stimulus provides the animal reassurance that the trainer is still focused on them despite the fact that the behavior is in process. In systems where there is no means to communicate that the animal is doing something wrong, silence will occur when the animal is on the wrong track. But during prolonged behavior, silence will also occur when the animal is on the right track. Thus, after prolonged silent effort, the animal may lose confidence and the KGS can reassure the animal that they are still on the path to success. *Primarily this signal acts to acknowledge and extend behavior that is occurring for a prolonged period of time.* I use a softly spoken, extended "good" sound to help distinguish this signal from the terminal bridge.

Drawbacks of the KGS. The KGS is a relatively weak signal that is generally not necessary to maintain behavior if the appropriate size approximations (steps) have been made to support the behavior previously. Often the KGS can also distract the animal from completing the behavior by disrupting the flow with unnecessary additional information.

It can also disrupt the behavior by being confused with a terminal bridge, in which case, as with the IB, the trainer will need to reestablish the behavior before proceeding on. The tendency to confuse the KGS with a terminal bridge will be mitigated by the fact that the animal does not get reinforced and will ultimately end up putting more effort into the behavior before getting reinforced. The KGS is then best used as the trainer notes that the behavior threshold is being approached and that the animal is beginning to mildly hesitate.

THE NO REWARD MARKER (DELTA) STIMULUS

The 'delta' is a term apparently erroneously adopted by animal trainers to represent what should be called a 'no reward marker (NRM).' This is a signal that indicates to the animal the complete opposite meaning of the bridge stimulus; it indicates incorrect behavior that will not receive reinforcement. The word "not" would be a reasonable example of a NRM.

This should be distinguished from a 'stimulus delta' in psychology which is a stimulus under whose presence a behavior will not be reinforced. A stimulus delta precedes the unreinforced behavior, and it is essentially the wrong answer to a question if there are multiple options to choose from. The term 'delta' that has been adopted by some animal trainers to mean a NRM clearly came from a misapplication of the original psychological terminology. I presume the similar terminology carried over from the limited practical value of the antecedent stimulus described by psychologists and came instead to represent the more applied consequence as a matter of practicality. Despite this confusion, I include the term here in both ways that it is used in order to be inclusive, since the use has become pervasive in many training circles.

While the true stimulus delta precedes a behavior, the NRM follows it as a conditioned consequence to undesirable behavior. It is used and trained as essentially the opposite of a bridge. The aptly named no reward marker is conditioned through association with a meaningful stimulus, in this case a punisher. The NRM is a secondary punisher by nature since it is associated with punishment. Typically it is associated with negative punishment (the withholding of reinforcement), but it can also be modified and associated directly with some form of physical positive punishment.

➤ The benefits and drawbacks of the no reward marker stimulus

Benefits of the no reward marker

The biggest advantage to the NRM is to be able to give the animal information not just about what is right in their behavior, but also about what is wrong. Without being able to tell the animal when they are wrong, you are stuck with silence, which becomes a weak form of secondary punishment by default. In the game of Hot-and-Cold, if the bridge is the 'hot' then the NRM (or the Redirecton stimulus, see later this chapter) functions as the 'cold.' To see why both the animal and the trainer might want such a stimulus, try playing the game with only a hot and then separately with both stimuli to work with. Which do you find easier? Try this as both the animal and the trainer. Most people find it clearly more satisfying and faster to play with both the bridge and the NRM for both parties involved. Why is that?

The cold information helps the animal make better decisions about how to get its behavior on the right track faster by knowing what behaviors it is doing that are wrong, enabling it to stop wasting energy on fruitless behavior. In school, we are given feedback about our successes as well as our failures in order to help us improve. So this is clearly a *valuable communication tool in defining correct behavior*. Unfortunately, to train this as a no reward marker, it has to be conditioned and maintained through an association with punishment, which nobody likes. What is needed, therefore, is a stimulus that gives the meaning to the animal that they are wasting their energy on the wrong track without having to imply that a bad outcome is necessarily imminent (see Redirection stimulus in this chapter).

Drawbacks of the no reward marker

Punishment by definition is anything that decreases the frequency of the behavior it immediately follows (see Chapter 6 for a full discussion on this). In the case of providing information that enables the animal to be more successful and no longer wasting fruitless energy in the wrong direction, most individuals are not averse to this form of 'punishment.' However, in the case where it is directly associated with a certainty of bad outcomes (aversive stimuli or no opportunity of forthcoming reward), punishment can be quite unpleasant and upsetting. Thus, the traditional no reward marker, indicating a certainty of aversive or no reinforcement, is a very harsh stimulus to many animals. In those cases, animals are very often frustrated; this can lead to aggression easily depending on how strong and unpredictable the punishment is. Anything *leading to aggression* can be considered highly undesirable. Associating yourself with such a stimulus does also take a toll on your relationship bank account. By *associating yourself with punishment you come to represent punishment*, which is not ideal for your animal's motivation to work for you or in your system. For this reason, most people avoid the use of this tool or at least limit it severely.

The reason this stimulus is associated with punishment is to find a way to explain to the animal that their behavior is wrong or 'fruitless,' but that information per se is not what is so bothersome to the animal. What causes the trouble is that to get this meaning across - it must be associated with punishment. So to find a way to permit the valuable and ultimately positive information about where the animal is wasting time performing useless behavior (or behavior that doesn't lead to reward), we need to create a stimulus that gets the meaning across, but also empowers the animal toward the hope of reward not the fear of punishment. It is for this reason that I have developed the redirection stimulus.

THE REDIRECTION STIMULUS (RS)

The redirection stimulus (formerly called a communicative delta) is a term I have defined as a signal that indicates the animal is on the wrong track and they can receive reinforcement by stopping or altering their current behavior. In the game of 'hot and cold,' if the bridge gives the 'hot' information, the RS gives the 'cold' information. Most often the word "no" is associated with this stimulus, but obviously any signal can be used. What distinguishes this signal from the traditional NRM is that it does not merely signal no reward. The *RS signals that reward is available by changing behavior, but not by continuing it.* Where the NRM simply says, "no" to the animal, the redirection stimulus says, "no, try again."

This is how it works: when the animal receives the RS, any change or altering of its behavior different from the previous, results in a bridge and can result in reinforcement. This is the principle of differential reinforcement of an other behavior (DRO), which is a technique to eliminate undesirable behavior through the alternative reinforcement of any other behavior (see Chapter 6). But, in this case to get the meaning across clearly, failing to alter behavior after the RS will result in some form of punishment. This is typically negative punishment like the withholding of both the trainers attention and the loss of opportunity to earn reinforcement (a time-out) of some magnitude. Generally, I choose negative punishment because these forms of punishment are much milder and are not associated with the same level of fear and aggression as positive punishment. This includes the use of the 'LRS (Least Reinforcing Scenario)' which is a form of time-out that lasts only two to three seconds and is designed to cause a behavioral reset. These tools will be further described in Chapter 6.

It is critical that this stimulus most frequently leads to some reinforcement opportunity (preferably on a variable schedule) through the animal changing its undesirable behavior. To condition it, I prefer to create the choice for the animal between punishment and reinforcement which helps stack-the-deck in favor of appropriate response all the more strongly. Thus, they learn to respond to the RS by stopping or altering undesirable behavior leading more quickly to reinforcement opportunity.

This can be as simple as a strongly stated "no" as the animal heads in a direction you do not want (like toward the wrong target). Done correctly, the stimulus and behavior of the trainer will frequently cause the animal to pause at this moment, in which case he has responded 'correctly' to the RS by altering his behavior. This pause can then be bridged and reinforced further depending on the circumstances. If the animal does not alter its behavior in an acceptable manner, the trainer can then use some period of time-out in order to drive home the point and draw the animal's attention to the implications of the stimulus. Similarly, in novel behavior training, if the animal adds an inappropriate behavioral 'flourish,' it can quickly be tagged by the RS. As soon as the animal aborts the added 'flourish' they are on a better track to the successful behavior and can be bridged and reinforced depending on the situation. This can help clarify to the animal the exact particulars of the criteria for the behavior.

By associating the stimulus with both reinforcement and punishment, it maintains a delicate and mostly neutral value that offers the choice to the animal of what consequence it will have.

It is worth noting that it may be possible to condition a similar stimulus that simply indicates to change behavior without associating it with punishment in any form. For me this would inherently weaken the message and the usefulness of the tool, although potentially it would be more reinforcing. This could theoretically be done by opportunistically reinforcing only the correct responses to the stimulus and doing nothing when the animal fails to alter its behavior.

➤ The benefits and drawbacks of the RS

Benefits of the RS

One major advantage of the RS is *to give information to the animal about the quality of the behavior* as it is in progress without having to halt and interrupt the behavior. This immediately allows the animal to try an alternative and more successful topography and thus receive reinforcement. The RS *pinpoints in time when the animal has done something incorrectly*. In this way, the animal does not toil on, needlessly wasting energy and time on behavior the trainer knows is fruitless, but has no way to point this out to the animal. In a situation with highly motivated animals, this waste of energy, in well-intended effort to produce desirable behavior, is sad and frustrating to both the trainer and the animal. It is a blessing to be able to help the animal through these mix-ups with information and support instead of watching helplessly in silence.

By explaining to the animal what it is doing wrong and giving it reinforcement for not doing that behavior, the RS provides both enhanced communication and increased opportunity for reinforcement. In these cases *it functions just as a differential reinforcement of any other behavior (DRO) would, but with more information and clarity* involved (see Chapter 6 for more on DRO).

By emphasizing the path to reinforcement opportunity, the punishment is not necessarily bad. It reduces the frequency of the behavior it follows, certainly, but that may be a good thing by directing the animal towards success, and as a result they are closer and faster to receiving reinforcement.

The RS can also be *used to teach an animal not to do something* that might be undesirable (like aggressive behavior) or help it to avoid something that is dangerous like a hazardous area. I have used my RS many times to *save an animal from dangerous circumstances* by quickly asking them to stop. In the case of teaching an animal not to do something, this stimulus helps explain to the animal the reason behind any punishing consequences that might arise and thereby empowers them to make what choices they prefer depending on their predominant evaluation of the many drives involved in the scenario. The least harmful and least stressful scenario in which to receive punishment is that which comes as result of informed and deliberate choices. Random and unpredictable or uncontrollable punishment is the type of punishment that is most damaging, as we will discuss in Chapter 6.

The RS also *teaches the animal a healthy attitude about the process of learning.* It helps to teach the animal that it is ok to 'fail' at a behavior, because other avenues to reinforcement will be available if the animal pays attention and awaits further instruction. This can drastically reduce the frustration threshold and often increases the desire of the animal to continue to work to figure out what behavior the trainer wants.

Drawbacks of the RS

Many people feel this type of stimulus or in fact *any use of punishment is unwarranted* and will cause animals to feel upset and frustrated. It is certainly true that frustration can *lead to aggression.* So this is a very valid concern, but not all punishment leads to frustration. That will depend on the control that an animal has over the situation and also the level of punishment. We will discuss these issues further in the Motivation Chapter; however, it is inaccurate to claim that this tool regularly causes frustration, when used correctly. Most of the people who profess this position have never actually tried to use an RS and may be confusing it with a NRM.

If abused, this tool *can harm your relationship* with the animal by being negative and associated with the use of punishment. Overuse can easily create a very negative discouraging environment which does not have adequate reinforcement to maintain healthy behavior. Think of someone repeating over and over "no, no, no, no, no" and how discouraging that would sound. This situation would deplete your relationship bank account. So the judicious and very limited use of this stimulus is a key to its effectiveness. If overuse is likely, it may not be worth the risk to your relationship. Personally, I consciously try to avoid using the RS more than approximately two times in a row and more than roughly five times in a given training session, although this will, to a certain extent, depend on the number of times that the RS results in reinforcement as opposed to a lack of reinforcement. Generally limiting the number of non-reinforced uses of this tool in any training session is a good idea. When deciding about the use of the RS, it is important to evaluate why the animal is on the wrong track and to what extent information will possibly aid them to altering their behavior. If the scenario is not likely to be improved with more information being provided (in the form of the RS), then some other technique may be better chosen or used in addition to the RS to address the situation. Counting on the RS as the only tool to repair bad behavior is a dangerous and a fruitless mindset that will bring about the worst aspects of this conditioned stimulus. The "first line of defense" should always be to endeavor to set the animal up for success.

Alternatively, since the alteration of behavior may lead to reinforcement, it is possible that a cunning animal may choose to misbehave in order to alter their behavior and provide the opportunity for reinforcement. This is why I recommend using this stimulus followed by a variable schedule of additional reinforcement even when the animal has correctly altered its behavior, so that if the trainer perceives this pattern, they may choose not to reinforce the animal. Further, they may also choose to stop using the RS in this situation in order to limit the opportunity for DRO.

Finally, this stimulus *requires excellent judgment* to train properly and to maintain since it will be associated with wrong behavior and punishment. It can be tricky to pick the right situations in which to condition it. This requires an advanced animal savvy and good knowledge of your individual animal and species. Thus, this tool does not lend itself easily to novice trainers or large systems with lots of training staff where consistency may be difficult to maintain. I have successfully used the RS with a staff of several dozen people. In these cases, however, the stimulus has nearly always been initially conditioned by me or another highly advanced trainer and then permitted to be used by my staff under careful instruction.

THE END OF SESSION STIMULUS (EOSS)

This controversial conditioned stimulus tells the animal that the training session is over and that their attention is released. Effectively, this is the training equivalent of "goodbye," and in fact many people choose that exact word as their EOSS. However, since many people include all or nearly all the reinforcement within the training session, this signal can come to mean to the animal that the opportunity for reinforcement is gone (or a stimulus delta in the psychological sense). In that case, it is a type of secondary negative punisher and may therefore lead to frustration, anxiety, and in the worst case scenario, aggression. For this reason, this stimulus is hotly debated, especially within marine animal training circles.

Whether or not the stimulus comes to represent a negative punisher depends on whether or not it does in fact predict no reinforcement. It is possible to vary the session times randomly and provide post-session reinforcement delivery that will contradict the conditioning of this stimulus as a stimulus delta; however, doing this requires careful planning and effort. One solution is to routinely provide post-session reinforcement to the animal after the trainer's departure and the EOSS. Leaving food in the enclosure would be an example. Another solution is to also frequently return repeatedly after varying lengths of time (a technique I call 'multiple sessions') to disassociate the EOSS with any predictability of a lengthy absence or loss of reinforcement opportunity.

It should be pointed out that without a specifically conditioned stimulus to say such a thing, the animal will naturally associate the various activities that the trainer does in preparation and associated with leaving, as an EOSS that they come to recognize from an associative learning process à la Clever-Hans. So, in some sense, whether or not you deliberately condition this stimulus, the observant animal will generally learn one or several activities of the trainer that are effectively a type of EOSS. This truth makes a heated debate over the evils of the EOSS rather silly in my opinion, since in all likelihood there exists some form of EOSS in any case. Ultimately, the real evil is found in the predictable association to a period of no reinforcement that should, in either case, be mitigated by prudent counter measures like those described above or other means to lessen the negative implications of departure.

➤ The benefits and drawbacks of the EOSS

Benefits of the EOSS

The primary reason that I have utilized an EOSS with some of my animals is to *release them from their full attention* on me which I would otherwise expect and condition during a training session. In my intensive and focused training system, the EOSS enables the animal to relax and go on about its business, when my attention needs to be elsewhere. Many trainers feel it is simply rude to walk away from an engaged animal without any explanation of what is happening.

Secondarily, if you want to maintain the option of using a time-out form of punishment to reduce undesirable behaviors (where the trainer leaves for a period of time removing the opportunity for reinforcement), the EOSS helps to clearly delineate the two situations in which the trainer might be leaving the animal. This *makes the time-out more effective and clear* - since in only that case does the trainer leave without an EOSS - helping to hit home the point that the animal's personal behavior is the cause of the end of session, not something that would have happened either way. This potentially enables the animal to take responsibility to control this outcome in the future should they wish to do so.

Finally, I have occasionally found this stimulus to be highly valuable for use with blind animals that cannot otherwise easily recognize the signs of the end of session and may therefore sadly wait attentively at an empty fence for further interaction from the trainer. In this rather heartbreaking situation, I find the EOSS does its best work at informing an otherwise challenged animal.

Drawbacks of the EOSS

Since most people and facilities do not make an effort to vary the consequences of the EOSS by providing post-session reinforcement or variable return times, this stimulus can *become a stimulus delta* and lead to unhappiness at the certainty of no further opportunity for reinforcement. This is often *associated with aggression* and so-called 'end of session anxiety' which are undesirable outcomes. For that reason, many people choose not to use this stimulus. As I stated earlier, the EOSS does not have to accurately predict no reinforcement opportunity, as long as you provide post-session reinforcement and reduce the predictability of the inter-session interval by returning on a variable schedule, sometimes immediately.

It can certainly be argued, especially by those who do not intend to use time-outs as a form of punishment, that the EOSS is simply unnecessary and not worth the potential negative consequences, since by and large the animal will not need this stimulus to recognize the end of a session.

CHAPTER 5

COMMUNICATION: OPERANT CONDITIONING

Having thoroughly covered the subject of classical conditioning and the most prominent of its associated conditioned stimuli, let us now move on to the meat-and-potatoes of communication techniques: operant conditioning.

The definition of operant conditioning

Operant conditioning is the learning mechanism by which most behaviors are created in animal training. In fact, it is so important in this regard that most people consider the term synonymous with the very idea of animal training. Other synonyms for operant conditioning include: instrumental conditioning and shaping.

An 'operant' is a voluntary behavior which acts on and produces a change in the environment; what happens as a result of that behavior then determines how likely or unlikely it is that that behavior will be repeated. ***"Behavior is determined by its consequences"*** is the hallmark phrase originally coined by B.F. Skinner that characterizes learning through operant conditioning. These consequences fall into three basic categories described by the motivation continuum: punishing, neutral, and reinforcing. Obviously if the consequence is punishment the behavior will be less likely to occur in the future, and the opposite will be true if the consequence is reinforcement. Neutral consequences, by definition, have little effect on the predictability of future behavior.

Another way of looking at this is that behavior occurs through a three-step process: the antecedent, the behavior, and finally, the consequence (determining future behavioral probability). This way of looking at the process is often called the ABCs - for *Antecedent, Behavior, and Consequence*.

The antecedent would be the situation under which the behavior is first emitted, or the scenario and its associated causal properties. Once the behavior is trained and under stimulus control, the antecedent becomes the S^D. Prior to that, the antecedents would include the trainer's use of operant conditioning techniques and/or anything the trainer or the environment has done to instigate the likelihood of the behavior emission. The behavior is the 'operant' that is acted out on the environment, followed by an outcome or the consequence. This process occurs naturally but in the case of animal training, the trainer is often setting up the antecedent and, of course, the consequences as well. Simply put, if the animal does something right, it should be rewarded. In the opposite case, when the animal's behavior is undesirable, it should at minimum get no reaction (a neutral response) or alternatively, punishment.

It is worth noting that in the Communication section, we are discussing ways to explain something to an animal. Primarily this is how to perform a novel behavior. As such, communication does not deal much with techniques to eliminate unwanted behavior, except in so far as to mark or tag for the animal that the behavior is unwanted. This alone will not generally cause a change in bad behavior. For that to occur, one must change the motivation of the animal, since the animal is fully versed in the performance of this behavior and simply needs to be convinced to change it. Therefore, the subject of communication is primarily about behaviors you want to occur while motivation deals with both desirable and undesirable behaviors.

Most of what we will discuss in the rest of communication are all the techniques used by trainers to provide the best antecedent situations to promote the desired behavior. I have broken this down to six fundamental operant conditioning techniques used to create behavior you would like the animal to do.

Types of Operant Conditioning Techniques:

- Scan and capture
- Imitation or mimicry
- Negative reinforcement
- Manipulation or Sculpting
- Baiting or Luring
- Target training
- *Language??*

There are six basic techniques of operant conditioning for animal behavior modification which we will cover in the coming text: scan and capture, mimicry, negative reinforcement, manipulation, baiting, and target training.

A seventh technique - *language* - is not widely used with animals and so I do not consider it one of the basics, but it is obviously very important with humans. In animal training, the use of language to explain something to the animal is only applicable in very rare situations (*i.e.*: some apes and cognitive laboratory animals) where the individual is first taught a type of language and then the language (symbolic communication) can be used to further teach behavior, as well as communicate with the animal. It could be argued that to a certain extent, the entire behavioral repertoire, especially in very elaborately trained animals, can become functionally *similar* to language in how it can be used to explain novel combinations of existing behavior. I find this a very defensible argument; however, practically speaking is not particularly different than demonstrating stimulus control over behavior.

Nevertheless, true use of language to 'talk' to an animal - using nouns, adjectives and verbs - is extremely rare and exceedingly time-consuming to condition. While this has been done with a handful of animals, it is restricted to the laboratory environment and for this reason we will leave language off our basic list, although technically I think it is a unique and definable operant technique.

Generalities of operant conditioning

Before we delve into each technique in detail, let us discuss briefly some of the universal concepts common to all techniques.

Before beginning any behavior training, it cannot be overstated how important it is to set up the circumstances, environment, and approach in such a way that it makes it more likely for the animal to emit the desired behavior. *A good trainer will always engineer environmental antecedents to influence the behavior to occur. This sets the animal up for success making the entire process faster and more effective.* This strategy will be useful regardless of the basic operant technique you choose to employ to begin to sculpt the behavior. For example, if you want to train an animal to go into a cage, you can place the cage, open at both ends, in a pathway as a thoroughfare; this arrangement precludes passage without entering the cage. This will make it more likely that the animal will enter the cage merely because of the constraints of the environment, since it is not possible to go around the object. Then you can additionally choose to influence the animal to enter by any or all of the basic operant techniques such as using baiting by placing food on the other side of the cage or by placing a target in a similar location. Simple things like merely pointing the animal in the right direction to start off a behavior will also be highly effective and basic, yet important, considerations. Some people will list environmental arrangements like these as an operant technique, but in my perspective this is a mischaracterization. Setting up the situation for optimal success is common to every technique used, just as using a bridge or a basic process (see the next page) can be or is common to all techniques.

It should be pointed out that *the bridge stimulus can be used with any of these techniques* or it can be omitted in favor of simply delivering reinforcement (in the latter case, with the potential associated timing-related disadvantages already discussed). Either way, in the case of any creation of behavior, by definition, some form of reinforcement is utilized as a consequence to the desired behavior. This can be either positive reinforcement (the delivery of something the animal desires) or negative reinforcement (the removal of something the animal finds aversive). Both negative and positive reinforcement are tools that create behavior.

It is worth noting that one does not need to choose to purely stick with one technique or another. Indeed much of the art form of behavior modification is to fluidly and astutely determine which techniques might work best in which situation, and how to combine or modify them based on the individual and the results as they occur. Picking techniques can depend on species, type of behavior and individual personality, and there is certainly no single right way to do so. I usually go into a training session with several ideas in mind as to what might work, preparing to switch on the fly or combine techniques depending on the results of my initial attempts to explain things to the animal. Of course, everyone is going to have their preferred strategy and tools, and some people will feel so strongly about this that they may present an entire system of how to go about training a particular species or type of behavior. However, my preference, as I have stated, is to allow the practitioner to explore and understand all their options by weighing the costs and benefits to each technique. That having been said, there is a vague form of common truth to all approaches and systems of behavior formation, which I would describe as 'the basic process for training a behavior.'

THE BASIC PROCESS FOR TRAINING A BEHAVIOR

Regardless of the operant technique or techniques chosen, there is a kind of general 'process', if it could be called that, for training any behavior that has the following components:

- Choose one or multiple operant techniques and form a behavior
- Repeat over and over until predictable by the animal
- Phase in predictive S^D by associating it using classical conditioning

- Phase out any tools used to train the behavior (targets, touch, bait, pressure, etc)
- Test the understanding of the S^D against other cues for discrimination
- Test in variety of situations and with different trainers if appropriate

As we will discuss, the arrangement of these steps can change depending on the practitioner and circumstance, so the above order is just a starting point for discussion and should not be taken as a sacred sequence. Before beginning the training process, it is ideal to *have a training plan* outlining your intended steps. Of course this must be fluid and changeable to circumstances, but ideally it includes alternative steps to be tried if something is not working. It is particularly helpful for beginning level trainers to write this down to make sure that they have given the process a certain amount of thought and contingency planning, but even after decades of training, I always focus my thoughts on my training plan before I start training the animal.

Shape the behavior

The first step is to pick your technique or techniques from the basic operant techniques that I have already listed and I will describe shortly in detail. Using these tools, you will begin to mold and shape your behavior with your animal. In fact, this process is described by many as 'shaping.'

In order to shape the behavior, the trainer needs a keen concept of the exact *behavioral criteria*. This is a description of exactly what the goal behavior will look like down to which parts of the body are to be used, in what sequence, and for approximately how long. It is ideal to clearly visualize the behavior before embarking on the training process. Of course these criteria can be shifted as the trainer learns more about the animal's capabilities, but this is definitely suboptimal and may cause some confusion when the trainer suddenly changes what is required.

Successive approximations

Generally, when shaping a novel behavior, the procedure that is used is called *successive approximations.* Successive approximation is a term that describes the process of taking small increasing steps in the direction of a goal behavior. *Focusing on a single exact criterion for reinforcement at each approximation is necessary to guiding an animal clearly through the shaping process.* The exact choices and 'size' of each approximation or step is up to the trainer. Making the right choice in this regard accounts for much of the difference between highly skilled and amateur animal trainers.

Unfortunately there is no right way to universally describe how to choose the optimal approximation, since much of what contributes to these choices are case-specific and dependent on individual, species, behavior, and what the trainer is able to understand about the animal's current level of comprehension. This last component is a skill and an art in and of itself which many refer to as 'reading' the animal. We will discuss this aspect of the training conversation at the end of the chapter, but needless to say, insight of this kind is highly valuable and can require years of study to learn.

In terms of making the best decisions about approximation size and type, the optimal arrangement is to train as fast as the individual will allow without risking overreaching this goal and frustrating the animal. All other things being equal, it is preferable for the animal to be successful throughout the process, since this will associate the behavior and yourself with a reinforcing experience and will result in the least rehearsal of incorrect behavioral components. *Generally it is ideal to train quickly until you hit the behavior's* **threshold** *(the point of the edge of the confidence of the animal) and then very slowly using more minute approximations once the threshold has been established.* Training quickly to the behavioral threshold and slowly thereafter optimizes the approach by reducing the time spent on confident steps while minimizing the risks of going too quickly on less confident ones. Training should go as fast as possible, but as slow as necessary.

I have heard this referred to as splitting versus lumping, where splitting describes the minutest steps of successive approximations, and lumping, the larger approximations that combine many steps. *All other things being equal, taking smaller steps concentrating on a single criterion at a time will generally be the safest if not the fastest course of action.* And when a trainer finds a behavior plateauing or inconsistent in its development, it may indicate that too many imprudently combined approximations have been attempted. When choosing to advance from one criterion to the next, it can be necessary to relax the previous standard somewhat until the new criterion has been met and then continue by combining the two criteria in approximations. To what extent this is necessary is again subject to the user's judgment and represents more of what I would describe as the art form of training.

Chaining behaviors

A chain behavior is a behavioral sequence made up of recognizable distinct behaviors that occur in uninterrupted succession upon the instigation of a single S^D. Each behavior acts as both the reinforcer for the previous and the cue for the next. Chain behaviors are most frequently seen in show environments where, for example, a raccoon might come out onto the stage, retrieve a coin from a chest, move to another area of the stage, place the coin in a slot which raises a flag that the animal grabs, and carries off the stage. The entire sequence has a single antecedent S^D and a final reinforcement consequence.

To a certain extent, any aspect of a complex behavior can be considered a module or a part of a chain. Essentially this concept is really just an expansion of any elaborate behavior, and it remains a mostly semantic question as to which behaviors are chains and which are not. For me, these behaviors exist on a continuum from the most simplistic to the most elaborate. Regardless of this intellectual point of interest, when *training a large chain of distinct behaviors, most people train the last behavior first and then work backward add-ing behaviors.* This way, the behavior that finally results in reinforce-ment is the strongest and most frequently rehearsed, and the other behaviors are sequentially added on before it. Thus, the animal gains enthusiasm as the chain progresses and it can see the light at the end of the tunnel.

Rehearsal

The basic process of conditioning any behavior involves repetition and practice. These are fundamental to all learning. People under-stand that practice makes perfect and studying and reviewing is how something is generally learned. There is even a philosophy that quan-tifies approximately 10,000 practice hours for an average person to become a master of something. Even for what we might consider simple tasks, the need for repetition is even greater in animal learn-ing. Generally people grossly underestimate the number of repeti-tions needed before the pattern begins to be clear and predictable for the animal. It may take many trials before an animal is perfectly and, most importantly, confidently performing the behavior. Along the way, I usually like to see at least two to three perfect, confident repeti-tions of any given approximation before moving forward, although there is no hard and fast rule. The goal in this case would be to have the animal confidently predicting what is occurring and demonstrat-ing this in their eager, fluent and unassisted behavior.

Establish stimulus control

In order for a behavior to be fully conditioned, it needs to be under stimulus control, or in other words put on S^D. We have already dis-cussed that this process is accomplished using classical conditioning by predictably associating the cue with the onset of the behavior you are creating (and its subsequent reinforcement).

Exactly when you decide to introduce the S^D is entirely optional, and there is a great variety of thought in this regard among practitioners. Some people believe that the cue should not be introduced until the behavior is fully completed so as not to inadvertently associate the cue with any failed approximations or difficulty encountered in the learning process (the so-called 'poisoned cue'). Other people will introduce the cue once the animal is showing intermediate level understanding of the behavior in order to aid in the process by identifying this behavior as a unique 'entity'. Still other situations suggest the use of the cue very early in learning process in order to solicit operants (or guesses) from the animal, by indicating this is a novel behavior and not one they already know.

Myself, I use all three of these strategies depending on the situation. Generally, I favor the intermediate approach of naming something once it has some identity to the animal but not waiting until it is fully complete. However, in the case where I can anticipate great evolution or difficulty in the learning process, I will hesitate to name the behavior until most of this period is past and the animal is largely confident with the basic form of the operant. And in the contrary case (especially when I am using the scan/capture technique, see later in this chapter), if I want the animal to understand that we are working on something new that they should try to figure out, I will occasionally introduce the S^D very early in the process of scanning for the behavior I am seeking.

However you choose to do this, you will achieve success so long as the cue reliably and repeatedly predicts the behavior and its window of opportunity for reinforcement. In order to achieve stimulus control, the opportunity for reinforcement for the specific behavior should be available only with the antecedent S^D precursor and not merely at any time that the animal chooses to display the behavior. This is part of the principle of differential reinforcement that will be discussed further in Chapter 6.

Phase out any tools used to train the behavior

Involved in most of the operant techniques are training aids, props or tools that help focus the animal's attention on the task and guide the behavior. In fact, this is the case in all the techniques except for scan and capture, and to a certain extent, the application of these tools describes the differences between these techniques. Examples of training tools are bait or food to lure an animal into a behavior, pressure or touch to mold an animal into a behavior, or a marker target to guide the animal through a behavior. Whatever the case, these tools will initially support and promote the behavior but generally should be phased out to give the behavior its full form and to *require the animal to take responsibility* for the action. This removal process should begin to occur as early as possible in order to prevent too much rehearsal of the behavior contaminated by a dependence on the training aid. Indeed, depending on the animal, the removal of the tool can cause sincere confusion and loss of understanding of the behavior. Keeping in mind this dependence and approximating the removal of the aids as early as possible will optimize the use of these tools while insisting that the animal independently manage the behavior without guidance. I try to begin this process early and use the minimal nuance of each tool possible in order to maximize the animal's responsibility for the behavior and ease of tool removal.

Discrimination

In order to have effective stimulus control, the animal must *distinctly recognize one cue from another*. This process is called 'discrimination' and describes how well an animal can differentiate between S^Ds. As it applies to the novel behavior training process, it is necessary to approximate this discrimination to increasingly similar S^Ds until the animal is confidently displaying the appropriate behavior on cue when they are mixed together in a random presentation.

During this process, it is wise to present the most similar cues and behaviors last, after the animal has built confidence with the discrimination from easier S^Ds and more dissimilar behaviors. This step can be performed before or after the context shifting, which I will cover shortly; however, it should not optimally be done until, in all other respects, the animal has displayed a confident and complete understanding of the behavior. I am often surprised by the poor choices that novice trainers make when choosing which S^Ds to be used first in discrimination. Failing to grasp carefully how animals or, more specifically, your species, may evaluate nuanced differences in S^Ds often leads trainers astray due to their very anthropomorphic view point. For example, for many species the nuance between a flat hand signal waving with palm up versus down or sideways can be very tricky to recognize. While in human communication these signals are quite straightforwardly as simple as the difference between waving, bouncing and beckoning, for many animals all of these motions appear to be the same thing: moving your hand back and forth. A good rule of thumb will be to consider behaviors that involve an S^D given in a similar manner, sounding the same, or a behavior involving the same parts of the animal's body, as potential discrimination problems. Approaching these discriminations *last* and more carefully will help avoid confusion for the animal in the initial stages of discrimination.

Context shift

Often for me, the final process in completing a trained behavior is to test to make sure it can operate in varying environments, and in a related sense, be performed by trainers not involved in the training process for that behavior. These steps are necessary as a result of a learning phenomenon called 'context shift.' *A context shift is the loss of a learned response when an animal is shifted to a new environment.* This is a psychological phenomenon that happens with humans too, but it is generally worse with animals. Context changes interfere with all categories of learning (communication and motivation). Even small, local environmental shifts can cause difficulty, like moving to a different part of the enclosure or onto a different substrate, such as from grass to pavement.

Many inexperienced trainers are often quite surprised to discover that their horse who was jumping perfectly in his own arena, failed miserably once taken to another location. By anticipating this problem and taking the necessary small approximations of changing the environment, orientation, and even the trainers themselves, the behavior will largely become strong and functional thereafter even in previously uncharted territory. Recognizing that this is the final step to a fully functional behavior is, in my opinion, a sign of a more advanced trainer. Whether or not the behavior is also finally transferred to alternate trainers depends on the situation. If this is a professional animal, then certainly this transfer should be completed; however for a companion animal, for example, this step may not be warranted since it will likely never present an issue.

It is important to note that regardless of the situation, environmental factors may cause motivational shifts due to desensitization issues. I will discuss how to approach and resolve these fears and distractions extensively in Chapter 7.

THE SIX BASIC OPERANT TECHNIQUES

The following operant techniques comprise all of the most basic and distinct *antecedent methods* used by trainers to form behavior. As I have mentioned, there is a seventh method, language, which certainly can and does deserve recognition as a basic operant technique; however, since you are reading this, I presume you understand most of the nuances, and regrettably, little of this technique is effective with the vast majority of animals.

Of the six techniques listed here, all but one involves the use of positive reinforcement applied as a consequence of the desired behavior. Reinforcement of some type or another is a necessity

of forming behavior, but this can be in the form of positive consequences or in the removal of aversive ones. Negative reinforcement
alone requires the antecedent application of an aversive stimulus,
allowing for the possibility of its removal as a consequence. For
this reason it should be recognized as a separate operant technique
whereas positive reinforcement, being only a consequence, does not
fit the definition of an antecedent method and so is not separated as
a particular methodology in this sense. It is also worth mentioning
that *the use of positive reinforcement is possible with all six techniques*, as
there is no reason why negative reinforcement cannot be augmented
by positive.

THE SCAN AND CAPTURE TECHNIQUE

For all intents and purposes, the scan and capture method is the
most fundamental and universal of all the operant techniques. This
is because, in some sense, it describes the very heart of the process
of operant conditioning: **the act of seeking and then reinforcing
desired behavior**. Scanning refers to the trainer's active searching for
a desired behavior to occur or, more typically, its earliest approximation. Capturing refers to the act of timely reinforcement being delivered following the production of the desired behavior (or approximation). Since reinforcement ultimately increases the frequency of
the behavior it follows, the behavior will begin to occur more frequently and therefore considered 'captured.' In many respects, this
is the true art of training - grabbing good behavior from the air by
reinforcing it. There is a certain amount of this in every one of the
operant techniques. All of the other five techniques do something to
cause the behavior to occur, so it then can be scanned and captured.
Scan and capture is distinct, however, in that it does not employ any
additional tool or aid to mold the behavior to occur. Although, as in
all operant conditioning, choosing the right situation and setting the
animal up for success is perhaps even more critical in scan and capture, since it fundamentally has no other device to rely on.

Scan and capture prowess is so critical to a trainer's skill that
many training systems teach their students to practice this method

by engaging in human-on-human drills called 'the training game.' The usual training game is merely the game of *hot and cold* practiced with only the *hot* (or as you now understand it - the bridge stimulus). The students take turns being the animal and the trainer, learning an increased appreciation for both roles as well as better timing and choices of approximation size (at least for humans). Additionally, some systems (including my own) use surrogate animals like chickens, pigeons, or rats for their students to develop their skills practicing on live animals.

➤ *The benefits and drawbacks of the scan and capture technique*

Benefits of scan and capture

As I have already stated, the scan and capture technique is *arguably present in all methods of forming behavior* and, as such, its usefulness is undeniable. It is especially convenient, however, when the desired behavior already exists fully as a basic *natural behavior* of the organism. Distinctive flight displays in birds and leaping in the air by marine mammals are two classic examples of common scan and captured behavior. In these cases, the complete (and often complex) operant can be anticipated in usually predictable situations and captured fully formed without substantial, if any, precursor approximations. This can save time and will usually result in a very fluid and natural appearing behavior.

Similarly, scan and capture is very useful in *small refinement* of existing behavior. Fundamentally, it is a good practice to (bridge and) reinforce for good behavior whenever it occurs, such as when an animal waits patiently at attention. I regularly use scan and capture to train my animals to default to attentive behavior, a process I call 'the attention game.' With service dogs that must be alert but calm at all times, you could call this process 'the patience game.'

The scan and capture method is particularly critical to train *non-mechanical behaviors* such as vocalization, urination, breathing, attention, or sneezing which must, by their nature, emanate fully formed from within the animal and can be almost impossible to train by any other means. Similarly, *training an animal to target* or touch a part of their body to a specific location or object is often trained by scan and capture. Then, the use of these controlled body targets moving in sequence becomes one of the more elegant basic operant techniques to be described shortly (although targeting can also be taught through baiting). Similarly, other verb or action behaviors are often trained through scan and capture, such as to put, to pull, to push, etc. The other operant methods can lead the animal close to these ideas but the final action is generally a guess that is captured by reinforcement, making scan and capture critical to this type of learning.

For most mechanical (especially not naturally occurring) behaviors, such as waving or tumbling, targeting could be considered, overall, the optimal technique. However, there are many situations, such as teaching a giraffe to lie down, where I find the use of targeting requires too many contact points and as such can be very difficult and time consuming. In these cases, working with the *creative 'guessing' of the animal may result in a faster* and more fluid outcome so long as the disadvantages (to be discussed) of the scan and capture technique can be effectively managed.

One of the recent advances in this regard that has become somewhat popular in marine animal circles is the so-called *innovative behavior*. Innovative behavior uses scan and capture to teach the animal to create new and distinct operants on cue. For those who like the scan and capture method, this can make their animals more effective by turning them into even more creative guessers. The secret to innovative behavior training is to make your reinforcement contingent on a new operant each trial. This effectively asks the animal for something distinct in order to be reinforced. The difficulty I have with this method is that it invariably encourages the animal to constantly guess instead of listen, creating a kind of 'free-shaping monster.' This annoying habit can be very disruptive and even dangerous, as over-solicitous animals offer a dizzying string of new operants any time they are eager for reinforcement. One way around this is to create very limited and specific contexts in which the guessing (innovating) is permitted, and hope that it can be contained effectively. In general, I have a clear objective in mind with my training and do not find much benefit other than amusement and enrichment for the routine use of innovative training.

I have often felt that in tricky desensitization scenarios where fear or distraction complicates the situation, *having the animal independently acting out on its environment* - rather than being influenced to do so by human ministrations - may give the animal confidence and focus. In these situations where the animal has competing motivations that might result in refusal or resistance to some of the other operant techniques, the use of scan and capture reduces the disadvantageous possibility of rehearsing refusal while still allowing the training process to potentially proceed. This is especially useful if the animal largely already understands the operant, but the trainer may be uncertain as to its motivation to perform the task at the moment. For example, an animal may understand cage training, but may feel somewhat reluctant to be enclosed at the moment. Using opportunistic reinforcement as the animal approaches and increasingly enters the cage can allow for a more positive choice-driven attitude toward the behavior. Similarly, sea otters love to investigate on their own, but can be nervous if pushed into a situation, making scan and capture an excellent technique for these type of situations.

Drawbacks of scan and capture

The biggest pitfall of the scan and capture only method is that the trainer is *not really explaining anything* except providing information about the timing of when the correct behavior is occurring. This *leaves the animal to guessing* what is wanted which very often can be *highly frustrating* for the uncertain creature. Frustration, at its worst, can easily lead to aggressive behavior, and, at minimum, will likely color the entire training session and potentially the relationship. Minimizing these effects by keeping the training sessions brief and focusing on discrete high probability approximations will help limit this disadvantage. Nevertheless, forcing the animal to guess your desires is, for me, rarely the most effective way of explaining something, and quite often one or more of the other techniques added in will help further illuminate the situation.

Since a lot is occurring at any given moment, very frequently the animal's mind and the trainer's mind will not be on the same thing. This can result in a *less well defined* or specific behavior and very often the inclusion of unwanted concurrent superstitious behavioral artifacts. Animals may frequently throw in undesirable flourishes such as waving or nodding in addition to the primary behavior (which might be backing up, for example) because these artifacts were inadvertently reinforced during the conditioning process. While this can be true using any of the operant techniques, scan and capture is generally the least specific and most prone to these problems.

Behaviors trained exclusively with scan and capture offer the *most difficulty should the behavior break down* for any reason. Behaviors will frequently deteriorate with context changes or from lack of practice, for example. In these situations, the trainer has no tools or props to put back in to help the animal reclaim an understanding or memory of the behavior, since none was used initially. While this may sound to the uninitiated like not much of an issue, in practice, this is one of the more frustrating aspects of scanned and captured behavior. In these situations, the trainer is helpless to remind the animal of the behavior except by means of returning to the identical context in which it was first learned (which, in many cases, may not be immediately possible). As a result, it is often necessary to give up for a time, which can feel like a failure to both the animal and the trainer.

Finally, scan and capture has the distinction of *needing to wait until the animal actually emits a behavior to begin with.* In certain slow moving or generally inactive species, like tortoises, this can be very time consuming and ridiculous. Usually in those situations trainers will resort to influencing the operant by means of baiting or one of the other easily available techniques.

THE MIMICRY OR IMITATION TECHNIQUE

The mimicry or imitation technique is very common in human teaching and is a type of observational learning. This is basically *learning by watching someone else,* like when a child learns from its mother by copying her behaviors. Generally, in this case, the operant comes out as a nearly fully formed replication of the original behavior. This technique uses another individual's behavior as a prop to elicit the goal behavior, then, using basic scan and capture, reinforces the newly produced operant. This can be done using another animal of the same species, or rarely, the animal mimicking the trainer.

➤ *The benefits and drawbacks of the mimicry technique*

Benefits of mimicry

There are *certain species which are hard-wired* to learn by mimicry and in such cases this technique is very effective at producing nearly perfect operants, often even on the first trial. In addition to primates, who are highly predisposed to observational learning, other species that show this predilection are flocking and schooling species like parrots and dolphins. Any time mechanical group cohesion is needed in the natural history of the species, you may find that the species has at least a rudimentary ability in this regard to learn from another member of its group. Imprinting facilitates this type of learning in species that demonstrate it. Konrad Lorenz famously demonstrated that imprinting in geese was transferable to humans, which allowed him to serve as a human model for his goslings to mimic, at least in respect to their gross movements.

In many species, *young animals will mimic parents* - in particular if that species rears their young for a prolonged period. In a captive population, this can mean that the already trained parents can be easily used to pass on important basics to their offspring, simple behaviors like gating or shifting from one enclosure to another for example. In neurologically complex animals with long periods of maternal care, these behaviors can even be quite elaborate, such as well choreographed high-flying jumps demonstrated easily through imitation in trained dolphins.

Even in animal systems that do not lend themselves to true mimicry (which most do not) there is a phenomenon I call *momentum transfer* that can be very useful. Momentum transfer is a lesser form of imitation, where the energy with which the trainer is acting will often have a corresponding effect on the ensuing behavior produced by the animal. In a simple practical application this means fast behavior: fast command, slow behavior: slow command. Many trainers will say, "life up or life down" according to your goal behavior. Of course this is not ultimately necessary, but can be a useful tool in influencing desirable behavioral outcomes. I believe in some cases this form of imitation may be related to the trainer functionally becoming a type of bait to the animal, where the trainer is followed intently as a result of the association with the delivery of food and information. This intensive focus can effectively lead to a certain amount of mimicry simply to pattern the trainer.

Drawbacks of mimicry

The successful use of this technique *depends* more than any other *on the social structure of the species* in question. Where it works, it often works beautifully (this technique is particularly useful with dolphins and primates). However, in species that are not predisposed to this type of learning, true mimicry will be a complete dead end. One interesting note in this regard: it is possible to teach an animal 'to mimic' as a behavior and then use this to help create further behaviors, but to my knowledge it has only been successful with a handful of species, all of which were fairly complex and generally predisposed to mimicry inherently.

The biggest problem with imitation is that the individual must have a way to generalize their body parts to ours. Although this sounds simple to most people, these analogies are very often beyond most animals' reckoning. In fact it is this difficulty that makes so much of mimicry limited, since it generally *transfers very poorly between species*. Individual body part analogies can be taught by other of the operant techniques and placed on mimicry S^Ds which may work for limited gross movement but generally deteriorate when pressed into any complex action. True mimicry in fact, by definition, requires perfect reproduction of the operant according to the strictest psychological definition. By that measure, very little that appears to be mimicry is actually so in the purest sense. Humans often erroneously anthropomorphize animal behavior that patterns them as intentional mimicry on the animal's part, while in fact most of it is merely caused by baiting. This misconception is encouraged by many animal performances, where cues are deliberately conditioned to create the illusion that the animal is imitating the trainer, while actually the behavior has been conditioned using one of the other operant techniques and merely associated with an apparent mimic S^D.

Since the mimicry technique is really a very limited modification of the scan and capture technique, it has in common many of the same pitfalls, especially as it applies to recovering lost behavior, which in this case would require the return of the original mimic. If the model is on hand, that may offer an easy solution, but if the original model was another animal no longer present, the behavior can be frustratingly difficult to recapture.

THE NEGATIVE REINFORCEMENT TECHNIQUE

Despite its reputation, negative reinforcement has historically been and remains one of the most prominent operant techniques. It is still in use today on almost every farm in the world with horses, cattle, and sheep for example. This technique uses *the application of an aversive stimulus to cause a desirable behavior* which effectively removes the animal from the aversive, thereby reinforcing it. The aim is generally to cause flight and avoid fight.

This type of learning often falls into the category of what can also be called 'avoidance learning' whereby an individual learns to do something in order to prevent the onset of something else that they don't like. Alternatively, 'escape learning' is the specific type of learning in which the animal learns how to get away from an ongoing event. Although this is a type of negative reinforcement, this is the less typical application for forming behaviors.

Figure 12: Sheepherding is one of the oldest forms of negative reinforcement. In this technique the dog is the negative reinforcer for the sheep (while the dog is generally being trained by positive reinforcement).
(Photo credit: Nichole Hartmann.)

In every situation where you see a whip or prod of some type pushing an animal forward (or backward), you are watching negative reinforcement (avoidance) at work. It is very important to distinguish that negative reinforcement always forms behavior, as opposed to punishment which extinguishes behavior. In negative reinforcement, the aversive stimulus precedes and causes the behavior in question, whereas in punishment the aversive is a consequence to undesirable behavior.

It is fair to say that this technique has fallen into wide disrepute in modern times, for a number of reasons, both emotional and empirical. As a result, most modern behavior modification specialists will avoid all discussion of this method except to warn against it in favor of the positive reinforcement techniques. I point this out so that the reader may include that cautionary perspective when considering this technique; however, as I have previously stated, it is not my intention to limit the reader's tools but to help explain the pros and cons of each technique to allow an informed decision. This is very important in the case of the negative reinforcement method since, in truth, this is typically what will be resorted to when all else has failed. Despite many people's aversion to this technique, I have never seen a system that did not resort to it from time to time. This technique comes up typically in medical or emergency situations where an animal must be forcibly restrained[1] or corralled, or alternatively, quite routinely in the use of a leash or lead rope, for example.

What is very critical in the proper application of negative reinforcement is to let up the aversive application as soon as the animal begins to perform the behavior, as this is the 'negative reinforcement' component of the technique. Continuing to pressurize a correctly performing animal effectively punishes them for behaving correctly and meanwhile pointlessly associates the trainer with a lot of undesirable aversive stimuli. Proper technique will involve the trainer using a very finessed 'on' and 'off' of the aversive, responding to the minute-to-minute reactions of the animal. This should be done while optimally keeping the aversive at the 'flight distance' instead of so close as to cause the animal to feel the need to fight (see Chapter 8).

Similarly, the best application will use the minimal amount of aversive necessary, which in many situations can make this technique much less undesirable than one might suppose. Very mod-

---

1 Note: This would technically be both negative reinforcement and manipulation for reasons that will shortly become clear.

est aversives are used regularly with humans and animals without the dire consequences that strong aversives can cause. Indeed, in a well-developed system of this type, the aversive is sculpted down to the absolute minimum where it remains merely a suggestion unless increased pressure is required. This can be small movements of the body or the hand of the trainer waving the animal away, which are very subtle and, to the untrained eye, appear innocuous.

Negative reinforcement can be accomplished without contacting the animal as in the case of a sheep dog and its sheep (the dog in this case is the aversive) or a lunge whip and a horse. Alternatively, the aversive can involve physical contact with the animal, in which case it can also be described as a form of the manipulation technique (the use of touch to form behavior) that will be further described shortly; this is the aforementioned case of restraint or the use of leashes or reins, for example. Aversives generally increase in strength the closer they are to contacting the individual, physical contact, therefore, being the strongest type of aversive. For this reason the techniques of negative reinforcement and manipulation overlap when the stimulus driving the behavior is aversive and in contact with the animal. I find this overlap regrettable and have considered combining the techniques but do not find that to be a more preferable arrangement. It is generally true, however, that in negative reinforcement the objective is more for the animal to move away, whereas in manipulation we do not typically have that objective. More on this overlap will be discussed in the section on manipulation.

➤ The benefits and drawbacks of the negative reinforcement technique

Benefits of the negative reinforcement technique

The primary asset of the negative reinforcement technique is that, although it is a technique of communication, it nevertheless has a *strong built-in motivator* to drive the behavior and encourage the animal to be responsive. Generally, *aversives maintain their value* in many more situations than positive reinforcers do, as they do not tend to satiate or desensitize nearly as easily. This is because survival is typically the ultimate motivational trump card and aversives work to a certain extent by playing on this instinctive drive.

For this reason, negative reinforcement is typically the inherent fallback option when everything else has failed. In this sense almost every trainer uses this technique, even if they don't want to admit to it. Largely, this rationale seems to be to ignore situations where, for whatever reason (often in the animal's best interest), the trainer feels the need to use forceful methods, while still claiming to use only positive reinforcement techniques. I find this outlook rather short-sided and convenient since it seems to suggest it is ok to use so long as you are officially opposed to it. It is precisely in those cases of last resort that a trainer should consider seriously how to best optimize the situation for the animal, while minimizing the negative repercussions such as injury and damage to the relationship. I feel this is better accomplished by acknowledging the use of the technique and focusing on its best applications. Part of the difficulty of being honest about the use of negative reinforcement has been created by overly stigmatizing these methods to the point that any use must be disavowed in polite society. While I generally agree that the use of aversives carries significant consequences (see The drawbacks of the negative reinforcement technique), exaggerated and misleading implications do not advance the cause of thoughtful, humane teaching.

One other important benefit of the negative reinforcement method is that it is instinctively *easy to use,* at least in the gross sense. An aversive is often at hand (or one can be easily created) making the training plan relatively simple to implement especially for *small animals* who can be very easily handled with this method, with minimal risk to the trainer from injury. Also, prey animals tend to respond easily to this method since reactive self-preservation is often top on their minds, which is why this technique has been employed for millennia with horses, cows and other farm animals.

About dominance and leadership. There are some interesting cases where it can be argued that carefully used negative reinforcement can effectively *place the trainer within the leadership hierarchy* of animals with instinctive leadership-based linear dominance systems. In these cases, the animals appear somewhat predisposed to following a dominant leader, due to their species-relevant natural history. Leadership is determined, to a certain extent, by being the one who drives (*i.e.* causes to move) the others around. In those (rare) situations, this technique, in addition to encouraging obedience, can allow one to maintain a respect from the animal by occupying an 'alpha position.' This can, therefore, have the surprising effect of reducing aggression to the extent that the alpha is not challenged by subordinates (see also Chapter 8).

It is important to note that many people do not agree with this perspective and feel uncomfortable with the use of terms like 'dominance' or 'alpha-position.' I respect these views; however, this seems to me to be more of a semantic discussion than a practical one.

The term 'dominance' has a negative connotation for people that 'leadership' does not carry. Dominance has been defined variously throughout the literature and there is not a clear consensus opinion. Burgoon et al. (1998) described the problem that the idea of dominance, for many, implies submission and forceful conflict, although this is not necessarily the case. Dominance is best described by having an unfettered access to resources. In many species, like dolphins or humans for example, the negotiation of dominance occurs through a variety of subtle mechanisms, both social and physical, and often does not involve substantial conflict. Leadership, on the other hand, is related to who is choosing the direction of the group. Leadership has a more positive potential connotation, even though many leaders are, in fact, dominant.

Whether or not dominance infers leadership depends enormously on the species-specific organization. In some species like wolves, certain sheep and primates, the leader is the dominant. This has also been demonstrated in non-territorial wild horses; however, there is no apparent relationship between dominance and leadership in most birds, goats, and cows for example.

Precisely how far these concepts can be applied to humans working with animals is uncertain, although there is a considerable successful history of the use of these methods with both dogs and horses. Many animals are routinely guided around by a rope attached to their neck. In addition to being a lead, the rope also serves to limit and constrain the animal's access to anything that the human chooses. In this case, it is hard to argue that the human is not in both a 'leadership' *as well as* a 'dominant' position.

What dominance does *functionally* is establish preferred access and control over resources (food, mates, territory, etc). In captivity, this control is inherently in the hands of the human. Most of the time, we choose and control the animal's access to territory, food and mates. Therefore, *functionally*, we are dominant (and from a training standpoint, we must also be leaders, see Chapter 8).

I think for many people, the acceptance of this technique depends on how much bullying and force is involved in the application. Generally, as we have discussed, the use of aversives has potentially very bad outcomes and must be managed carefully (for more on this see below and also Chapter 6). So the style of leadership or dominance is critical to maintaining this balance, and the *application of this concept is generally one of degrees.*

The use of instinctive leadership roles is the primary secret in the so-called 'horse whispering' technique made famous by Monty Roberts, although this type of 'natural horsemanship' has its roots in techniques that have been around for centuries (if not longer). To a lesser but similar extent, this method is a component of many successful dog training systems, since, like horses, dogs have a linear hierarchy with leadership at its center.

This method has been successfully employed with more dangerous animals like elephants, but in those cases there is a legitimate risk of fight. This risk can be very serious as, at least in the case of elephants, when it occurs, the situation is generally life-threatening to the human involved. Even if this risk is relatively small (especially when the trainer involved has been careful to apply minimal and appropriate use), death is, for me, too high a price and no one can expect to perfectly manage these methods at all times. The elephant trainer occupation used to be associated with the highest per capita mortality rate, until recently, when some people have stopped working in free contact with these mighty and potentially dangerous animals (see Protected contact in Chapter 8). Negative reinforcement poses less risk with less dangerous animals; however, these risks can still be very serious and should be considered carefully.

Drawbacks of negative reinforcement

Negative reinforcement uses the application of aversive stimulus; by definition, this can in many cases cause a certain amount of fear (to say the least). While this may provide a strong motivation, it carries a significant number of downsides, the most prominent of which is that fear very often *leads to aggressive behavior*. This happens when the aversive causes fight instead of flight or acquiescence. Aggression is almost always an undesirable outcome as it works against the very nature of a collaborative relationship and puts both the animal and the trainer at risk for harm. As we have discussed, depending on the type of animal, this harm to the trainer can often be life threatening. Given all the other available methods of training, this risk is generally too dire for my taste. Additionally the frightened animal who chooses to fight can often be injured in the struggle with the trainer, which is obviously equally undesirable.

Beyond the risk to life and limb, the routine use of significant aversives will inherently associate the trainer with these punishers. That association will *significantly damage and color the relationship* between the trainer and the animal, and will inherently weaken the trust that the animal can feel toward the trainer and the training process. Routine usage of aversives diminishes the learner's enthusiasm and can lead to a variety of psychological disadvantages. Thus, the penalties for the use of aversives can be quite drastic and counterproductive.

Additionally, it can reasonably be argued that whatever behavior the animal is doing at the introduction of the aversive will have been effectively punished. If the trainer is not very careful then, this may result in a certain amount of *somewhat random punishment*, which, as I will describe in Chapter 6, is the most damaging use of punishment. Being careful to produce the cue prior to the aversive will help to moderate this impact somewhat since if the animal responds properly, minimal if any aversive will be needed. In the alternative case where he fails to respond, the aversive will be, to a certain extent, punishing whatever behavior is not the goal, and this is less undesirable than the purely random application.

To reduce the harm to the relationship, it is prudent to limit the association with aversives in general by using the minimum amount of aversive that is effective to cause the behavior, and limiting the use of this technique in general to situations where it is necessary or optimal. It many situations of last resort, where negative reinforcement seems to be the best choice for whatever reason, I generally try to exclude myself from being the person that applies the aversive (such as in restraint or corralling for a medical procedure, for example). Often there are qualified people who will not be carrying on continuing relationships with my animals who can shoulder some of the burden of association with these negative events.

Furthermore, it is helpful to prepare the animal for these situations as much as possible to limit the level of fear that they might inspire. For this reason, I rigorously prepare my animals for all types of reasonably predictable and potentially frightening situations that they might have to encounter in their lifetimes. This is beneficial, whether or not the scenario involves the use of negative reinforcement, but negative reinforcement is often involved and the downsides can be mitigated with this preparation and forethought. Although this can require a great deal of time, as most of the work involves techniques of desensitization, it is something I find too often lacking, even in the most staunch devotees of positive reinforcement. It is well worth the effort, as most animals can learn to be calm even during painful procedures such as needle sticks. They can also be taught to quietly accept restraint devices (often called crushes or squeeze cages), making the risk of the procedure much less traumatic to the struggling animal, with a lower risk of injury to all involved. This often involves the counter use of positive reinforcement to augment the use of negative reinforcement. Indeed there is nothing preventing the prudent use of positive reinforcement following the successful completion of a behavior sculpted by negative reinforcement, and doing so helps to balance out the disadvantageous effects on the relationship.

Another major disadvantage of negative reinforcement is that the animal is so focused on the motivator, they often lose the message. This is a problem of all techniques of communication that involve built-in motivators of either type. In these situations it can be very tricky to get the animal to focus carefully on the specifics of the goal behavior while *their brain is primarily focused on flight.* Indeed, negative reinforcement systems must moderate carefully the application of pressure so as not to have the animal respond too reactionarily, while still incentivized to the behavior. It is very tricky to get a frightened animal to focus. Animals routinely involved in negative reinforcement systems are first taught to learn to give-in to pressure as a basic subset behavior that helps avoid the larger pitfalls of this method.

However, it still can be very difficult to get the animal focused on the specific nuances of the behavior in question. This is, in part, a result of the fact that applying pressure is *not a specific way of explaining the behavior* - making it still very hard for an animal to guess what you want. For example, asking the animal to move away is not as informative, as it is to ask the animal to move towards something specific (like a target). How challenging this is depends on the complexity of the behavior desired. This technique is therefore easier to use to develop simple movements of avoidance type behaviors, rather than nuanced and elaborate operants.

Ultimately, it is certainly possible to use negative reinforcement with limited troublesome consequences to the trainer and the animal, as almost all advanced horse training can demonstrate, but to do so certainly *requires an astute animal savvy and a great deal of finesse*. For many novices this might not be a good choice, and for others, at minimum, it is a choice that needs careful effort to manage properly with most animals.

THE MANIPULATION OR SCULPTING TECHNIQUE

The manipulation or sculpting technique is another of the ancient and historical methods that seemingly everyone intuitively utilizes. Manipulation is the operant technique whereby **the use of physical touch** is employed to mold or sculpt the goal behavior. Indeed I have heard this called the 'oldest trick in the book.' For example when asked, "How do you teach a dog to sit?" over 80% (of lay-people) respond with some variation on: "You push on its backside." (Professionals usually respond with some variation of scan and capture and/or baiting.)

The fact that touch is employed does not stipulate whether the touch is a form of positive or negative reinforcement, only that physical contact is used to achieve the goal behavior. This technique can be used equally well with touch that is pleasing or aversive, although the incentive may not be equivalent in these two cases.

In a situation where aversive touch (or pressure) is used, this technique overlaps with negative reinforcement and will be governed by all of the stipulations previously laid out. In that case, the application of the aversive will best be managed minimally and removed as the animal complies with the intention. In the most extreme cases of restraint, this technique is often used to perform medical procedures or to transport animals. Some may be tempted to argue that this is not an actual application of an operant technique as the behavior formed is not necessarily repeated nor put on S^D. However, generating a final and complete product does not define the training process. Many unfinished behaviors would easily be recognized as having undergone training which we have defined as behavioral outcomes brought about by human interaction. Further-more, I have witnessed many situations where animals are routinely, forcibly restrained for medical purposes or research, for example. In these cases, careful application of the technique regularly results in the animal submitting upon recognition of the situation (or effec-tively, the S^D).

In the case of pleasant or reinforcing touch, the stimulus is best applied to locations and in manners that instinctively result in the animal's relaxation into the goal behavior. In this case, the touch can often increase once the animal has performed the goal behavior as a reward for doing so. It should be noted that these two forms of touch (positive and negative) are often used in concert, or in alter-nation, and this results in a refined method in which touch may be largely neutral to the animal. As I have already pointed out, the use of positive reinforcement can easily mitigate and augment the use of negative.

Famously, one training system called the 'T-touch method' offered by Linda Tellington-Jones focuses on the uses of specific touching strategies to desensitize, calm and shape behavior primar-ily in domesticated animals that, by their nature, are bred to accept human touch, to a certain extent.

➤ The benefits and drawbacks of the manipulation or sculpting technique

Benefits of the manipulation technique

Assuming the animal is not afraid to be touched, the primary advan-tage to sculpting techniques are that, for the animals with which they work well, they are generally *easy and straight-forward*. So long as the animal is reinforced not to resist, this technique can quickly result in the goal behavior. This is in part because the goal behavior is gener-ally more obvious and it is inherently incentivized through a built-in motivation system. This is particularly true in *situations where physi-cal contact with the trainer is either necessary or inherently reinforcing.*

An example of the former would be any situation where the human is riding the animal. In such a scenario, physical contact cues would obviously be desirable. In these cases, teaching the animal to yield to pressure is fundamental to the cueing technique and, as such, will ideally be managed by using this conditioning method. For this reason, horse training has involved manipulation presumably since its inception.

Dogs and cats represent the relatively extraordinary case of where physical touch from a human is inherently a reinforcer (largely because we have selected for them to feel this way). Especially in the case of dogs, this drive coupled with their dominance hierarchy seems to predispose them to a more reinforcing attitude toward the use of manipulation. This dog view of the world certainly makes manipulation easier and more effective as a training tool. For these types of animals, manipulation techniques can also help to soothe an animal through any fear hurdles (desensitization issues) that trouble them in the performance of the behavior. Of course, this aspect of the manipulation technique requires that the animal perceive the touch as a reinforcer; for those who perceive it in the opposite way, the use of this technique would only increase anxiety, should they have other reasons to feel fear.

I often use modest amounts of manipulation with many species to add a little pressure to *emphasize the concept of staying or going* which I can then scan and capture more easily. Similarly, *animals in the water* can be relatively freely moved with gentle pressure due to the low resistance of the medium. This technique is therefore commonly used to move and examine dolphins taught to float out next to the trainer.

Another special case where I personally favor the use of manipulation is in the *training of the open mouth behavior*. Typically this behavior might lend itself naturally to being scan and captured, but I do not prefer this method for this behavior since in many species opening one's mouth is an aggressive threat display. I do not wish to condition my animals to offer aggressive behaviors toward me so scan and capture is not my preferred tool of choice. Small pressure offered on the inside corners of the mouth is generally enough to begin the process of the jaws parting in most animals. The jaws can then be placed on targets (see the Target technique in this chapter) once each jaw is separated from the muzzle (otherwise attempting this without manipulation - the target is the whole muzzle).

The implementation of *leashes or tethers* is one of the most common and fundamental usages of the manipulation/negative reinforcement method although most 'positive reinforcement trainers' do not acknowledge this fact. Leashes are effective to the extent that they discourage (and prevent) by force an animal venturing further than a desired distance. What happens when the animal reaches this distance is that they feel the increasingly strong application of aversive pressure until the situation becomes unbearable to the point of compliance (or, when done incorrectly, the animal breaks free). Many will argue that optimally the tether does not need to act as such a restraint if the animal has been properly conditioned. Of course this is true to the use of all negative reinforcement systems - where if used effectively the aversive diminishes to a minimal warning of the potential incentive. Still, if the behavior were not being negatively reinforced by the leash, it could be trusted to occur without the leash, such as in the case of scan and capturing a heeling behavior. Once again, it is possible to combine these techniques effectively to minimize the negative downsides to any particular approach while maximizing its effectiveness. For example, the heeling behavior could be primarily conditioned using positive reinforcement techniques (such as baiting or scan and capture) and the leash utilized only to provide the stop-gap measure of last resort to prevent the animal from fleeing.

The use of the leash to prevent an animal from fleeing aversive stimuli (like fireworks) or chasing desirable stimuli (like a dog chasing a bird) is a technique of increased response effort utilized to aid desensitization (see Chapter 7). In either case, the leash helps to reduce the reinforcement and rehearsal associated with these undesirable behaviors. However, forcing an animal to endure aversive stimuli can cause serious damage to the relationship, so care should be taken to moderate this use.

Drawbacks of the manipulation technique

Where manipulation is using negative reinforcement as its incentive, it carries all the same inherent problems therein associated (see Negative reinforcement in this chapter). Furthermore, since manipulation always involves physical contact with the animal, this increases the fear associated with it and the associated *risk of injury to both the human and especially to the animal*. Restraint induced injuries are not uncommon and frequently result from the animal struggling so severely as to injure itself in the process.

One counter-intuitive reason for this struggle is if the animal has been permitted to succeed in freeing itself by struggling or resisting in the past. This would inherently negatively reinforce the behavior of resisting and could result in considerable effort and persistence in this disadvantageous behavior. For this reason, it is critical at all times and in any situation when using negative reinforcement to always choose to release the pressure only when the animal has stopped struggling. I cannot emphasize this point strongly enough, and it is one of the reasons I wish more people would admit to themselves that they are occasionally using this method. *Learning to resist pressure is one of the more dangerous behavior patterns in a captive animal's life, for all concerned.* Prudent attention to prevent accidental reinforcement of this behavior is a characteristic of excellent trainers in my opinion.

A further pitfall of the manipulation technique is that it can be a particularly *difficult technique to give the animal responsibility for the behavior* while the tool is approximated out. This is primarily due to two problems. The first is that the animal generally learns to give in to the pressure and allow the manipulation to occur. Once they have done this, the behavior is then created by the trainer. Unfortunately, it can be very difficult to explain to the animal that they are not finished with the behavior by accepting the manipulation. Getting them to take personal responsibility, especially for complex action, can be very challenging and involves using the technique minimally and then quickly withdrawing its use to encourage the animal to take responsibility to perform the operant independently. The second problem that makes this process challenging is that, to a certain extent, it is not a mental activity for the animal to be forced into something. Generally, the animal's mind is either on resistance or relaxing, but rarely do they focus on, or even notice, the nuances of the movement involved. The mind is effectively on the motivator and this (as I have already described) interferes to a certain extent with the animal's ability to grasp the concept or learn the behavior.

Obviously, *many behaviors cannot be formed* using sculpting alone. Behaviors like leaping into the air for example could only be comically imagined using this method (throwing the animal into the air?!) and would in such cases be very difficult to convince the animal to perform independently using only manipulation. For this reason, manipulation is very often coupled with scan and capture for full effectiveness.

THE BAITING OR LURING TECHNIQUE

The operant technique of baiting or luring is the special case *where a strong positive reinforcer (usually food) comes out before the behavior occurs in order to lure the animal into performing the behavior.* Although food ('bait') is the most common example, any strongly desired motivator will work as a 'lure' (a favorite toy, for example). While in many techniques positive reinforcement is used as a consequence to behavior (including in baiting), only in baiting is it also used as an antecedent or a means to form behavior. Wherever you see someone holding out a blob of meat or laying out a trail of bread crumbs, you are watching the technique of baiting.

Although it acts as the antecedent, the bait will also function as the consequence when the trainer finally delivers the reinforcer after the animal has performed the desired behavior. Alternatively, the bait is simply waiting in the desired location where the trainer wishes the animal to be, in which case they have performed the operant by arriving, whereafter, they are free to enjoy their reward. This technique is widely used with carnivorous animals and frequently seen at dog shows, for example, where the trainer often holds the bait right in front of the nose of the running hound. Likewise, it is by far the most prominent technique used with predatory birds, where meat is almost always found clutched in the grasp of the trainer's waiting glove (see Figure 13).

In many ways, baiting is the mirror opposite of negative reinforcement. In both cases, the method uses one of the two basic drives (reinforcers or punishers) as the antecedent at the front end of the behavior to increase its probability and drive it forward. As such, both systems of communication have built-in motivators which have the benefit of making the behavior more likely and the disadvantage of clouding the message. By saying this, I do not mean to suggest that these techniques are inherently equal (which depends on how you evaluate their strengths and weaknesses), but merely to comment on the structural similarities.

Figure 13: Keepers Carmen Sepetka and Jennifer Gale using baiting with a Swainson's hawk during a flight training session at CuriOdyssey.

(Photo credit: Melanie Echanique.)

➤ *The benefits and drawbacks of the baiting or luring technique*

Benefits of the baiting technique

As I have already pointed out, baiting has the significant advantage of a *motivator built-in* to the communication system, and this motivation is positive reinforcement! That means that the trainer is inherently associating themselves with a reinforcing stimulus. As a result, baiting associations generally help the relationship and therefore the motivation of the animal. However, this effect will depend on whether or not the trainer is baiting the animal into an aversive situation. Luring an animal into an aversive situation can build distrust and seriously damage the relationship (think Hansel and Gretel).

My favorite quality of baiting is that, since it offers something important that the animal wants, it is an inherent attention grabber. *There is no technique that is better to focus and hold the animal's attention* than baiting. If I am in a high intensity or critical situation, I will almost always use a lure to help ensure the animal's full attention stays solidly focused on me and that the animal stays with me. Choosing to bait at the right moment has many times in my career made the difference between failure and success in distracting or challenging situations; for example, bringing an exotic animal without a leash onto a chaotic Hollywood set.

It is worth noting that there is another technique - targeting - that shares this quality of focus of attention (see the Targeting technique in this chapter). In fact it is from baiting that targeting is derived. Some people even feel that targeting is a form of baiting. Targeting certainly got its start from baiting, but conceptually targets do so much more than lures that I choose to look at them as separate strategies, and where attention holding is concerned, targets are good, but bait is better and stronger.

If the trainer is a proponent of positive reinforcement, the history of association with positive reinforcers effectively makes the trainer a positive reinforcer as well. Thus, in these situations the *trainer functionally becomes a type of bait* and the animal will orient and follow the trainer where he or she goes. This is especially true of imprinted or hand-reared animals. The trainer, acting as bait, is valuable across many training goals, and often makes basic behaviors easier to accomplish as the animal 'patterns' the trainer. As I have already mentioned, it is this quality that leads to a type of mimicry where the energy of the trainer can often be parroted by the animal (see the Mimicry section in this Chapter). To the extent that this baiting is recognizable in the reaction of the animal to the trainer, it can demonstrate the value of the relationship bank account. Having said that, I am mindful that the trainer is often carrying additional positive reinforcers such as food or toys, but the effect can be demonstrated even when such things are left deliberately apart. In fact, this can be used as one of the best tests as to the value of the trainer or the strength of the relationship.

Owing to its relatively simple and singular focus, baiting is also excellent at accomplishing *basic gross movements,* often called A to B movements. These types of basic obedience behaviors are necessary to the daily husbandry and care of animals, such as moving from one enclosure to another (called gating or shifting) or entering a cage for example. In this capacity, baiting is often used at the rudimentary level to begin to establish a repertoire while investing in a positive relationship bank account. This will offer a good preliminary foundation of behavior and relationship, so long as the trainer avoids the pitfalls of 'tricking' the animal by luring them unsuspectingly into a trap that causes fear or stress.

Drawbacks of the baiting technique

One of the difficulties of using bait or a lure is that careful attention should be paid to the distance between the animal and the reinforcer. If the distance gets too close, many animals will aggressively steal the lure, irrespective of the human parts attached. Additionally, this method is very much like teasing, so in many situations this technique can further *frustrate the animal and encourage aggres-*

sive behavior. To reduce this likelihood, the bait must be *kept at a distance* where it encourages the animal's performance, but not so close as to incite a risk of mauling. Of course, how much risk this is depends on the size and species of the animal. This technique can be used with much more impunity with a poodle than a lion, although the method is regularly used with both species. Even a relatively harmless creature has teeth though, and the desire to just take what is so blatantly waved about can be counter to the healthy cooperative relationship between the animal and the trainer. Not to mention that any technique that inspires aggression and involves teasing the animal should be cause for concern and careful implementation. *There are a lot of methods to reduce aggressive behavior but the best of these is to avoid inspiring it in the first place.* Since I consider aggression my first priority, I generally limit the use of this technique to its best applications and favor less risky methods for most of my behavior formation.

One of the reasons for this is that baiting is also *not particularly useful to train most complex movements.* Anything that requires multiple moving body parts generally is not trained through baiting. While baiting can inspire an animal to produce vigorous behavior in an attempt to beg for the reward, any selection and shaping from these offerings into more elaborate behavior would be the process of scan and capture. That said, many people do use baiting to inspire a kind of guessing effort from an animal in order that they may find the preliminary approximations to capture the behavior they are seeking. I admit that this may occasionally be desirable but, on balance, the mental state of frantic guessing is not the attitude I feel is most productive and enjoyable for anyone. So at best, this technique should be kept to the minimum needed to establish the beginning path for the behavior, or to change things up for animals who enjoy the challenge of guessing.

Similar to other techniques with a built-in motivator, one pitfall of baiting is that the *animal's mind is primarily only focused on the food,* not on the trainer or what they are doing. This restricts the mental engagement of the animal on the task and distracts and divides the attention between the bait and what is required to acquire it. As we have already outlined, this can be a plus in that it encourages performance and a minus in that the performance is linearly aimed at the reward.

It goes without saying that baiting *requires food and food motivation* (or the equivalent) in order to be effective. While this can be said of all positive reinforcement techniques, baiting tends to depend rather singularly on a particular motive of this type. In other positive reinforcement systems, however, a wider variety of motivators can more easily be utilized, and to a certain extent, this untold variety can be part of the inspiration to cooperate. There have been many occasions where my animals have lacked a food motivation due to illness, but this has generally not discouraged them from cooperation with me. In these situations, the cooperation is often lost, however, once the animal is offered food for their efforts. Food in these cases - being rather more of a punisher than a reinforcer - tends to be discouraging (and maybe even nauseating). (Exactly why the animal will perform as long as no food is offered is not precisely clear, but I attribute it, in part, to the significant positive relationship that has been developed.)

Food dependence provides another problem in *establishing a rather fixed feeding ratio* that originates from the virtual promise of reinforcement derived by this technique. If the animal is tempted into a behavior through the lure of a given reinforcement, that reinforcement is reasonably expected as a consequence. Failure to deliver the promised 'payment' will seriously undermine the credibility of and the trust in the trainer, and in many cases this broken 'promise' may lead to aggressive behavior. Such a type of aggression is called 'schedule induced' aggression where an animal who expects reinforcement at a particular ratio may respond to any change with frustration and violence. This can be easily avoided by proper payment for every behavior, however that does limit the trainer to this continuous reinforcement schedule. As we will discuss in Motivation, there are a variety of advantages to variable reinforcement schedules that are inherently precluded by the use of this method. This may not seem

Figure 14: Various body targets. The primary target for both the dolphin and the sea lion in the upper photo is the nose; however many other target points are also useful. Trainer Stefani Skrovan is seen here demonstrating a forehead target, a rear flipper target, a chest target and jaw targets with a California sea lion.

(Photo credit: ATR International.)

to be a disadvantage to those who favor continuous reinforcement schedules, but for those who do not, baiting would not be ideal to rely on as the primary operant technique.

The final limitation I find with baiting is a practical one: this technique *frequently limits you to having food in hand*. While this might not be problematic in many situations, imagine the trainer who has a leash, a clicker and a blob of meat…where do they get the extra hand? This method is also often a bit messy, since the longer you grasp something, the more slathered in it your hands become. While this last point is a very minor one, it does promote the use of baiting with more dry food forms (although they may not always provide as much incentive as the moister alternatives).

THE TARGET TECHNIQUE

I have saved the target technique for last, as it is arguably the most modern and elaborate of all the operant methods (unless you consider language, which is by far the most sophisticated method). Targeting describes the process of **using points that the animal has learned to touch, moved in sequence to define any physical behavior**. The contact points (or targets) can be between any part of the animal's body and any object that the trainer conditions (see Figure 14). The targets are then sequentially directed to create the movement that the trainer desires. In this sense, target training can work very similar to a puppeteer with a marionette or, more simply, to a game of twister.

As far as I am aware, routine use of target training originated in the marine mammal industry which has only been around since the 1950s, when aquaria first became widely popular. The primary reason for this development was that the traditional technique of negative reinforcement was not nearly as easily accomplished within the three dimensional fluid environment where these animals lived. Baiting, as the other traditional method, was employed successfully with marine animals (think of the trainer leaning over the pool with

a fish in his mouth), but its limitations encouraged further development of the tool of targeting.

As I have already mentioned, the target concept grew out of
the useful qualities of the lure to focus an animal's attention on a particular place. Baiting primarily only focuses and moves the head (or
where appropriate – the hands) of the animal since that is the part
that consumes the food (although frequently moving the head also
moves the entire body). Alternatively, targeting is capable of drawing attention to any part on the animal's body, by asking that part to
make contact with a designated location. In some sense, *targets pinpoint in space where the correct behavior is occurring*, and this, coupled
with the bridge stimulus providing information about timing, allows
the animal highly specific references to the desired behavior. For this
reason, in practice, the use of the target technique is almost always
accompanied by the bridge stimulus. Graphically this could be represented as such:

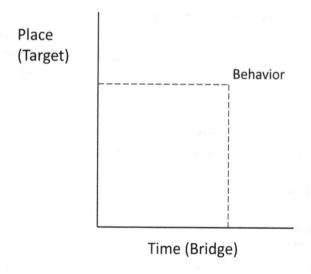

Thus with the target technique, the all-important *specific
location* of the behavior can at last be easily identified and brought
quickly to the animals attention. Combined with the bridge stimulus
providing an understanding of exactly when the behavior is occur-

ring, the target technique enables the animal to most easily identify the exact behavior.

Semantically, it should be noted that a target can be a both a noun and a verb. As a verb, it consists of an animal's action to touch a designated spot with a particular part of their body. This 'specific touching' is seen most frequently as the animal touching its muzzle to the trainer's hand, but further targets are defined by the animal touching its paw to the trainer's hand, its tail to the trainer's hand, or even its belly, to name just a few common examples. While the trainer's hand is most frequently available, anything can be a target. The noun form of target is often a prop which pinpoints a spot for the animal to touch such as a target pole or a target plate (see figure 23 page 253). In the previous examples, the trainer's hand also represents a target even as the animal is actively targeting on it. To be most effective, the animal should maintain contact with the target until told to do otherwise by the bridge or another S^D.

The targets are points that the trainer chooses. Anything can be conditioned as a target, and we can establish any point on the animal's body to touch it. Targets are trained by using one of the other techniques of operant conditioning; most frequently either scan and capture or baiting is used to form the target concept. For example, using scan and capture to form a target, the trainer reinforces for the animal getting closer and closer to the target until it finally makes contact. Using baiting, the animal is lured towards an area where it might incidentally contact the target en route to the bait. This moment of contact is bridged before the animal arrives at the bait and the animal learns to touch the target to receive a bridge.

Once the target is created, its use to form other, more complex behaviors is the technique of targeting.

➤ The benefits and drawbacks of the target technique

Benefits of the target technique

Targeting is by far *the most specific form of communication* of all the six basic operant techniques. This no-guesswork system makes it much

less frustrating to the animal. From the animal's perspective, as long
as they follow the target, they are engaged in the correct behavior.
Through targeting, the animal is nearly always doing the right behavior and is on the path to success. That knowledge is both reassuring
and highly rewarding in comparison to the alternative of guessing
what the trainer wants. Animals who have learned to target often
default to targeting when under any doubt or confusion. Through
this process, the animal also learns how to control any frustration
from confusion, since they have a proven and successful fallback
behavior. The reassurance and confidence provided by targeting,
coupled with the association with positive reinforcement, makes targeting one of the most successful methods of *establishing a positive
relationship* with an animal.

Overall, targeting an animal through the approximations to
train any physical behavior is *typically faster* than alternative methods, all of which involve the animal guessing what the trainer wants.
This is especially true for any rare or unnatural behavior which will
have less chance of being guessed or offered by the animal. However,
for abundant, naturally occurring behaviors, targeting may not be
best, and scan and capture may offer a faster and a more fluid choice
in those situations, as I have pointed out previously (see the Scan
and capture technique in this chapter).

Second only to baiting, targeting provides an excellent
means to focus an animal's attention. Further, since this focus is not
clouded by food as the prominent thought, targeting provides an
unparalleled means to give the animal further instruction or to introduce them to a new situation. Targets act in this sense as the start
to many other behaviors and the primary station from which an
animal will operate. The primary target or station is generally either
the muzzle or (for animals that have them) the hand. This is because
these are the parts of the body that the animal first uses to explore its
world. Thus the primary target is formed and typically maintains as
the strongest default station from which to receive further information.

Of all the techniques, targeting is perhaps the *easiest for retraining any behavior that falls apart* from confusion, context shift or memory failure. As I have noted, scan and captured behaviors have the highest difficulty with this issue, since they have no tool to fall back on to jog the animal's memory. The other techniques do have tools that can be reimplemented to influence the animal to return to the behavior, but targeting - being as it immediately draws attention to a particular part of the animal's body doing a particular movement - is usually the easiest way to retrace what has been lost.

Teaching an animal through target training helps them *to become active and avid learners*. It teaches them to take responsibility through their actions to figure out what the desired behavior is. This ultimately leads to a more motivated and engaged animal, and a better learner.

Drawbacks of the target technique

Targeting works very well to describe most gross physical behaviors, but it is *less proficient at the nuanced conceptual behaviors or internally originated actions*. Conceptual behaviors such as take or pull can be prompted by targeting leading the animal in the right direction; however the final leap is generally made by scan and capturing the concept once the animal offers it. Targets can only get the behavior to the doorstep and the rest is a guessing leap. As I have mentioned previously, targets are even more useless for any 'internally' generated behaviors, like spitting or vocalizations, which do not involve external target points and, as such, are very hard to target train. Scan and capture or mimicry are really the only viable methods to train these types of behaviors.

Another downside to target training that many trainers feel is a significant consideration is *the time it can take* to train anything. Before you can even get started, the animal must be conditioned to understand typically several different target points on their body. After which, the targets must then be used to mold the behavior and then approximated out, leaving just the physical motion. This whole process can be considerably more time consuming than capturing a fully formed or nearly fully formed behavior in progress by one of the other methods. However, once the initial investment in the creation of body targets is made, they are useful for countless further behaviors, so the effort cannot be fairly judged for a single behavior. Ultimately, the targets (analogous to letters in the alphabet) enable so many new behaviors (or, in the analogy, words) that the investment in creating them pays off many fold and is well worth the effort!

Additionally, the animal's reliance on and affinity for the targets often impede the trainer's ability to remove them from the behavior. This *target dependency* can be such a hurdle to get out of behaviors that the experienced target trainer will begin to sculpt out the targets almost as soon as the basic form of the behavior has been developed, in order to give the animal responsibility for the action on their own and not rehearse too much use of the target in the behavior. It can take considerable skill and practice to remove targets elegantly, and this can be very difficult with elaborate multi-target behaviors that take a while to build. Once the behavior has been repeatedly rehearsed with the targets holding it together, the animal may have difficulty conceptualizing it without the target points. Smooth, continuous repetition can help in this process, but it is another factor that often results in target training being somewhat time consuming.

Certain animals might instinctively aggress towards a pole or object to be conditioned as a target, particularly if the target involves the mouth. For animals and species that have this tendency (birds for example), it is possible to select out the biting behavior by asking for a target that does not involve touching but merely looking at the target. Using body parts other than the mouth area will also help eliminate this problem and better develop the target capability. With horses, for example, I often target the front top of the nose instead of the mouth region.

UNDERSTANDING IS A TWO-WAY STREET

I have now described all of the basic tools used to explain to someone else what you want them to know, or as I am putting it, the subject of Communication. As I have said, these techniques can be used alone or in any combination that the trainer dreams up, and to a certain extent, these choices make up some of what could be described as the art of training. We will now transition to the category of issues that will most determine your success or failure as a trainer: Motivation, or what drives and convinces someone to cooperate. If you can both explain how to perform a behavior and convince someone to want to do so, then surely you will succeed. Of critical importance to this success is to be able not only to communicate to someone else, but also to *hear* what they are communicating as well, since understanding is a two-way street.

READING BEHAVIOR

Listening to the animal will tell you about their understanding as well as their motivation. Many human beings, having been dulled by their verbal abilities, often find it challenging to rely on non-verbal communication to understand what someone else is feeling. The ability to 'listen' to what the animal's behavior indicates is called *reading the animal*. Needless to say, this ability is one of the attributes of the most talented and successful trainers. Unfortunately, this is something that does not translate well to text.

Largely this empathic nature stems from a *constant awareness of the non-verbal information* available from someone's body language and responses. This awareness is moment to moment, non-verbal feedback. To 'hear it' requires a sensitivity to the thoughts and feelings of others, rather than merely a focus on one's own objectives and desires. It can be taught, but for many people it is an inherent talent brought about from their upbringing or an element of their intrinsic personality.

While much of non-verbal communication can be highly nuanced and difficult to generalize, there are some simple indicators that are helpful to be aware of. Watching the direction of the animal's eyes or ears (or alternatively the angle of the head) will almost always indicate what they are focused on. This is probably the most important tool to indicating what is on the animal's mind both in terms of their understanding and their drives. Tension or fear is sometimes indicated by overly wide-eyes, a sign that the fight or flight response has been activated and the animal is attempting to take in more sensory information. Likewise, in certain species sniffing will indicate a similar distraction. Body tension, posture and breathing rate can also indicate the level of comfort and emotional response that the animal feels, and may warn of important drives that the animal is experiencing that should be taken into account and neutralized. Postures that are relaxed and not poised and ready to flee generally indicate an animal is comfortable in a situation. Whether or not an animal approaches or retreats is important to understanding their interest and appraisal of a situation. Avoidance of something is almost always an indicator that the animal views some aspect of the situation as punishing or undesirable, or at least potentially so. While these simple guidelines will be useful across a wide variety of circumstances, it is important to stress that each is a merely fleeting indication, and as time goes by, the animal's feelings and thoughts can and do change constantly (see Chapter 6 for more on this).

For many people, the talent to read behavior is only cultivated with a particular species they happened to be well exposed to. This exposure created an affinity for the nuances of a species-specific body language. These people are often so attuned to the specific language and customs of their particular species that they find it difficult to generalize and understand any other group. This phenomena falls under the category of 'subject-matter expert syndrome', and can result in brilliant trainers who are completely limited to a particular species. Many people consider this quite natural. However, someone who has a true understanding of the general principles of animal behavior modification should not be limited by their ability to read a particular species. That said, it is certainly necessary and important to cultivate a deliberate understanding of each unique species as well as each unique individual with whom you will be working.

KNOW YOUR SPECIES

Each species has instinctive and specific body language, as well as auditory and scent cues that are used to communicate basic information. If the species is highly social and cohesive, these patterns may be very elaborate and difficult to fully understand. The best place to start is with a basic natural history understanding of the species: how it lives, where it lives, what it eats, etc. This investigation will reveal critical insight into the basic nature of the animal: if it is predator or prey (or both), whether it maintains stable social bonds or group cohesion, and which senses it relies on most to navigate its world. Generalities can then be loosely inferred, prey animals are more flighty whereas predators more aggressive, while smells are more likely to distract cats than birds, for example.

Next, gross observation of intraspecific interactions and their consequences will begin to acquaint the careful observer with a host of important behaviors to be aware of. These are the basic instinctive ways the animal interacts with others of its kind in its own environment. Seeking out a specialist in that particular species can also be used as a key to unlocking important interpretations. It is especially critical to understand behaviors related to feeding, territory and sexual activity, as these highly instinctive areas will often be responsible for the vast majority of the animal's repertoire. Additionally, these instinctive behavior patterns will be subject to the least modification and may routinely dominate an animal's outlook on any situation. The Brelands (1961) famously described this problem as *instinctive drift, where conditioned behavior inherently drifts toward instinctive behavior* wherever the two have something in common to begin the pattern. This phenomenon is particularly important in the most basic instinctive animals that are without the complex social systems which engender more plasticity of response and learning.

Among animal training professionals there is a saying: "Always think of your animal by the species first and as an individual second." This important reminder is intended to prevent some of the most dangerous mistakes that arise from the comfort of knowing a particular individual for so long that you tend to forget the potential species-specific hazards they may pose.

Dangerous species are usually highly predatory, territorial, and/or very large animals. In those cases it is critical to always recognize the inherent instinctive dangers that these species will pose, and not to allow familiarity to dull your skills. In many of the most well-known and tragic cases of trainer casualty, the trainers fell victim to the comfort that familiarity and experience can bring. This can happen despite being highly experienced and accomplished trainers.

I am often concerned by the risky choices people are willing to take with dangerous animals. The fact that they can get away with these risks encourages people to believe, erroneously, that they are manageable. Please believe me that wild dangerous animals, however well trained, can *always* cause serious injury! It behooves any one working with them to take any past pattern of aggression or any current sign of danger *immediately* to heart and avoid and prevent that outcome by whatever means necessary. Or, ultimately one day, that individual may show its true 'species' and the outcome can be very grave.

KNOW YOUR INDIVIDUAL

Although for safety's sake, knowledge of species characteristics should always trump individual familiarity; knowledge of personal habits, interests and talents is particularly useful and critical to the training process as well. Just like people, each animal has its own distinct and unique personality brought about by a combination of genetics and past experience.

While getting to know the animal is very important, one of the best overall guides to predicting and understanding its behavior will be its past behavior and experiences. *How an animal behaved in a previous context, is very likely to predict feelings and issues in any similar context in the future.* This understanding is the most readily available information that a trainer has, and should guide a preemptive appraisal of future issues, and where training effort will need to be applied. Understanding contexts in which an animal might be afraid, playful or aggressive, based on similar displays in the past, can save lives and prevent problems through careful and proactive training. To aid in this endeavor, I maintain careful training logs with my animals that allow a record of important events to be recorded for posterity, to be passed on to other trainers.

In addition to past experiences, knowledge about what any given animal likes or dislikes enables the creative trainer to find ways to use these as reinforcers and punishers in the training process, rather than being merely restricted to a generic species-specific diet. Understanding the aversives can also help avoid or neutralize them to prevent their interference in training goals and objectives.

One newer way of understanding an individual is to try to categorize his or her *personality type* somewhat, which can lead to generalizations, but may help interpret and anticipate which techniques may be most appropriate. Some general categories that help understand individuals grossly could be how extraverted or bold an individual is versus how introverted or timid they are. Bold individuals (sometimes called 'bomb proof' animals) will have more issues with aggression, but much fewer with desensitization, for example. Timid individuals may not respond well to indelicate use of aversive technique and will need a heavy focus on desensitization principles.

COMMUNICATION, *IN SUMMARY*

Techniques of communication are engaged to explain to individuals what it is that you want them to learn. The tools fall primarily in the categories of classical and operant conditioning - two fundamental types of learning. The process of classical conditioning forms associations and, as such, creates symbolic language and cues. The most basic of such conditioned stimuli are the bridge stimulus that is used to indicate the moment of correct behavior and the redirection stimulus that indicates that the animal should change behavior. The techniques of operant conditioning develop behaviors. The process of training behaviors involves selecting and/or creatively combining operant techniques, but all techniques fundamentally involve the use of successive approximations, reinforcement (both positive and negative) and rehearsal. While techniques of communication involve what the trainer is doing to alter the antecedents to behavior, all behavior is fundamentally controlled by its consequences or expected consequences. These consequences are the techniques associated with motivational issues and will comprise the majority of the rest of the book. Managing to 'read' the animal's body language is a critical ongoing challenge that must parallel the trainer's interest in their own objectives. This will enable a meaningful and appropriate management of the techniques of both communication and motivation, by assessing the moment to moment impact on the animal.

CHAPTER 6

MOTIVATION

*Figure 15: The author working in free-release in the open ocean with
a trained sea lion wearing an underwater video camera to capture
images of wild whales (seen in the distance). Working in free release in
the natural environment of the animal provides one of the most direct
indications of the true motivation of the animal, since it has
the option of choosing the wild over captivity.*

(Photo credit: ATR International.)

Now we have come to the most critical issue of behavior modification - what drives behavior! Where communication was largely focused on antecedents, motivation is largely the subject of consequences. This is the subject of how to influence someone to do behavior that you want them to do and, just as important, how to convince them not to do behavior that you don't want them to do. Any goal behavior you want will require explaining it to the animal using the 'tool bag' previously described in the Communication section, as well as the appropriate tools from within Motivation to drive the behavior. With limited exception, however, getting an animal *not* to do something involves *convincing* much more than explanation. They clearly and readily understand how to do the behavior; they simply need incentive to stop doing it. So curtailing unwanted behavior becomes largely a motivational problem.

Thus, I will break down the motivational tool bag into these two fundamental objectives - methods to encourage behavior and methods to discourage behavior. In each case there are fundamentally only two issues: opposing drives (reinforcement versus punishment) and opposing experiences (rehearsal versus prevention).

But before we get into the details of these tools, let us first discuss some particulars of the general topic of drives and motives, which, for the purposes of this text, we will consider synonymous terms.

Drives

What motivates or drives someone is *unique to each individual's perception*, their current status, and events both past and recent. As such, what motivates someone is personal and varies widely between individuals. It is forever changing and only exists at a moment in time, and it can change at lightning speed. Therefore, it is hard to measure and nearly impossible to fully understand. Factors driving behavior will include both external stimuli and internal drives.

To understand the important mechanism of drives in creating behavior, it is helpful to remember the basic tenant of operant conditioning: *Behavior is determined by its consequences*. As we have already discussed, there are two fundamental motivators or drives: reinforcers and punishers. Both of these come as a consequence to behavior and later result in behavioral frequency change. **Reinforcers** are things that increase the frequency of the behavior they (immediately) follow. While **punishers** are things that decrease the frequency of the behavior they (immediately) follow. **Note that a punisher or**

reinforcer is only defined by its effect on behavior, not by a prop-
erty of the stimulus itself or how the trainer is inclined to view the
stimulus.

It is also very important to recognize that these drives generally must follow immediately after the goal behavior in order to
have the strongest potential to influence the operant and be seen as
linked to the production of the behavior. This timing is critical to
effective behavior modification. The bridge stimulus, for example,
works to improve the trainer's timely delivery of reinforcement,
making communication about the operant even more precise. Alternatively, **latency** or being late in delivering consequence to behavior
can confuse the animal. Latent delivery can easily result in reinforcing or punishing the wrong behavior. Thus, one of the qualities of a
good trainer is good timing.

It is worth noting that there are ways around the necessity
of immediacy of consequence, of which the bridge stimulus is but
one example. All that is actually necessary is the mental perception
of the link between the behavior and the consequence, not the actual
fact. However, nothing will be as strong as the direct consequence.
Mental perception can make a real and effective substitute depending greatly on how strong this perception is and the ultimate value
of the motivator associated with it. This is (regrettably) how much
of human behavior is driven, by an understanding and expectation
of future incentive or perceived costs. For humans, language can
explain an intended future reinforcer (like a paycheck) to be associated with a current behavior (work). Too much reliance on these
frequently low-value mental substitutes is very often where human
motivation falls apart. For example, there is considerable evidence
that providing timely praise to a hard-working employee, will have
a greater impact on her productivity than a raise at the end of the
month. With animals, these same mental connections are possible
but enormously more difficult to cultivate and depend on with certainty. Thus, it is best to be guided by the principles of immediacy of
consequence for most behavior modification purposes.

The motivation continuum

There is a third value that a stimulus can possess – neutral. However, neutral stimuli cannot be considered drives as they have no effect on the frequency of behavior. Together, these values are depicted on the *motivation continuum*. Every stimulus falls somewhere on this line for each individual at any given moment in time:

Punishing ———————— Neutral ———————— Reinforcing

Any particular stimulus' value is typically moving up or down on the continuum regularly, depending on a wide range of factors including: context, time, exposure, association, and physiology. For example, when you are hungry, food is highly reinforcing! Then when you eat, your motivation for food satiates to neutral (like during Thanksgiving). If you are then forced to continue eating, food can rapidly become a punisher. In fact, anything in excess will often become punishing. The astute trainer must carefully pay attention to make sure the reinforcer being offered is still, in fact, reinforcing to the animal.

Changing the value of a motivator

It is also possible to attempt to alter the value of a motivator using environmental changes or context changes that will alter the priority and access to certain drives. These environmental manipulations will depend greatly on the trainer's complex understanding of the nature of the drive for that individual. They may or may not be possible, or even ethical, depending on the drive in question. These mechanisms can be used to both increase or to depress the value of a certain drive.

Deprivation is certainly the most obvious mechanism to drive up the value of a reinforcer, particularly primary or innate reinforcers (see the Definitions section in this chapter). Deprivation is accomplished by preventing access to the reinforcer until its value increases as the desire for it builds.

The opposite of deprivation, the processes of satiation and habituation, will both depress the motivational value of either a drive or stimulus through exposure over time. Another way of neutralizing drives that we have discussed already is counter-conditioning, whereby motivators are associated with drives of the opposite value using a classical conditioning type model (see Chapter 4). More on the subject of how to reduce the value of motivators will be discussed in the Desensitization chapter.

A final mechanism of effectively altering the value of the motivator is to change the effort required to achieve it, by making it either harder or easier to acquire. This idea is called *response effort*. By making a reinforcer harder to acquire, you, in that moment, reduce its relative value to the animal since there is a cost of effort that must be 'subtracted', in a sense, from the value of the reinforcer. An example of *increasing response effort* is to have no junk food in the house. Therefore, considerably more energy will be required to eat poorly, than if these foods were found in the cupboard. An animal example would be to contain the animal's food in a raised container, instead of on the ground where stealing would be much easier and more tempting.

Reducing response effort is the opposite case, where something is made very easy to acquire. Since there is no significant behavioral cost to invest, its value is somewhat exaggerated momentarily. An example of reducing response effort is to have your gym bag in the car, making it easier to go directly to the gym after work, instead of facing the hurdle of going home first. An animal example would be to locate or position the animal in-line and proximate to the goal behavior. This prevents the animal from having to cross great distances or change directions to achieve the desired operant.

Changing the motivational value of available drives is only a small portion of the process of behavior modification. Most behavior modification is accomplished by understanding and providing appropriate consequences at the appropriate times.

Drive state analysis

Much of what makes training (and motivation) so challenging is the fact that it can be very difficult to understand all of the complex and discordant motives affecting someone else at any given time. Motivators generally describe how an individual values different stimuli, opportunities, and feelings. The best trainers work hard to create particular scenarios that will motivate the animal to choose the goal behavior. This is done in part by limiting the stimuli in the environment and driving up the stimulus value of what is being done and what is being offered, and then, most importantly, by providing the ideal consequences at the right moment.

We would, however, be much more successful if we had a guide to the animal's particular drives at the moment we are training them. (I have often thought how useful this would be interacting with people as well ☺.) Such an analysis could be called a drive-state analysis and would incorporate the motivation continuum with a list of relevant drives affecting the individual in question, at a particular moment in time. For example, a simple drive-state analysis of a ukulele-playing, thirsty person might look something like this:

The Drive-State Analysis of a Thirsty Person

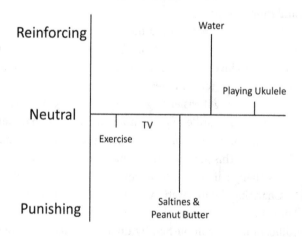

This silly example is a picture of a single moment in time of how one particular person might value things - the list of stimuli and drives could go on forever. Stimulus value is also called **salience** by psychologists and describes *the relative importance of any given drive by comparison to another*. The higher salience of any given drive permits it to *overshadow* any competing drive with lower value.

From this depiction we can recognize another important property of motives: they can stack up to increase the drive value or cancel each other out to neutral. To drive the behavior you want, it is best to have as much in the reinforcement column as possible. At minimum, to be successful, you must have more reinforcing the behavior than the value of the alternative motives punishing it. For example, although it is a reinforcer to the imaginary person in the drive state diagram, the opportunity to play the ukulele could not be used to drive this person to eat saltines and peanut butter, which, at the moment, represent punishing stimuli. However, the combination of the ukulele and water could be used to convince this person to eat the saltines and peanut butter since the motivational values of the two reinforcers added together is greater than the punishing opposing value.

Figure 16: A tiger relishing his milky treat enough to accept an injection at the Downtown Aquarium in Houston. The animal's cooperation demonstrates the salience of the reinforcer over the punisher.

(Photo credit: Patti Shoemaker.)

As trainers, we, quite reasonably, tend to focus on the external stimuli we can see and control, that may be effecting behavior; however, it is important to recognize that many internal drives motivate behavior as well. These so called self-reinforcing or automatic reinforcing behaviors can be especially challenging to identify and control. Generally, if there is no other explanation for a certain behavior, I often suspect an internal drive that I cannot recognize. I once had an animal that, when things were quiet, often used to spend some of her hours peacefully suckling her own stomach. This surprising behavior produced no outward benefit that could be recognized, yet nevertheless seemed to provide comfort and happiness that was born from an internal satisfaction unique to her.

Further description of drives and motivational principles regrettably necessitates a more thorough review of some relevant psychological lingo. I will try to keep this to a minimum; however, a detailed understanding of these ideas is central to the informed discussion of motivation. To make the process more bearable, I suggest using a little counter-conditioning on yourself and permit yourself some nice treat, like chocolate or candy, as you read and digest the next sections.

Definitions

Certain drives are called **primary motivators** because they *have an intrinsic value* (inherently punishing or reinforcing) that is based on some physiochemical process and is unlearned. These primary motivators will therefore be expected to rebound should their value wane for some reason, such as from exposure. In this sense, primary motivators can be seen to be relatively reliable, and this makes predictions about their effectiveness to drive behavior less problematic. People debate exactly what is and what is not primary for all species or individuals. There is no way to know this for certain. This is another one of these myopic psychological arguments that has relatively little practical value and hence is of little importance to this text. If the drive is somewhat universal and rebounding, I suggest you consider it primary. Classic examples of primary motivators are food, water, sex, sleep, comfort, and pain. Note that some of these are stimuli themselves (like water), and others can be related to a variety of stimuli (like pain).

In contrast, **secondary motives** do not have any intrinsic value in and of themselves, but get their value through learning, or by an association with another motivator. Examples of secondary motivators are money, the bridge stimulus, applause, stoplights, and non-food objects such as jewelry or toys. Although many of these things have considerable value, this value is not intrinsic to the stimulus, and must be learned to be perceived. The fact that *secondary motives are learned*, however, does not mean they are less valuable or less powerful than primaries (as many people erroneously conclude).

Generally, the value of a secondary motivator is dependent on routine, maintained association with other motivators, through the process of classical conditioning (see Chapter 4), although this is the subject of some debate. Some secondary drives do appear to become functionally autonomous and no longer require associative maintenance; however, this is rare and somewhat uncertain. It *is* certain, contrary to popular opinion, that secondaries *do not require constant* maintenance (although, as we discussed in the section on bridging stimuli, they do require *routine* maintenance). I have regularly utilized a bridge stimulus to maintain behavior during metabolic research that otherwise prohibited primary reinforcement delivery for up to an hour. The bridge maintained its value without difficulty.

There is some semantic debate about what distinguishes these stimuli: whether or not they were learned (*i.e.* not intrinsically motivating) or whether or not they require a maintained association. People in the marine mammal and exotic animal industries tend to favor the view that if something is learned, it is secondary, whereas other psychologists may prefer the idea that the drive should be described by its need for maintenance. Both views seem equally valid to my mind. However, I tend to favor the view that if something is learned, and not initially intrinsically valuable, it should be described as secondary. This is mostly because I don't enjoy the idea that something can change back and forth between primary and secondary once the animal has learned to enjoy the stimulus for its own merits, and thus no longer requires a maintained association (such as playing a game, for example). Practically speaking, it can be difficult to determine accurately if something has become intrinsically motivating or not (and when that occurred). This, for me, blurs the convenient use of the term. Thus, in this text, we will be referring to secondary motivators as those that are learned and not intrinsic. This leaves uncertain whether or not they continue to require maintenance conditioning, although it should be understood that most secondaries certainly will.

By far my least favorite psychological terminology is the difference between positive and negative motivators. As these terms are used in psychology, they are inherently counter-intuitive and confusing to all but the most well-versed in the subject. Nevertheless, I feel obligated to explain these (poorly) chosen words because they are so central to operant conditioning. Psychologically speaking, *positive refers to adding something* to the environment; it does *not* suggest a value! Conversely, *negative refers to something being removed* from the environment, not to someone disliking it. It can help to think of arithmetic to understand the origins of this meaning.

Another way of understanding this difference is to recognize that positive drives are attractive or approaching drives, while negative drives are avoidance drives. So, the same stimulus applied differently can have opposite effects on behavior. Thus, something that is unpleasant that is removed by an animal's behavior is called negative reinforcement, whereas the same stimulus applied after a behavior is called positive punishment. Similarly something desirable earned after a behavior is called positive reinforcement, whereas the same stimulus being withheld as a consequence of a behavior is called negative punishment. Negative punishment sounds doubly bad although it is actually the most benign form of punishment. Examples of negative punishment include grounding or time-outs.

The most common point of confusion for many people is realizing that negative reinforcement and punishment are completely different techniques and have totally opposite effects on behavior (although they may involve the use of the same stimulus). Punishment always decreases behavior, while reinforcement always increases it. The following chart may help illuminate some of the differences, but remembering the earlier description of the operant techniques should also be helpful in keeping the differences straight.

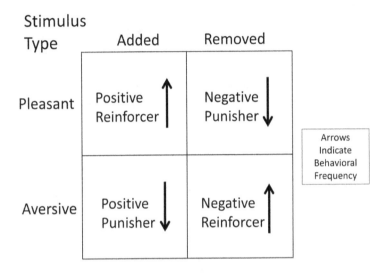

METHODS THAT DRIVE AN ANIMAL *TO DO* A BEHAVIOR: Reinforcement And Rehearsal

Now that we have covered the basic principles of motivation, let's turn to the practical discussion of methods that encourage behavior. As I have already indicated, there are only *two primary means to drive someone to do a goal behavior: reinforcement and rehearsal.* I will take these one at a time and discuss the principles and nuances of these critical concepts.

REINFORCEMENT

Reinforcement is, by definition, associated with the development of all learned, voluntary behavior. As we have discussed, this can be either positive reinforcement or negative reinforcement.

Positive reinforcement

Some of the operant techniques work only with positive reinforcement such as scan and capture, mimicry, baiting, and targeting where reinforcement is delivered to the animal after the successful completion of the behavior or approximation. This positive reinforcement can take the form of either a primary or a secondary reward. Generally, positive reinforcement training relies heavily on *food* which is the most easily delivered and predictable primary reward.

Primary reinforcers are inherently cyclical in nature, where the value changes with experience. Thus, relying on any particular and singular reinforcer to drive behavior is not optimal since positive reinforcers are especially prone to satiation. **Satiation** describes the condition of having had enough of a particular reinforcer and no longer wanting it. Conversely, **deprivation** is the technique of withholding something in order to drive its reinforcing value up.

The satiation point is where the reinforcer has become neutral, and consequently it cannot be used to drive behavior. Further exposure to the stimulus at this point can drive its value to become punishing.

Punishing ———————— Neutral ——————— Reinforcing

Satiation Point

We usually refer to a 'satiation point' with things that are primary reinforcers and as such, whose values generally rebound cyclically over time. For secondary reinforcers or punishers, a similar phenomenon also occurs and is usually just called desensitization (for more on this point see Chapter 7).

To avoid the satiation of any given primary reinforcer, it is optimal to utilize as many as are manageable to provide. Trying different food and drink options, prepared in a variety of manners will help reduce the satiation effect. Since this can be a relatively limited selection in some cases, depending on the species, it behooves the savvy trainer to also condition as many secondary (or learned) reinforcers to be used as possible, as well.

Perhaps the most powerful of the *conditioned secondary reinforcers* is the bridge stimulus (see Chapter 4). In some respects, it holds for animals an analogous value that humans might place on money. Being associated with a wide range of reinforcement that follows it, the bridge accumulates a value far above other secondary reinforcers. Of course, other secondary reinforcers are also very useful to have in the tool chest of available motivators. Examples of commonly conditioned secondary reinforcers are applause from the performance audience, being petted by the trainer (often called tactile reinforcement), and playing games such as with sprayed water or with toys.

Figure 17: Trainer Jennifer Gale using conditioned tactile reinforcement to provide therapeutic massage to an arthritic raccoon at CuriOdyssey.

(Photo credit: Rachael Rufino.)

I should note that for a few species, **tactile reinforcement** could be considered a primary motive. Dogs and cats most notably do not generally have to be conditioned to like being touched by people. It is important to realize that for most other animals, however, this is not the case. Human beings have deliberately bred dogs and cats to be motivated by human presence and human touch. Generally, most other animals have to be conditioned to enjoy touch from a person. Depending on the species this can be quite easy, as it is with dolphins, or with many other exotic animals, like sea lions, quite difficult.

The process of conditioning any secondary reinforcer will generally be done through classical conditioning as previously described. If the stimulus does not start out at a neutral value (*i.e.*: it is a punisher), it will be necessary to also first desensitize the animal to the stimulus before the reinforcement value can be conditioned. This is an especially prevalent problem in the conditioning of tactile reinforcement with many species. Great pains should be taken to do this carefully because the initial punishing value of the stimulus can easily cause aggression. I will describe, at length, the mechanisms of desensitization in the following chapter.

Principles of reinforcement

The delivery of reinforcement should be expected to affect behavior based on **The Matching Law,** which states that the effort expended on any given behavior will be matched with its history of reinforcement (in a given environment). Thus, the more something is reinforced the more likely the animal will be eager to perform that behavior (this is also a property of the effects of rehearsal to be discussed later in this chapter). Hopefully, this reality is self-evident and requires no fancy psychological lingo to explain. If you doubt this idea, it is only because in any given situation you will not understand all of the motivators at play that are driving the behavior. Thus, if you can't understand why your dog doesn't sit after so many treats for sitting, it may be merely that you haven't recognized how valuable the instinctive drive to investigate all the new and interesting smells around him is. To ultimately overcome these motivational juxtapositions, it is again helpful to have as many different motivators to drive your goal behavior as possible, not the least of which is your relationship to the animal, as I have repeatedly stressed. These motivators can add up and provide the needed edge to influence the animal to perform as desired, and often this extra push makes all the difference.

It is also important to realize that *behaviors themselves often have either learned or instinctive values to the animal and as such can be reinforcers.* If an animal likes doing a behavior, it can be used to reinforce another behavior you are trying to encourage, by delivering the opportunity to do the 'favored' activity as a consequence to good behavior. This idea is called **Premack's principle** which states that of any pair of responses or activities in which an individual freely engages, the more frequent (salient) one will reinforce the less frequent one. So you can use a frequently performed, familiar or 'favorite' behavior as a reward for a more difficult, less frequent or less well-loved behavior. Put more simply, your child is permitted to watch TV as a reward for having done her homework, or the animal is released to play after having performed well.

Since varying amounts of reinforcement produce varying amounts of effort, the principle of **differential reinforcement** naturally follows. As we have already discussed (see Differential reinforcement stimuli in Chapter 4), the concept of differential reinforcement is that *the net value of the reinforcement given is related to the quality of the behavior.* Differential reinforcement can be a very useful tool to shape and refine behavior by reinforcing differently one response over another, either by using a higher value reinforcer or greater amounts of reinforcement.

Greater quantities of reinforcement are more properly referred to as **magnitude reinforcement,** or, more commonly, jackpotting or bonusing. Jackpotting is when a large quantity of reinforcement is given to accentuate an especially excellent performance.

Many training systems incorporate a form of bonusing in their dictated reinforcement strategy, in part due to another important principle called **The Lottery Principle.** This principle largely explains why people gamble, for instance. The Lottery Principle states that if there is potentially a large payoff, even if it is very occasional, this will drive persistent effort of behavior. This works because sometimes you make little or nothing, but sometimes you may really cash in! The big payoff possibility is better than the knowledge of a constant reward. Thus, periodically using a magnitude reinforcement strategy can leverage this lottery principle to increase the motivation of the animal to perform overall.

In addition, magnitude reinforcement is a form of differential reinforcement, if it is used to reinforce a particular desirable topography of a behavior. Although it is not necessary to utilize differential reinforcement to condition behavior, it is certainly one of the most expressive tools to communicate the precise form, type or variant of a given behavior that the trainer desires.

Nearly the opposite of differential reinforcement is the important principle of **balance of reinforcement**. Balance of reinforcement is important when there are particular environments that the trainer would like the animal to freely move between. In order for an animal to desire to shift environments such as into a cage or a second den or enclosure, the reinforcing value of these environments needs to be reasonably equivalent. Thus, for shifting or gating animals in zoos for example, it is important to recognize how the reinforcement is available and distributed between the various locations. Difficulty moving an animal into a cage or trailer, for example, is often negated by making that location exclusively associated with a favorite food opportunity and, as such, increasing its reinforcement value to being more equivalent to the larger environments. Ultimately, in order to gate animals freely between circumstances, the trainer should offer similar reinforcement in each environment or, alternatively, compensating reinforcement if the environment itself has reinforcing properties beyond what the trainer provides. *If an animal is unwilling to shift easily between environments, the trainer should suspect a balance of reinforcement problem.*

Schedules of reinforcement

Rules governing the delivery of reinforcement are called *Schedules of Reinforcement* by psychologists and they generally fall into two basic categories – continuous and intermittent. Professional trainers often strongly prefer one or the other of these schedules, so it is worth comparing the pros and cons of each reinforcement delivery strategy.

> ### The benefits and drawbacks of different schedules of reinforcement

Continuous reinforcement. In *continuous reinforcement,* every desired behavior is reinforced. The trainer always reinforces every performance in some tangible way. Continuous reinforcement has the advantage of a strong drive for the immediate behavior producing *highly reliable and consistent performance.* As such, continuous reinforcement is generally the *preferred strategy for creating new behaviors,* where intermittent reinforcement might confuse or delay an understanding and enthusiasm for the newly developing operant. Additionally, behaviors under continuous reinforcement tend to be highly stereotypical or identical in presentation. However, continuous reinforcement also tends to produce behavior that is *less persistent* and will more easily exhaust or extinguish.

Additionally, the use of continuous reinforcement comes with the increased *risk of schedule-induced aggression* should the promised reward not be forth coming for some reason. Schedule-induced aggression, in this case, occurs because the reinforcement is essentially guaranteed by the schedule. Thus, if for any reason the operant is performed and not reinforced, the animal can feel intensely frustrated. Reinforcement may be skipped potentially due to the distraction of the trainer or due to a criterion change that the trainer has imposed that the animal is unaware of. In either case, the potential for the animal to feel a kind of righteous indignation is understandable. This flash of frustration in dangerous animals can easily become aggression. This type of aggression is of less concern in newly forming behaviors than with well-rehearsed 'known' operants whose reinforcement can be expected based on a long history. Additionally, continuous reinforcement *limits the options available for differential reinforcement* since every response is reinforced; however the reinforcement type and amount can still be varied as long as each response is reinforced.

Intermittent reinforcement. *Intermittent reinforcement* is the opposite of continuous reinforcement, in that not every correct performance is reinforced. One of the advantages of an intermittent schedule is the variety of ways it can be employed. Intermittent reinforcement can be provided after either a fixed or variable allotment of behaviors (called the ratio) or time (the interval), with either a fixed or variable reinforcement type or amount. Obviously this leaves the trainer with *more options of reinforcement.*

One of the best aspects of intermittent schedules is that they tend to resist 'extinction,' which is a decline in the frequency of behavior resulting from a lack of reinforcement. As such, they *tend to create more persistent, long-lasting behavior* and effort.

Fixed schedules tend to lead to more choppy response rates as predictable reinforcement makes the non-reinforced responses less energized and enthusiastic. Variable schedules create more moderate but consistent effort. All behavior on intermittent schedules tends to have *less consistently identically performed operants.* Extended reinforcement ratios or intervals can also lead to ratio strain if not managed properly. 'Ratio strain' describes the dampening effect on motivation as reinforcement becomes less predictable and associated with the behavioral effort. **Too much effort with too limited reinforcement is the slippery slope of intermittent reinforcement schedules.** If the responses are not reinforced with reliable enough frequency, the entire motivation of the animal may crash, even if it is still motivated for the reinforcer being offered. To avoid this ratio strain, the trainer is wise to maintain careful use of regular reinforcement and avoid the *pitfalls of overuse* of intermittent schedules.

A mixed approach. Clearly, both continuous and intermittent schedules have significant pros and cons, and I see no particular reason why these strategies cannot be used alternately depending on the trainer's objectives. These schedules of reinforcement are usually intended to describe only primary motivators; however, with the inclusion of a variety of reinforcement types, some of these psychological constructs become more clouded. For example, I generally reinforce each correct behavior with a bridge which is maintained with variable amounts of other reinforcers. From a certain point of view, this is a continuous reinforcement strategy since the bridge is a highly motivating secondary reinforcer. However, since the bridge itself is not reinforced by another reinforcer on each occurrence, the advantages of intermittent reinforcement such as behavioral persistence and highly nuanced differential reinforcement can also be leveraged. For example, I generally use continuous reinforcement with variable reinforcement type for creating novel behaviors, and switch to variable ratio with variable type to maintain behavioral persistence, avoid schedule-induced aggression and the lethargy of overly predictable reinforcement. Other trainers prefer to maintain continuous reinforcement to avoid the risks of ratio strain and the variability of response type but use variable type and amount of reinforcement to enhance the use of differential reinforcement and lessen the general satiation of reinforcers. Many people feel that novices should not be trusted with intermittent schedules because they will tend to abuse them and cause ratio-strain easily. I think that may depend a great deal on the 'novice.'

Reduced response effort

As we have already discussed (see Changing the value of the motivator in this chapter), one way to artificially drive up the frequency of behavior is to make it easier to do. In this sense, it costs less to perform and lower value reinforcers can be used more easily to motivate it. This idea is called, 'reducing the response effort', and it is an important consideration to increase the likelihood of behavior. This falls into the category of setting the animal up for success by making the operant more desirable. This is often very important in preliminary approximations of behaviors, where lower response effort enables the animal to perform the operant easily and then later the reinforcement history can further support the behavior as the response effort is increased. This can be done by leading the animal into the necessary posture or location before asking for the behavior to be presented. Lowering the necessary response effort will help maintain behavior when the available reinforcement is low in value, satiating, or overwhelmed by higher value competing motivators (overshadowed). It is essentially *a mechanism of enhancing the effective reinforcement value of performing the behavior (by subtracting a cost).*

Negative reinforcement

Negative reinforcement is, on its own, one of the main operant techniques, but it can also be associated with the technique of manipulation. As we have already described in great detail, negatively reinforced behavior occurs by avoiding something aversive (see Chapter 5). The negatively reinforced animal learns to perform those behaviors that successfully remove an aversive stimulus or situation. Negative reinforcement applies to a particular behavior, and there are often both negative and positive reinforcements influencing different behaviors in a given situation. For a classic example, a baby is crying. The older sister finds the crying punishing, and she tries different things. When she picks up the baby, the baby stops crying. The older sister learns to pick up the baby faster. So the behavior of picking up the baby has increased in frequency or it has been reinforced; it has been *negatively* reinforced by the removal of the crying. The baby has negatively reinforced its sister. The baby, meanwhile, has been *positively* reinforced for crying by being picked up (and is more likely to cry to be picked up in the future). The sister has positively reinforced the baby. For an animal example, a sheep dog approaches its sheep. The dog is frightening to the sheep, so they move away into their pen. The sheep dog stops chasing the sheep when they move to go into the pen. The sheep have been negatively reinforced for entering the pen. Incidentally, the dog is usually trained by positive reinforcement from both the shepherd and the satisfying movement of the sheep.

➤ The benefits and drawbacks of reinforcement

Generally speaking, there is really very little downside to positive reinforcement. I know that many proponents of negative reinforcement dislike the possible side effect of attraction-type aggression with positive reinforcement, especially food. Since the trainer is in possession of desired stimuli, the animal may be tempted to aggress in order to steal the reinforcer. As we will discuss (see Chapter 8), there are many ways to mitigate this issue, and in all likelihood this is a fundamental problem of captive animal maintenance, since feeding the animal is an inherent necessity. Fortunately, attraction-type aggression is among the most easily addressed forms of aggression. Learning to cope with aggression difficulties is one of the fundamental elements of this text, and necessary for handling larger or more dangerous individuals; not being able to do so will severely limit the use of many of the techniques contained herein.

Regardless of the limited risk of attraction-based aggression; most fundamentally, associating yourself with desirable stimuli will *enhance your relationship* and generally increase the animal's motivation to work with you. This advantage cannot be expressed strongly enough. ***There is no technique more promising to promote cooperation and well-adjusted animals than the use of positive reinforcement***. Thus, I endeavor to incorporate it wherever possible in all my protocols.

We have already covered the benefits and drawbacks of negative reinforcement - please see that section in Chapter 5.

REHEARSAL

The act of repeating something is inherently reinforcing. *Rehearsal or repetition of a behavior increases its frequency.* Thus, the more you have done something for whatever reason, the more likely you are to do it again. This is fundamental to all learning and has to do with neurologic connections being formed and enhanced in the brain through repeated use. Learning takes time, and time fixes learning. The effects of rehearsal are where habits and superstitious behaviors come from. The more you do something, the more likely you are to do that behavior again because of its long association with reinforcement and, according to the Matching Law, the more effort you will put toward it.

Behavior that has been rehearsed is always likely to occur again. For this reason you do not want bad behavior to be practiced (see Prevention in this chapter)! Due to the effects of rehearsal, it is much preferable to train things slowly and correctly with minimal practice of incorrect response types. This ultimately increases the chance of the correct response and decreases the chance of incorrect responses being demonstrated.

Desirable behaviors need to be practiced repeatedly to increase their future chances to generalize to other situations. *Generalization describes the ability of an animal to associate a behavior with a variety of S^Ds, or functionally, in a variety of situations or contexts.* This quality of a learned response is highly dependent on experience or rehearsal. Being able to make analogies between existing behaviors and other similar behaviors is very useful to both the trainer and the animal. For example, an animal is taught to target its nose on a beaded pole (called a target pole); however, now the trainer would like the animal to target on something else, for example, the animal's own body. By generalizing the target concept from touching the pole to touching their own wing, the trainer creates a new behavior of saluting. Generalizations become easier with increased familiarity with the operant and its function.

METHODS THAT DRIVE AN ANIMAL TO *NOT DO* A BEHAVIOR: Punishment And Prevention

Eliminating unwanted behavior is perhaps one of the most important and difficult issues of behavior modification. Since the animal is freely performing the operant, this subject is largely one of convincing or motivating them to choose differently. The practical tools to discourage behavior can be reduced down to *two primary means to drive someone not to do an undesirable behavior: punishment and prevention.*

PUNISHMENT

As you are, by now, familiar, a punisher is anything that has the effect of lowering the frequency of the behavior it follows. *Often the behavior is merely suppressed; rarely is it eliminated.* There are two reasons for this. The first is that the behavior in question is somehow being maintained through reinforcement because it is accomplishing something that the animal seeks. The second reason that behavior is hard to eliminate is the effect of rehearsal; once learned, there is always a slippery slope back to a previously rehearsed behavior. Thus, having well-behaved animals involves the proactive, prudent prevention of problem behaviors, as we will shortly discuss.

Punishment is generally inherently aversive. However, although all punishers decrease behavioral frequency, not all punishment is undesirable. For example, a good set of directions is effectively a punishment to the previous behavior of wandering lost, but few would lament this consequence. Thus, some forms of communication-based punishment may not be undesirable. But of course, most punishment works because it is an outcome that is unwanted. All punishment is applied to behaviors the trainer does not want to happen. Like reinforcement, punishment can be both positive and negative.

Positive punishment

Positive punishment is anything added to the environment that lowers the frequency of the behavior it (immediately) follows. Like reinforcement, punishment is relative, not absolute, since it depends entirely on the perspective of the individual. That said, however, many positive punishers are aversive stimuli that are intrinsically painful, obnoxious, repulsive, and/or scary to the individual in question. If they can be seen to do this innately - such as stimuli that cause pain or injury - these would be considered primary punishers. Secondary punishers are learned stimuli that decrease behavioral frequencies such as the no reward marker, the redirection stimulus (see Chapter 4) or a red stoplight for example. Debatably, most stimuli that cause fear are learned by their association with painful experiences in the past. As such, most punishers are actually secondary, not primary.

Physical punishment is anything that is done that contacts the body of the animal or is tactilely perceived which lowers the frequency of the behavior it follows. This type of punishment has the strongest potential to cause fear and aggression.

Any experience where an animal is restrained for medication or treatment amounts to a form of physical punishment. While the restraint involved may be merely the operant technique of manipulation, the injection or intubation serves no behavioral goal and is simply punishing. Most medical procedures done on most captive animals are performed this way. Despite the best intentions of the humans, to the extent that they cause discomfort, these procedures also amount to physical punishment unless the animal is willingly consenting and chooses to accept the procedure. Regrettably, since the animal can neither predict nor prevent these procedures based on any merit of its own behavior, these punishments would be considered 'random' from the animal's point of view. While these procedures are understandable and necessary in many situations, that does not change the reality that the animal has no way of understanding their benefit and may justifiably resent and fear the situation greatly.

From the animal's perspective, this random physical punishment is the most dangerous and stressful type of punishment because the individual has no way to predict the outcome, nor a mechanism to avoid it through their behavior. Animals in these situations will often learn to avoid whatever behavior or situation preceded the procedure, and potentially the individuals involved.

It is very possible to train animals to cooperate with almost any type of medical procedure, voluntarily, using the methods described in this text, by investing the time and energy in the necessary desensitization and behavioral conditioning. This practice has become increasingly prevalent in recent history in the exotic animal field, originating primarily with marine mammals being conditioned for everything from blood samples to dental extractions. This trend is certainly ideal, in my opinion, since there is nothing good that comes from random physical punishment. All the worst disadvantages of punishment are magnified by its random application (see later in this chapter for Benefits and drawbacks of punishment).

Negative punishment

Negative punishment sounds terrible but is actually the more benign form of the two. Negative punishment lowers the frequency of the behavior it follows by the removal of a reinforcer. Common examples of negative punishment include grounding or time-outs.

A *time-out (TO)* is a period of reduced stimulus and no response from a trainer. Used properly, a TO is the removal of the opportunity for reinforcement. This can be by placing the individual in a situation where there are limited stimuli (and hopefully no reinforcers) or by removing the trainer or teacher's attention for a period of time. Leaving the animal in a reinforcing environment, like a graze field for a horse, would not qualify as a time-out.

A word of caution: time-outs can be dangerous to use if your animal does not value your presence. In this case, instead of punishing the animal, you are, in fact, reinforcing them by leaving. For this reason many people fear to use TOs with animals, since they risk accidentally reinforcing *the behavior they are trying to punish*. This risk is greatly reduced if the trainer has been able to maintain a highly positive relationship with the animal by careful decisions about technique use, and by choosing to associate with predominately reinforcing stimuli. Thus, the ability to utilize TOs effectively is just one more reason to value and preserve the training *relationship*.

There are several magnitudes of time-out from very brief to very prolonged depending on the trainer's preference and the severity of the behavior in question.

Very popular in the marine mammal community is something Sea World has controversially termed the **Least Reinforcing Scenario or the LRS**. The LRS is a two to three second period of no attention or reaction from the trainer in response to an undesired behavior to reduce its frequency. The trainer should suddenly freeze (completely cease all movement and sound) and wait utterly unresponsive while silently counting the three second duration. If the animal reacts to this 'non-stimulus' stimulus with attentive behavior, this attentive behavior may be followed by reinforcement on a variable schedule. Despite the use of the word 'reinforcing' in this term, this is clearly a negative punisher that acts as a cue for attention which can then be reinforced. The LRS has many properties in common with the redirection stimulus (RS) except that it lacks a deliberate stimulus and is only associated with the differential reinforcement of attention as opposed to any other desirable behavior. Despite being a negative punisher, by definition, it is understandable to include the term 'reinforcement' in this concept since it clearly can effectively lead to reinforcement, again very similar to the RS. Unlike the RS, the LRS unfortunately lacks any mechanism to draw the animal's attention to its use. So, in many cases, it will fail to tag the undesirable behavior or even be recognized by the animal at all.

Standard time-outs tend to occur for various durations, usually just a few minutes of time, depending on the situation. For children they are often the same duration in minutes as their age, for example. With animals I find it helpful to distinguish between these relatively brief TOs that might occur within a training session, and a more dramatic punishment where the trainer will not return within the period of a standard training session (at least 20 minutes for my purposes) and often won't return for the entire day. These lengthy time-outs are called *Extended Time-outs or ETOs* and are generally used in cases where the animal has displayed some form of aggressive behavior which can be accompanied by an adrenaline rush. As will be discussed in the chapter on Aggression, it is suboptimal to interact with animals that are under the influence of adrenaline, as it will color their responses and generally make them more dangerous and reactionary. For this reason it may be preferred to avoid interaction with the animal after an aggressive encounter. Rarely, ETOs are also used for non-aggressive behaviors that the trainer feels warrant a prolonged break. Through deprivation, the TO will also have the potential effect of increasing the value of the reinforcers being offered. However, prolonged deprivation amounts to abuse, therefore an ETO should not be used for this unethical purpose.

➤ *The benefits and drawbacks of punishment*

Correctly applied punishment will be of moderate intensity and immediately follow the undesirable behavior. Optimally, this will be on the first presentation of the behavior in question. Repeated scientific research with both animals and people has demonstrated that ramping up punishment, instead of using moderately high intensity on first presentation, is a formula for creating tolerance of the punishment, and should be avoided. This is effectively a desensitization phenomenon that results from incremental increasing exposure to the stimulus ultimately causing little or no reaction to it (see Chapter 7 for more on this). Thus, for punishment to be effective, it is best to use moderate intensity, so as to have a strong impact, but not maximum intensity which might cause sensitization and extreme behavioral trauma. Additionally, continuous schedules of punishment are drastically more effective than intermittent schedules. It is prudent to attempt to punish every performance of the target behavior to effectively eliminate or suppress it. Consistency is key.

Furthermore, the most effective punishment is offered in conjunction with an alternative behavioral option, ideally one that involves the reinforcer that the behavior is driven by. For punishment to be most effective then, the animal is given a choice to perform an alternate behavior that will result in reinforcement or the undesirable behavior that will result in punishment. **Choice and understanding are the central elements that distinguish good punishment from bad.** Bad punishment may cause severe behavioral backlash such as aggression or depression, while optimal punishment will cause successful calm reduction of the undesirable behavior. This comes from choice and understanding leading to an empowering sense of control. As we have already discussed (see Chapter 3), control is fundamental to the needs of all creatures.

Unlike many tools, the use of *punishment can be associated with disastrous results* including aggression, depression, behavioral suppression, learned helplessness, escape or avoidance behavior. Additionally, the event will be associated with the user and will therefore *damage (potentially severely) the relationship* with the animal. These risks are very serious and must be weighed carefully before any punishment is used. As I have already stated, the most debilitating form of punishment is random, so avoiding unpredictable punishment should be the goal of every good trainer.

Some people fear the effects of punishment so much that they claim it is ineffective. This is simply incorrect. Contrary to what is currently popular (a complete opposition to the technique), Matson, Van Houten and numerous others have demonstrated that there are both effective and ineffective punishments, and many treatments are far more successful if they include some punishment contingencies. Additionally, it is worth noting that several studies by Hanley and others have demonstrated that, in children with severe behavioral problems, punishment contingencies (in addition to reinforcement ones) are more preferred by the children involved than extinction contingencies (non-reinforcement). This preference for systems that include punishment is hypothesized to be because, in those systems, the children understand both what they should and also what they *should not* be doing. This gives them a greater opportunity to receive reinforcement.

However, determining when punishment may be more helpful than harmful presents a challenge not worth the risk for many trainers. For this reason, *many modern trainers do not recommend punishment be used, especially by novices.* Ironically, successful use of punishment has the tendency to reinforce the user into further implementation and dependence on this form of behavior modification. This self-perpetuating nature of effective punishment can quickly lead to routine aversive interactions that severely damage the relationship and threaten the entire motivation of the animal to perform for the trainer. So at best, punishment must be used with the utmost caution and restraint, and never for vindictive or other personal motives.

PREVENTION - AVOIDANCE OF REHEARSAL

Where punishment is a direct and oppositional force that provides aversion to performing a behavior, the techniques of what I call 'prevention' are approaches to circumvent the undesired behavior. These techniques seek to alter, or ideally, eliminate the antecedent circumstances to the unwanted behavior, or failing that, to alter or eliminate the driving reinforcement consequence.

The easiest way to have a well behaved animal is to never allow them to walk the 'dark path' or practice behaviors that would be detrimental in the long or the short term. This is due to the profound effects of rehearsal on behavior. Once something has been reinforced (rehearsed), it is always lurking in the background, ready to resurface as a behavior. Preventing this process from taking root is the most dependable key to having a well-adjusted animal. Thus, *understanding where an animal (according to species) might make mistakes, and preventing them from rehearsing disadvantageous behaviors, is one of the most advanced ways of training.* I believe that true professional trainers distinguish themselves by this method frequently: understanding where the animal may go wrong and instead steering them, during their critical early life development, away from problem areas of behavior. The result is well-trained and adaptive creatures that will rarely consider classic misbehavior because they have grown up their whole lives not doing so. This *proactive prevention is routinely accomplished by controlling the environment or situation by preventing or altering the antecedent* using the techniques of redirection and desensitization. Alternatively, but *less effectively, behavior can also be circumvented by eliminating or altering the consequence* by using the techniques of extinction or increased response effort (see Table 1).

TECHNIQUES TO PREVENT REHEARSAL OF AN UNDESIRABLE BEHAVIOR

	Antecedent	Consequence
Alter Value	DESENSITIZATION Reduce value of whatever is driving the behavior	INCREASED RESPONSE EFFORT Where cost of effort significantly diminishes the value of the consequence
Eliminate	REDIRECTION Prior to behavior onset perform an incompatible / different behavior	EXTINCTION Ensuring no possibility of reinforcement for the behavior

Table 1: The four basic methods to prevent rehearsal of an undesirable behavior by either altering or avoiding either the antecedents or the consequences.

Redirection: Prevention of the antecedent

Redirection is a technique to eliminate behaviors through reinforcement of alternatives; it functionally prevents the antecedent of the unwanted behavior by imposing a substitute behavior prior to its presentation. Thus, if an animal is likely to do something undesirable, you set up another behavior which is reinforced, so it does that instead. I often think of this rather tongue-in-cheek as the "Look, there's Elvis" technique: following the old ploy of trying to get someone to become distracted elsewhere. This technique primarily falls into two basic options:

- *DRI: Differential Reinforcement of Incompatible behavior* (a specific behavior)
- *DRO: Differential Reinforcement of Other behavior* (reinforcing for any other behavior than the unwanted behavior)

In DRI, a specific alternative behavior is chosen and reinforced when presented before the onset of the undesirable behavior. This behavior should be one that cannot be done simultaneous to the undesirable behavior. Thus, it is called 'incompatible' since its presentation should be mutually exclusive to the undesirable behavior. It is possible to either scan and capture the incompatible, or more effectively, to cue it, if it is an already conditioned behavior. Targets or stations are often chosen as incompatible behaviors. For example, when a trainer is coming and going, the animal is asked to station at a distance to redirect it from rushing the gate. Holding an object in one's mouth (which is incompatible with biting) would be another common example of DRI.

In DRO, the trainer opportunistically chooses to reinforce any behavior that is not the undesirable behavior. This could include choosing to reinforce so-called 'no behavior', although technically there is no such thing. Generally this is accomplished by pure scan and capture, and the trainer will be looking for the smallest unit of any other behavior to reinforce (see Chapter 5). These preliminary approximations can be as simple as reinforcing the animal for merely looking away or even just pausing in their behavior, anything that is not the undesirable behavior. Thus, DRO is not necessarily as contrary to the undesirable as DRI and may therefore not be as strong a deterrent to its presentation. Or worse, there is the risk that the animal might get reinforced for the DRO while simultaneously performing the undesirable behavior.

It is worth noting that the previously described Redirection Stimulus is effectively a cue for DRI or DRO and works to enhance the use of these techniques by asking the animal to perform an alternate behavior (see Chapter 4).

➤ The benefits and drawbacks of redirection

In terms of techniques to eliminate or suppress unwanted behavior, *redirection is clearly optimal wherever possible*. This is for two reasons. The first is that, done correctly, redirection effectively prevents *any* rehearsal history of the undesirable behavior, whereas punishment, extinction, and response effort involve consequence to the undesirable presentation, resulting in at least some rehearsal. Alternatively, as we will discuss, desensitization techniques can be very time consuming and may be difficult depending on the driving stimulus.

The second benefit of redirection is that it is, essentially, a technique that manages to use reinforcement to eliminate bad behavior. Thus, the trainer enhances the relationship by associating with the reinforcer(s), while reducing the target behavior - a great accomplishment in my opinion. The downside to redirection is that it can *be a bit time consuming and off topic* to constantly be forced to maintain alternative behaviors in order to suppress unwanted ones. For this reason, some trainers may choose to incorporate punishment with the use of redirection to stack the deck in favor of the alternative without as much maintenance of the DRO or DRI.

Desensitization: Lowering the value of the antecedent

One possible method of altering the frequency of an undesirable behavior is to change the value of any stimulus or situation that might be driving the behavior. This is primarily the subject of competing motivations and all of Chapter 7 is devoted to this subject. However, a brief description of the techniques is outlined here.

Habituation and counter-conditioning are typically used to reduce the value of an antecedent stimulus or scenario that is causing avoidance-type, undesirable behaviors. Let's imagine you have a horse that is refusing to enter a stall due to the presence of plastic bags (that cannot be removed) in the environment. The plastic bags are an antecedent to the undesirable behavior of bucking and running. What must be done, in this case, is to concentrate on changing the value of the plastic bags, and then the behavior of bucking will reduce.

Habituation employs prolonged exposure to desensitize the stimulus, such as tying up a plastic bag to blow harmlessly in the wind near the animal's enclosure. Eventually the horse, who was at first concerned with plastic bags, will come to ignore them. Alternatively, counter-conditioning, as we have discussed (see Chapter 4), uses reinforcement to change the punishing value of the disruptive stimulus. In this case, that could include feeding the animal near the plastic bag or even from it, for example. The applications of these techniques of desensitization are designed to reduce the antecedent stimulus (*i.e.:* the plastic bag), and in doing so, neutralize its salience and resulting drive of the undesirable behavior.

Extinction: Prevention of the consequence

Extinction is the halting of reinforcement for a particular behavior that was previously reinforced. Thus, where redirection seeks to prevent the antecedent to behavior, extinction seeks to eliminate the consequence (between them effectively addressing both reasons for behavior to occur). Technically, extinction is largely a peculiar psychological construct where behavior in the laboratory is first reinforced and later refused reinforcement deliberately.

In a practical sense, since few people would deliberately condition a behavior and then attempt to eliminate it, extinction is the scenario in which the accidental reinforcer that is promoting an unwanted behavior is uniquely identifiable, and therefore can be withheld to suppress the behavior in question. This obviously requires an understanding of what is driving the behavior, and the ability to control that drive. From a functional standpoint, most typically extinction is the specific case of 'no response' when presented with an undesirable behavior.

In slight contrast, *negative punishment* occurs when an undesired behavior is demonstrated and available reinforcement is therefore removed. It may not be apparent what is reinforcing the undesired behavior or it may be that the reinforcer is internal. However, the removal of other reinforcers will suppress the unwanted behavior, even if those reinforcers are not inherently driving the behavior in the first place, so long as the reinforcers being removed are of greater value than that which is driving the behavior.

Thus, extinction and negative punishment are related, but not identical ideas, although both techniques impose the cost of withholding of reinforcement in order to suppress unwanted behavior. In the case of extinction, this occurs through no response from the trainer, whereas in the case of negative punishment this occurs through the removal of other reinforcers. Thus, extinction could be considered a particular form of negative punishment in my view, but this is not the conventional perspective, so I have chosen to present it as a separate approach to avoid confusing the reader.

Putting undesirable behavior on stimulus control and spontaneous recovery

There has supposedly been some success in putting unwanted behavior on stimulus control and then never again requesting that behavior, but I have never heard of a verified case of this technique being truly effective at eliminating the behavior in the long term. This is because, regardless of the extinction that the trainer is applying to the behavior, there was originally, and presumably still is, some personal motive that the animal had for performing the behavior in the first place. Far from eliminating this incentive, if anything, the reinforcement and rehearsal history can only serve to enhance the long-term likelihood of this behavior.

The phenomenon of behaviors going through extinction only to later re-emerge is called *spontaneous recovery*. For example, a parrot is taught to repeat after its owner when a gesture is made. The parrot demonstrates this behavior well for some time. However, after a period with no reinforcement for this behavior, the parrot stops responding to the gesture. Later, for no apparent reason, the parrot one day begins to talk again after seeing the gesture. This is the process of spontaneous recovery, and it makes true extinction always uncertain. So the technique of deliberately conditioning and then attempting to extinguish undesirable behavior is at least fraught with pitfalls, if not completely counter-productive.

➤ The benefits and drawbacks of extinction

In the real world, *the savvy trainer should avoid, at all costs, deliberately creating behavior they later want to eliminate*. The effects of rehearsal and reinforcement are too powerful, as already discussed. Therefore, most of the practical use of extinction comes in the form of a common and proactive strategy consistent with the concept - *when in doubt it is generally wise to default to ignoring unwanted behavior*. This reaction (or rather, non-reaction) is intended to prevent the accidental reinforcement of the unwanted behavior by the trainer's reaction, which might provide reinforcement in the form of attention. Even if the behavior is not being maintained by the trainer's attention, the trainer's attention might still reinforce it further, making matters worse. Thus, the idea of non-reaction is warranted until further analysis can be applied to best decide how to approach the problem. If the trainer's reaction is the reinforcement that maintains the unwanted behavior, this will be demonstrated by the behavior undergoing extinction and therefore being suppressed or eliminated. If, on the other hand, the trainer's attention is not what is promoting the undesirable behavior, it would be expected, in that case, to expand and continue unless the trainer enhanced the technique by further negative punishment (such as leaving, for example), redirection or increased response effort (see Increased response effort in this chapter).

There is an interesting phenomenon associated with a behavior undergoing extinction called the *extinction burst* which can actually be used to enhance existing behaviors. The extinction burst describes the animal's last ditch attempt at increased effort toward the target behavior being extinguished. The animal, having been previously reinforced for this behavior, responds to the lack of reinforcement with a surge of effort ('the extinction burst'). This type of increased effort is a component of all intermittent strategies of reinforcement (in a sense the behavior is initially on an intermittent schedule prior to extended non-reinforcement causing extinction). During this burst, the animal can be expected to put in desperate and often variable effort toward the behavior that had previously paid off. For example, during discrimination training, an animal who is having trouble learning to recognize the difference between several different S^Ds corresponding to various similar flips and jumps, may start to demonstrate extremely high jumps of the wrong type after receiving no reinforcement on prior trials. This effect can be both terribly sad to watch and oddly useful to creating new variants of the original operant to choose from. This is a somewhat mixed bag that must be considered carefully. Generally, using an extinction burst to push through to a new level of an old operant is a technique that should be used only by advanced trainers, and done with a good deal of caution. The extinction burst is by nature a frustrating and frantic experience for the animal, and not one that enhances the relationship with the trainer. The frustration can easily become so great as to lead to aggression or depression, as extinction nears and ratio strain presents. Threading this needle and using this technique sparingly is necessary to avoid damaging the animal's overall enthusiasm for the learning process.

Increased response effort: Lowering the value of the consequence

The final technique of avoidance of the unwanted behavior involves the reduction of the reinforcement value of the consequence through an imposed cost to acquire whatever is driving (attraction-type) undesirable behavior. If it is possible to make access to the reinforcer that is driving your unwanted behavior more challenging, you effectively impose an additional subtractive cost from whatever salience it had that was driving the behavior. For example, a dog is barking at a squirrel in a tree. The barking is the undesired behavior in this case (being driven by the squirrel). Moving the dog so that it is farther away from the tree will increase the response cost to get to the squirrel and reduce the barking behavior.

This response cost minimizes the value of the reinforcer driving the behavior, such that other reinforcers (or punishers) may more easily overcome it and consequently limit the behavior. This is a way to avoid or alter the consequence. Increasing response cost can be as simple as making the reinforcer more distant from the animal or making more behavior necessary before gaining access to the reinforcer. Trainers regularly remove animals from distractions to create this effect, but other forms of environmental manipulation can similarly accomplish increasing response effort such as working in protected contact (see Chapter 8).

MOTIVATION, *IN SUMMARY*

Motivation is the complex subject of what drives behavior. It is unique to each individual at a particular moment in time and space. There are two fundamental drives, reinforcers and punishers, each having an opposite effect on the behavior it follows. Reinforcement and rehearsal are the two basic mechanisms to encourage desirable behavior, while punishment and prevention are the two basic mechanisms to discourage unwanted behavior. To create desirable behavior, techniques from Communication should be combined with motivational tools to encourage behavior. To avoid undesirable behavior, the antecedent is optimally prevented or altered, or alternatively, the consequence can be prevented or reduced. It is best to prevent undesirable behavior to eliminate rehearsal history and escape the downsides of punishment. Punishment should be used with caution and, when used, it is optimal to use moderate intensity, immediate punishment on each presentation of the undesirable behavior. Among punishers, negative punishers are the most relationship-friendly techniques, while random punishment is the most damaging. Further sub-categories of motivation are the special cases of competing motivations: desensitization and aggression which will be covered in detail in the upcoming chapters.

METHODS THAT DRIVE AN ANIMAL TO DO A BEHAVIOR
- Reinforcement
  - Positive or negative
  - Primary or secondary
- Rehearsal of behavior

METHODS THAT DRIVE AN ANIMAL NOT TO DO A BEHAVIOR
- Punishment
  - Positive or negative
  - Primary or secondary
- Prevention
  - Redirection
  - Desensitization
  - Extinction
  - Increased Response Effort

CHAPTER 7
DESENSITIZATION

*Figure 18: Els van der Zanden desensitizing
a horse to an intimidating situation.*
(**Photo credit: Marlon Stapert.**)

Having covered the basic principles of motivation and what drives behavior; we will now move on to commonly occurring special cases of motivational difficulty. These are very often the real juggernauts of behavior - desensitization and aggression. Indeed, most of the times that I have been faced with a very difficult behavioral dilemma, it has been as a result of one of these problem areas: how to teach the animal to be calm and accept a situation, or equally vital, how to convince them not to harm me.

For the purposes of this text, *desensitization issues are the special cases of stimuli in the animal's environment competing to drive the animal from the goal behavior*. Desensitization, then, is a special sub-category of motivation. From a behavior modification standpoint, desensitization training is needed primarily *to eliminate and prevent fears and to teach an animal to ignore desirable distractions* as well. Thus, the techniques may apply to both avoidance and attraction type motives; however, the primary focus is to minimize the salience of fear-provoking stimuli. This effect is accomplished by neutralizing the competing stimuli and their associated motivations, leaving the animal motivationally more open to the drives offered by the trainer. The techniques of desensitization are designed to *make environmental stimuli and experiences have reduced or neutral value* so that the animal focuses on the desired behavior and not on the alternative influences of the situation. So if your horse is afraid of running water, you must first teach them to be calm when crossing a stream, and *then* take them trail riding, or else you may end up doing an unscheduled dismount and walking home!

On the Motivation Continuum, desensitization is any process which drives a stimulus' value towards neutral. Neutral stimuli have no effect on behavior and therefore will not compete and drive the animal's attention off the task of the trainer.

The Motivation Continuum

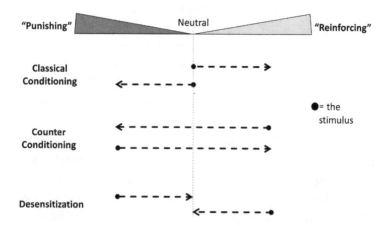

Desensitization could be considered the opposite process to traditional classical conditioning which gives value to a neutral stimulus (see Chapter 4). Alternatively, counter-conditioning initially drives a value toward neutral; however, it will become classical conditioning with continued association.

The novelty effect

Desensitization issues begin when an animal first notices an environmental stimulus. During this initial exposure, there is an introductory period called the 'effect of novelty' in which the animal considers the value of the stimulus. The *novelty effect* describes a characteristic set of mammalian responses to the introduction of a novel stimulus and is an important part of the fight or flight response in animals. It is loosely defined as the innate fear-provoked response associated with exposure to a novel stimulus. The novelty effect can be described with the following set of responses: animals will respond initially with an *orienting response*, accompanied by a variety of behavioral and physiological changes as well as arousal and suppression of appetitive behaviors. This reaction helps the animal to assess and react to potential danger – it rouses them to alertness.

As it is with all issues of motivation, after initial orientation and evaluation of the novel stimulus, the individuals' environmental context and unique perception of a stimulus will significantly influence the resulting response. For example, a mother with a pup or a sleeping animal will exhibit an increased startle response when exposed suddenly to new stimuli. Conversely, an alert, confident individual may show little response to the same stimulus.

The *effects of context changes are particularly profound with issues of desensitization,* altering the value of stimuli rather dramatically in many cases. Thus it is important to anticipate the possibility of increased fear and distraction with the addition of stimuli or with any change in the environment, and work to counter-balance these effects by careful proactive desensitization training.

Sensitization

The opposite of desensitization is called sensitization. *Sensitization* is defined as the enhancement of a response solicited by a stimulus with repeated presentations of that stimulus. Sensitization heightens and increases an animal's reaction to a stimulus by increasing the motivational value of the stimulus or its salience. Remarkably, sensitization is the condition described in part by the novelty effect. In this sense, sensitization universally precedes all other behavioral reactions to novel stimuli, at least momentarily. What happens next will depend on numerous factors; however, if the assessment of the animal leads to sensitization, further interaction with the stimulus should be expected to cause increased reactivity. Since this response is intended to protect the animal from potential danger, generally sensitization *causes highly undesirable reactions that intensify fears and produce over-reactive behavior. **Of all the things I would choose to avoid as a trainer, undesirable sensitization would be top on my list!***

Preventing sensitization is a sign of an advanced and adept trainer, in my opinion. Avoiding sensitization will save considerable time and effort in the future, since this reaction will cause distracting and often paralyzing effects on the animal's performance. These effects can be very long lasting and amount to an ever-present paranoia that the trainer must constantly strive to nullify. I had an animal that was so traumatized by early life experiences associated with going into a cage that it presented a life-long struggle to overcome. While the animal did successfully accept the cage after careful desensitization work, the behavior was never as fluid and dependable as with other animals. The smallest additional stimulus - like an inadvertent sneeze - could easily disrupt the behavior and visibly weaken the animal's resolve. Thus, careful and constant effort was needed to maintain the animal's perception of the cage and prepare for the confounding effects of environmental stimuli. Painstaking work was needed to slowly increase the animal's tolerance of sneezing, wandering, and sputtering stimuli while performing the caging behavior. To say the least, a lot of time and effort could have been saved if the initial exposure to caging had not resulted in sensitization.

It is worth noting that in those rare cases where use of aversive stimuli is desirable in the training process, such as in the techniques of negative reinforcement or punishment, a certain amount of sensitization would be considered advantageous. In those cases desensitization would be undesirable and the techniques in this chapter therefore should be avoided or applied in the reverse.

Stimulus strength

In the beginning stages of exposure to a stimulus, there is a delicate stage where an animal can become increasingly sensitized instead of desensitized. The resulting effect is primarily based on the initial stimulus strength. *Stimulus strength* is another way to describe the potential value of the stimulus to the animal, or its *salience*. Where this applies to sensitization, this is generally *the potential punishing value* of the stimulus.

There are many factors that can typically suggest an increase in stimulus strength. Stimuli that are very *loud* or that emit intense sound are often highly sensitizing, for example. Similarly, objects that are very *large* (or sometimes, very small) generally cause increased reactions. It is easy to understand that loud and large stimuli may inherently pose more risk. Likewise, the *closer* an object is to the animal, the more potential it has to do harm, and thus the greater its stimulus strength. Loud, large and close stimuli could be considered the most basic stimulus qualities contributing to increased stimulus strength, but there are several other similar qualities that regularly suggest higher value stimuli.

If the stimulus is apparently *reacting meaningfully to the animal*, its stimulus strength will increase. Thus, a stimulus erratically moving, but in no way oriented towards the animal, has lower value than one whose movements appear directed at the animal in particular. Directed movements seem to provoke the not-irrational fear of the object being "out to get the animal," increasing the potential stimulus strength. Also, stimuli that touch the animal are usually more threatening than those that the animal chooses to touch. *Significant, fast or erratic movements* are generally more sensitizing than calm movements. Additionally, stimuli which *cannot be seen* or are behind the animal are typically more threatening than those in full view but this will depend somewhat on the animal. Finally, animals may react more dramatically to any stimulus if the animal feels it is in a *vulnerable position,* such as lying prone, in an unfamiliar environment, or in cases of physical restriction, when the stimulus is presented. Of course, there are many other reasons why an animal would perceive increased stimulus strength, but these are the most common examples to be aware of.

The lower the stimulus strength, the less worrisome the new stimulus is, and the lower the response. It follows that a weak stimulus, introduced slowly, will not invoke a strong sensitization and will thus be more easily desensitized. Therefore, it is *extremely important to keep in mind the possible sensitizing effect from the intensity of a stimulus, especially upon initial exposure.* All stimuli can be eventually desensitized; however, there will be a lot more work involved to desensitize an animal that is initially sensitized.

Introduction to the techniques of desensitization

There are three primary means to neutralize the value of a stimulus: habituation (exposure over time), counter-conditioning, and increased response effort. In addition, there are two fundamental approaches to stimulus exposure: systematic desensitization (using approximations) and flooding (unrelenting exposure). These techniques can be combined and intermixed based on the choice of the trainer; however, there are some distinct advantages and disadvantages to each approach that warrant comparison.

TECHNIQUES THAT NEUTRALIZE THE VALUE OF THE STIMULUS

HABITUATION[1]

Habituation (also called *passive desensitization*) is the most funda-mental process to all desensitization. It describes *the reduction in response to stimuli as a result of exposure over time*. It is a relatively pas-sive process that results from the animal's acclimation to a stimulus after there has been enough time to conclude that the stimulus value is low and not warranting a response.

The word habituation appears to have first been defined in the psychological literature by J. Donald Harris (1943). At that time, habituation was becoming increasingly recognized as impor-tant to the analysis of learning. There were many terms circulating to describe the decrease in magnitude of an unlearned response: accli-matization, extinction, inhibition, accommodation, and stimulatory activation. Harris chose the word habituation to describe instances of decrement in the magnitude of unlearned responses that occur in whole organisms and were due to repetitive stimulation. Habitua-tion is distinguished as a type of learning, distinct from other types of response decrement which occur as a result of the physiological processes of sensory perception.

In general, it should be recognized that the process of habit-uation serves an important role in the adaptation of an animal to its environment. The ability to habituate to new stimuli associated with environmental changes is critical to the fundamental needs of the animal to minimize energy waste. Habituation is a learned and rea-sonably persistent reduction of response to a stimulus after repeated exposure and not as a result of any form of reinforcement or fatigue. It is further characterized by being specific to a particular stimulus.

---

1   The following is partly an extrapolation from a paper I co-authored with Nicole Holmes in 1998.

This is significant in that it recognizes the habituation process as being driven predominantly by the stimulus rather than any resultant reward or benefit.

Thompson and Spencer (1966) specified that habituation can usually be distinguished from other types of response decrement because it is reversible. They outlined the following common characteristics that have subsequently served as a detailed operational definition of habituation, and serve to illuminate many important aspects critical to the understanding of desensitization in general. (*I have interjected an example for the purposes of clarification.*)

1) Habituation is the process by which, given a particular stimulus that elicits a response, repeated applications of that stimulus result in a decreased response. (*For example, the feel of a harness to a sea lion will initially cause a strong reaction but will subside with repeated exposures (see Figures 2 and 15 on pages 1 and 149 for pictures of sea lions wearing harnesses).*)

2) If the stimulus is subsequently withheld, the response tends to recover over time - called 'spontaneous recovery'. (*In the example, if the sea lion has previously been trained to accept a harness placed on its body, and the behavior has not been reviewed for a considerable period, the animal may initially balk at the sight or feel of the reintroduced harness.*)

3) If a response is habituated and allowed to recover, the future habituation of that response becomes more rapid - called the 'potentiation of habituation.' (*For the reintroduced harness, the time and training necessary to return to the desensitized state will be much shorter than the original training time taken to desensitize it.*)

4) Other factors being equal, the greater the frequency of exposure, the more rapid and more pronounced is the habituation. (*The more times a sea lion is exposed to a harness the sooner it will become desensitized. In other words, if a trainer works with the harness five times a week, versus only once a week, the sea lion will become desensitized to the harness at a faster rate.*)

5) Additionally, the weaker the stimulus, the more rapid and more pronounced is the habituation. Strong or aversive stimuli may yield no significant habituation. (*If the harness is uncomfortably constricting causing breathing difficulty or is associated with manipulative punishment, it will be more difficult to habituate the animal sufficiently to promote its cooperation.*)

6) Additional habituation training after the response has disappeared or reached a stable habituated level will result in a slower recovery of the original response. (*This indicates maintenance level training and periodic review of wearing the harness is highly useful in promoting continued desensitization to wearing the harness.*)

7) Similar to other forms of learning, habituation of a response to a given stimulus also exhibits 'generalization' to other similar stimuli. Additionally, animals with long histories of desensitization to a wide variety of different stimuli will generally be easier to desensitize to any particular novel stimulus. (*For example, if a sea lion is desensitized to carrying an EKG monitor on its back, the transition to wearing a camera or other objects will be relatively smoother than the initial desensitization process.*) This quality of habituation results in what is commonly referred to as 'bomb-proof' animals. These are animals who are so accustomed to stimuli that you may even be able to set off a bomb in their midst and they wouldn't react substantially. This is a highly desirable quality for many animals working in chaotic environments, such as police dogs and horses, or animal actors working on sound stages.

8) Presentation of another very different stimulus frequently results in recovery of the pre-habituated response. This process is called 'dishabituation,' meaning the loss of the habituated response or the return to a fearful state with presentation of additional stimuli. This happens because the new stimuli represent a context shift. As we have already discussed, context changes effect both communication and motivation based issues. Context shifts are particularly prevalent in desensitization-related issues because the new context inherently

necessitates a re-evaluation of the safety and value of the stimulus, from a survival standpoint. (*If a sea lion is confronted with a crowd of people and has not previously been desensitized to crowds, it is likely that the sea lion will be wary enough of the crowd to refuse to allow its harness to be put on, even if the harness was previously desensitized.*)

These principles of habituation help to guide and inform the process of desensitization training. Clearly habituation functions with exposure over time and requires maintenance to be effective. The better desensitized an animal is to a variety of stimuli, the easier it will be for that animal to accept additional new stimuli, and most importantly, the initial stimulus strength will determine the ease with which an item can be effectively desensitized.

Habituation of both punishers and reinforcers

It is worth noting that the process of exposure over time works to desensitize both reinforcers and punishers, although when it is applied to primary stimuli the effect will be inherently temporary. To what extent habituation accounts for *satiation* is not clear, especially for drives that are not physiological in nature; however these processes have a similar result and functionally can be seen to be related (see Chapter 6 for more on satiation). Thus, if an animal is highly motivated for exercise after being cooped up, for example, it is very often a good choice to exhaust them with running around a bit before trying to get them focused on other behavioral objectives. In this example, the competing motivation was a reinforcer (exercise or impulsive energy) and the desensitization process involved habituating this drive first through satiation before proceeding with the training plan.

Conversely, most of the training challenges associated with desensitization involve nullifying punishing stimuli. In this way, the animal learns that the stimulus which was seemingly harmful or deadly is actually harmless. Initially frightening stimuli are eventually recognized as innocuous, once the animal has lived with the object for a time, through the process of habituation. Many horses, for example, are irrationally phobic of plastic bags; leaving a bag or two tied to a wall of the paddock is a simple way of promoting habituation to these stimuli, so long as the trainer is careful to avoid the initial exposure at high stimulus strength to prevent sensitization.

➤ *The benefits and drawbacks of habituation*

Habituation, as a technique to reduce the value of environmental stimuli, has the primary benefit of *requiring no additional intervention from the trainer*. It is a passive process that occurs whether or not the trainer is even involved, but merely by the exposure to the stimulus. Thus, it is possible to passively desensitize an animal to stimuli left in their environment without expending further effort. While it is unclear if habituation is a process of satiation, it nevertheless functions similarly *allowing desensitization of both reinforcing and punishing stimuli* in a relatively benign, *relationship friendly* manner.

However, this process *can be very slow* and inherently requires time and experience to change the value of the stimulus. This process can be rather painstaking to endure if the trainer has need of the stimulus for a pending behavior that cannot be completed until the animal willingly accepts the object or environment. To speed up the process of desensitization, counter-conditioning can be very useful, particularly for punishing stimuli.

COUNTER-CONDITIONING

As I outlined in Communication, counter-conditioning is a classical conditioning process that works by *associating stimuli of opposite value*, the combination of which acts to nullify one another and drive the stimulus value toward neutral (see Chapter 4). By contrast with habituation, counter-conditioning requires the active ministrations of the trainer and so is also called *active desensitization*. Although this process can be used to negate either punishers or reinforcers, the technique is primarily used to reduce the disadvantageous effects of fearful stimuli rather than to suppress the attraction of reinforcing stimuli.

Therefore, counter-conditioning is most frequently performed through the use of food reinforcement combined with an aversive stimulus in order to drive the value of the aversive from punishing towards neutral. For example, a lion is nervous to enter a new room, so the trainer supplies small meaty treats to help increase the value of the room while the animal assesses the other qualities of the environment. Continuing to reinforce the lion in the new room will, over time, make this a preferred area, so long as there are no real dangers waiting within or additional sensitizing experiences.

Of course, as the value of the room increases, the opposite may be occurring to the value of the meaty treats. One advantage of using this technique with primary reinforcers (as opposed to secondaries) is that, generally, their value rebounds naturally. It is possible, however, that certain food preferences may be altered by counter-conditioning if these foods are sufficiently associated with highly punishing stimuli. Therefore, it is preferable to use a variety of different foods in counter-conditioning and also to attempt to combine this technique with other methods of desensitization (such as systematic desensitization, see later in this chapter), to mitigate any disadvantageous effects on the reinforcers involved.

Obviously, if continued, counter-conditioning will become classical conditioning as the stimulus ceases to be punishing and moves to a reinforcing value by continued association with a high value reinforcer.

Most of the time this effect is desirable, since increasing the reinforcing value of the stimulus or environment involved will usually only benefit the trainer. Rarely, however, neutrality is preferred, in which case halting the ongoing association would be necessary.

Approach conditioning

Approach conditioning teaches the animal to run after the aversive stimulus. This special form of counter-conditioning associates the reinforcing value of chasing something and acting out on the environment with the aversive stimulus. This can have an empowering effect. Similar to the advantages of the scan and capture technique (see Chapter 5), this method leverages the value of the animal taking control, versus the environment controlling the animal.

Aversion conditioning

Generally counter-conditioning is not commonly employed *to reduce the attractive effects of reinforcement*. This is because doing so would require leveraging a significant and repeated amount of aversive stimuli. The film "A Clockwork Orange" famously depicted such an attempt to associate aversives with the desire to harm or cause mayhem, and in the film the conditioning failed. This kind of aversion conditioning has been used to treat chemical dependencies and other so-called deviant behavior in humans with mixed success. For example, in humans, this technique has been used to create an aversion to alcohol using medications which induce nausea when alcohol is consumed. Psychologists have employed this strategy for scientific research, but the laboratory is not similar to real life situations, where, thank goodness, electrified floors are not commonly available. To the extent that aversion conditioning is used to attempt to reverse the effects of primary motives, it will generally fail, although it may be more successful with secondary motives.

Aversion conditioning is best employed with moderate intensity consistent application that ideally does not involve the trainer, but instead is a fixed response of the environment or stimulus. For example, if gnawing on the cage is undesirable, painting the cage with a bad tasting liquid may result in an aversion to performing this behavior towards the cage, if the taste is reliably associated. However, the desire to gnaw may still resurface with other stimuli.

Using strong aversion conditioning, like any application of punishing stimuli, *can cause aggression, depression and severe distress, not to mention a dramatic negative effect on the relationship between the animal and the trainer.* Increased response effort or redirection techniques are generally more palatable techniques to address the effects of attractive stimuli that compete with desirable behavior, and these approaches have far fewer downsides.

➢ The benefits and drawbacks of counter-conditioning

The primary benefit of counter-conditioning is to *expedite the process of habituation* which can otherwise be very slow. It is best used to *negate fear-provoking stimuli* and ameliorate an animal's view of a situation by adding reinforcement. Care should be taken not to permanently damage the value of the reinforcer used. This should be accomplished by using a variety of mostly primary reinforcers, as well as other techniques of desensitization.

One situation where people can run afoul of the association with reinforcement is related to the animal becoming aggressive after learning to covet the reinforcer. This attraction-type of aggression could be considered a disadvantage of the use of positive reinforcement in general, but should pose only modest difficulty to the experienced trainer utilizing proper anti-aggression training (see Chapter 8 for more on these techniques).

Another issue of association with reinforcement might be to accidently condition a preferred environment. If a particular environment or scenario has a substantial history of association with reinforcement, this may pose a *balance of reinforcement* problem which prevents freely shifting the animal about (see Chapter 6). This is a common problem with show tanks, for example, where dolphins may receive so much of their reinforcement in one pool, they often do not wish to leave it. Solving a balance of reinforcement problem, as we have discussed, involves applying adequate reinforcement to the alternative environments.

Counter-conditioning has been *used in the form of aversion therapy* to reduce the reinforcement value of stimuli, but this involves significant use of aversives and a resultant damage to the relationship, as well as, *potentially traumatic psychological effects.* Thus, counter-conditioning should be used minimally, if at all, to change the value of reinforcing stimuli.

RESPONSE EFFORT

As we have discussed, requiring an increased effort to obtain distracting, desirable stimuli effectively alters the motivational value of these reinforcers making them less motivating to the animal (see Chapter 6). This is because there is an increased difficultly or cost to acquire the reinforcer and this cost must be 'subtracted' from whatever value the stimulus had. For relatively weak stimuli, increasing the response effort is often sufficient to reduce the salience enough that other competing drives, offered by the trainer, may easily prevail. *Increasing the distance between the animal and the desirable stimulus is the simplest and most common method of increasing response effort.*

Much of the use of *increased response effort* simply falls into the category of creating the optimal circumstances for success. For example, if the trainer wants to practice dog agility work, it may be best to do so in a separate field from the dog park, in order to avoid the tantalizing draw of socializing with so many other dogs. A more complex use of the technique would involve placing blocks or barricades to reduce the animal's desire to move forward to acquire reinforcers. Later, the blocks can be sculpted out, once the animal has sufficient reinforcement history with staying put. Many techniques of manipulation, like leashes, would technically also fall into the category of increased response effort, insofar as they create physical barriers that make acquiring the reinforcer much more difficult, but not technically impossible. Many dog owners routinely experience this effect, as they are pulled about by their dogs on the leash; the leash makes it more difficult (but not impossible) for the dog to chase the squirrel.

Increasing response effort is an excellent approach to neutralizing the value of distracting stimuli in the animal's environment but, in order to apply this same technique to diminish the effect of punishing stimuli, it requires making the desirable response easier to do and effectively costing less (*decreased response effort*). This may result in the animal choosing to perform the desired behavior but generally will do nothing significant to the value of the punishing stimulus that is causing fear. This fear will continue to plague the trainer until habituation or counter-conditioning more deliberately address the issue. However, this use of 'overshadowing' of motives can help the trainer to begin the process while the animal is otherwise engaged, focusing on something more salient. Thus, this technique of setting the animal up to most easily perform the desired behavior offers only a small advantage, where it applies to frightful or punishing stimuli, and will generally require a further combination of techniques.

TECHNIQUES OF APPROACH TO STIMULUS EXPOSURE

Having covered the various methods to alter the motivational value of environmental stimuli, let us discuss the two basic training methods of introducing these stimuli: *systematic desensitization and flooding. Each of these techniques can be paired with any or several other methods to reduce stimuli value, creating a mix-and-match option of* methodological combinations suitable to most situations requiring desensitization.

FLIGHT PREVENTION

For particularly flighty animals, it may be best to limit the chance of the rehearsal of fleeing, since this is somewhat reinforcing and highly likely. For this reason, people often employ a leash or tether during exposure to novel stimuli for prey animals, like horses, or inexperienced animals that are more likely to be reactionary. This approach which could be called 'flight prevention' can be used in conjunction with either systematic desensitization or flooding. It is fundamentally a technique of manipulation and increased response effort (see Chapter 5). The use of this technique with either flooding or systematic desensitization should be carefully managed with the advantages and drawbacks of that application (see below).

SYSTEMATIC DESENSITIZATION

Systematic desensitization refers to the practice of *reducing stimulus strength by breaking the stimulus into smaller components and using incremental steps of exposure to increase an animal's tolerance of an aversive stimulus.* Systematic desensitization uses successive approximations to break a stimulus into smaller units and sequentially desensitize each one and then combine them for full stimulus strength. By systematically limiting stimulus strength, the risk of sensitization is minimized, enhancing the potential of desensitization and improving what can be ultimately accomplished. This method has been used successfully to desensitize numerous animals to even very painful and frightening medical and transport procedures. It is *key to most of the elaborate training associated with human-animal partnerships.*

Figure 19: A sea lion trained to exit a transport vehicle, enter a restraint cage in an animal hospital, insert its head into a cone mask and inhale in order to cooperate in an anesthesia procedure. This process involved considerable systematic desensitization to many frightening components.

(Photo credit: ATR International.)

General model of systematic desensitization

Establish a baseline

Systematic desensitization can be accomplished with either habituation or counter-conditioning or both, but counter-conditioning will generally be faster. In order to determine when to proceed with increasing the approximation, it is best to first *establish a baseline of the animal's behavior in the situation, without the stimulus.* This can then be used as a helpful guide to reading the behavior of the animal and determining if there is a frightened reaction. Generally this should be performed for each desensitization session. It is best not to rely on previously obtained baselines, as each day is a new context and the animal's behavior may easily have shifted.

Analyze the stimulus variables

The *stimulus is then analyzed to break it into component variables.* It is often helpful to consider the separate senses of sight, sound, smell, and touch to make this analysis (usually taste does not come into play with most stimuli, unless they are to be swallowed or carried). Sight often has the sub-categorization of movement that must always be considered seriously. Both the movement of the object and the movement of the animal will have to be considered. Optimally these component variables will be prioritized from least frightening to most frightening based on general principles of stimulus strength described earlier in this chapter. Each stimulus component would then be (ideally) desensitized separately. By *desensitizing each variable separately*, the stimulus strength is inherently reduced, lowering the risk of sensitization. Once each variable has been desensitized, they are *then combined* until the stimulus is fully articulated.

Use distance

To further reduce stimulus strength, it is helpful to start out far away and then move closer, as the animal is comfortable. *Distance inherently reduces stimulus strength* by making the potential for harm less likely. Taken to the extreme, this idea means that anything touching an animal will be more fear-provoking and significant. Thus, touch is almost always the final variable to address. Furthermore, it is very helpful to first allow the animal to touch the object, and second, to touch the object to the animal. This is because acting on the environment generally inspires more confidence than the environment acting on you.

Choose the optimal context

An additional element controlling the stimulus strength is the context. As we have discussed, *context affects the perception of the stimulus considerably* and will contribute to the perceived strength or weakness of the exposure.

Choosing the context carefully when first approaching the desensitization of a novel stimulus is very useful. It is important to consider any safe zones that allow the animal to feel more comfortable due to familiarity or the ability to flee. For example, marine mammals generally feel safer in the water than on land, and providing access to water can readily reduce stress and anxiety. Similarly, it is best not to begin by impacting the safe zone of the animal; keep the stimulus out of the territory where the animal may want to retreat. For the marine mammal, this would mean to expose the animal first to the stimulus in air, and later, to it submerged.

In addition, making sure the animal is in a comfortable position that does not make them feel inherently vulnerable is important to reducing stimulus strength and proceeding in an approximated manner. For many animals, this will mean standing up as opposed to lying down or rolled over. In those prone positions, it is harder to flee if they feel fear, and this increases the anxiety, similar to a bout of claustrophobia.

Finally, since you are trying to make the point that this stimulus has no value, it is helpful not to have the stimulus react specifically to the animal. The stimulus should be presented more obliquely, as if it is occurring regardless of the animal or its behavior. Many times when the stimulus in question is a human being, for example, it is helpful to adopt the attitude of wandering or milling about rather than walking directly towards the animal at first.

For reasons of practicality, it is generally preferable to desensitize only one animal at a time, since it can be challenging to read and react to the behavior of multiple animals at once. On the other hand, some animals are inherently much more confident and calm in a group context. This may override the concern of practicality, especially if you have a very calm 'guide' among the group. For example, calm dog breeds are often employed as companion animals for trained cheetahs, to act as a kind of 'pace horse' whose presence offers a solid and calm attitude (see Figure 20).

Figure 20: A calm dog is raised as a companion animal to a
cheetah at the San Diego Wild Animal Park.
(Photo credit: ATR International.)

Read the animal

In order to decide when to proceed from one approximation to the next, it is necessary to 'read' the animal's behavior and compare it to the baseline. The *animal's reaction determines whether or not you are ready to move forward.* As long as they are demonstrating baseline behavior, and they have definitely perceived the stimulus, moving forward to the next approximation is warranted. If, however, you see apprehension, it is best to back up and proceed more slowly, by reducing the stimulus strength to avoid the potential of sensitization. When in doubt, it is generally better not to proceed than to risk sensitization, but that will depend on the experience of the trainer and the animal.

There are several typical generic *signs of stress and fear to watch for.* Orienting on the stimulus is the first reaction of the effect of novelty and is to be expected; however, obsessive and prolonged focus on the stimulus is likely to be a sign of concern. *Increased sensing* of the environment by sight, smell, or touch can indicate the animal is wary and seeking more input. Wide-eyes are a general sign of increased effort to see, for example, and usually indicate a hyper-alert condition. Any change in behavior can indicate a sign of stress, but not always of course. Nevertheless, it is prudent to be aware of *any change* and evaluate further what the behavior might indicate. *Avoidance,* or putting a lot of distance between themselves and the stimulus, is almost always a sign of fear and is the most direct indication that the animal is uncomfortable with the situation. I always respond immediately to signs of avoidance to react to a potentially sensitizing experience.

It is just as important to recognize that just because you do not perceive any signs of stress does not mean that the animal is not experiencing any. Very frequently, animals may show little or no outward signs, though all the while they feel adrenalized and their heart rates are increased. Therefore, allowing enough time and exposure throughout the desensitization process will always be a prudent move.

Blood sampling: an example of a systematic desensitization procedure

To help further explain the process of systematic desensitization I have chosen the difficult and complex scenario of blood sampling, and have broken it down into possible approximations. Please note that in all behavior modification, the choice of exact approximations is part of the art form of training, and there is no such thing as a 'right' and a 'wrong' choice. Thus, the following is merely one simplified example and *not* intended as a precise and exact approach.

There are many elements involved in taking blood from an animal: there is the veterinarian, the smell of sterilizing alcohol, the extraneous supplies needed to collect the blood such as tubes or slides, and of course the needle stick (see Figure 22 page 234 for a voluntary blood draw example). In order to train an animal to accept the procedure of blood sampling using systematic desensitization, each of these components must be reduced to the minimal stimulus strength possible, approached separately and then combined.

Some of these elements, such as the extraneous tubes or the smelly alcohol, can be desensitized relatively easily using habituation, by exposing the animal to these stimuli passively over time. To further reduce the stimulus strength on initial exposure, it is optimal to keep these stimuli at a distance and reduce the distance over time as the animal becomes comfortable. However, this can be a tedious and time-consuming undertaking. So, wherever possible, using counter-conditioning will expedite the process.

Depending on the animal's past history, the veterinarian may pose a problem since the animal often has no relationship with the vet, or more commonly, an aversive one. The vet can be desensitized by devising numerous innocuous visits where he/she is counter-conditioned by being the bringer of goodies, for example. To speed up this process, those with whom the animal has a positive relationship can mimic the vet's dress and general actions first, and then later non-veterinarian strangers can be recruited to approximate the same function. Pretending to be a veterinarian is a common pasttime of many students and visitors to my facility. Eventually, all of these aspects can be combined with the actual veterinarian.

The needle is clearly the most worrisome component and will certainly require substantial desensitization since it is inherently a pain-inducing object. To reduce the stimulus strength of the syringe and needle, it is helpful to separate the visual aspect of the needle from the pressure, pricking, and sticking sensations and then combine these.

To simulate the process of taking blood, the trainer can first desensitize the animal to pressure at the appropriate location using the trainer's hand, and eventually, a stand-in object such as a pencil. Once this is tolerated, increasing amounts of tactile stimulation should be simulated such as pricking with a pointy object like a paper clip or flicking with a finger. Once significant tactile sensation is tolerated, the implementation of a very thin (high gauge) needle is used to introduce minimal pain while still approximating to the penetration of the skin. This needle can then be inserted farther and for longer, in each case, increasing the effective stimulus strength until the thin needle can be used to simulate the exact procedure of the blood sample but with a much less painful sensation. Generally, all of the above approximations are done in concert with counter-conditioning and the use of considerable positive reinforcement. Finally, the introduction of the larger needle is approximated once the animal freely accepts the smaller versions, and the process repeats itself until the full needle and syringe are accepted.

Once these stimuli have been approached separately, they are then combined in approximations until the entire process is tolerated by the animal. Finally, the veterinarian is able to arrive, supplies in hand, and collect a voluntary blood sample from the animal, which now fully accepts each aspect of this process.

➤ The benefits and drawbacks of systematic desensitization

The tremendous advantage of systematic desensitization is that it is *very safe from the debilitating effects of sensitization*. As such, it is relatively *relationship friendly* and generally only a mildly uncomfortable, or even a positive experience, for the animal. Unfortunately, systematic desensitization *can take a great deal of time* and effort to work through all the needed approximations. While time is a general property of desensitization, nowhere is the process more time-consuming than using systematic methods. Additionally, this technique *can lack enough motivation to conquer certain phobias* based on irrational fear or sensitization. In such cases, where the animal often needs a push to get over an imaginary hurdle, flooding may be the faster and preferred technique.

FLOODING

Flooding is an extreme method of stimulus exposure where the *animal is heavily and unrelentingly exposed to a frightening novel stimulus or environment until they give in and decide not to react any further and/ or become habituated (ideally)*. Generally, this is the stimulus at nearly full strength. However, a more refined use of the technique would involve some approximations of increasing stimulus strength so long as the exposure is unrelenting until the stimulus reaction is habituated for that approximation. What is key to a successful process of flooding is not to remove the stimulus until the animal has become desensitized to it. If the stimulus is removed prior to that point, it is likely still within the sensitization phase, and will result in the opposite of desensitization. This is one of the major areas of difficulty with this technique, since it is impossible to predict how long it might take to habituate and, if the exposure is relented prior to that point, the trainer will have made the situation considerably worse as a result of the flooding. Flooding is accomplished by leaving the animal trapped in the presence of the stimulus or environment until they become normalized and behave naturally without particular concern for the stimulus.

The most common uses of this technique involve introducing an animal to a novel environment, cage or enclosure (typically done with full stimulus strength). Most people don't think twice about bringing their dog or cat into a new house, and correctly assume that the animal will eventually accept the situation. This is an everyday example of flooding. An alternative, more approximated approach would be to expose the animal to one room at a time while minimizing the activity and stimulus in the environment. Exposing them to the new environment with familiar furniture in place could also reduce the stimulus strength and provide a more systematic method. Of course, this is rarely needed with most dogs that are generally easily desensitized because of their domesticated nature. More so, cats have retained a wariness that makes systematic approaches helpful.

Another common example of flooding is in the equestrian world, in the form of *breaking a horse*. 'Breaking a horse' refers to the practices of forcing the horse to endure the saddle and rider until it is calm. This is how most of the horses in the world today are trained to accept a saddle, in fact. This form of flooding involves the animal being trapped in the saddle until their behavior becomes more relaxed and normalized. This process usually involves only days to accomplish, but sometimes produces horses that are so sensitized and traumatized by the experience that they are not considered useful thereafter. These animals are generally then considered untrainable and left to a life of breeding or to become dog meat. Many horse specialists believe this is the only method to training a horse to saddle and rider. However, I know of animals trained successfully by more systematic methods. I am happy to report that it is increasingly common to use a combined form of flooding and systematic desensitization to accomplish this process more gently and with less trauma.

➤ The benefits and drawbacks of flooding

Flooding's best advantage is that, where it works, it is *relatively fast and easy*. The stimuli that it works well for are generally not truly harmful stimuli, but they nevertheless tend to cause great anxiety and reluctance, which makes using systematic desensitization even more painstaking than normal. In these cases *the animal may have hit a plateau* of phobia that is not rationally related to the properties of the stimulus in terms of any real harm posed by it. This can be especially true for *new environments* that the animal may at first be very reluctant to experience; however, once they have accepted these environments they can quickly even become preferred, depending on their attributes. Dolphins will frequently hesitate to gate into a new pool, but once they have gotten accustomed to the new environment they happily move freely from one tank to the next. I have heard this referred to as "Pulling-off-the-Band-Aid desensitization" or even "Get-over-it desensitization," as the immersion is often effective at overcoming irrational reluctance.

Another benefit of flooding is that it is *usually very long lasting,* once the animal has overcome their fear using this technique, it is not as likely to resurface.

Of course the downsides to flooding are quite numerous and quite serious. This is a very traumatic method and should be done with caution and deliberation, as well as, used minimally, if at all. A highly frightened animal is *dangerous to everyone involved,* including itself. It is quite easy for a panicking creature to become harmed physically and mentally. The panic comes, in part, from *enduring an initial sensitization* from the experience which, depending on the severity of the situation, can cause great distress. If this experience is associated with the trainer, by the trainer presenting the stimulus or being otherwise associated with the event, this type of aversive experience will have a *disadvantageous effect on the on the relationship* between the trainer and the animal, and will damage the trust. Some things, particularly genuinely painful stimuli, are very hard or nearly impossible to flood through. A *learned helplessness* may result in that case, where the animal is so traumatized that it becomes apathetic and unresponsive, even when given the opportunity to flee. These events cause permanent and lasting damage to the animal and to the training relationship that cannot generally be repaired. Thus, attempting flooding for truly harmful stimuli is unwise. Finally, the *unrelenting effort needed* for true flooding can be inconvenient in some cases if the process goes on for hours and days. This should be considered prior to embarking on this technique since, once begun, you are in for a penny, in for a pound!

When choosing to use flooding, a combination of techniques is probably most helpful to minimize the potential debilitating effects while utilizing a small occasional push once the animal has hit a plateau. Significant flooding of frightening stimuli should only be attempted by experienced trainers and not by beginners.

DESENSITIZATION, *IN SUMMARY*

Desensitization is always a function of time and experience. Like all issues of motivation, it is dependent on the individual's perception of the stimulus. It is vitally important to recognize the potential impacts of exposure to new stimuli or situations, because a little care in the beginning can prevent the animal becoming sensitized. If sensitized, it can take a long time to recover the animal's perception of the situation or stimulus. There are three ways to alter the value of a stimulus: habituation, counter-conditioning and response effort. Habituation works well for stimuli that can be left around the animal and thus slowly desensitized; however counter-conditioning is very useful to more rapidly reduce the value of fear-provoking stimuli. Counter-conditioning is generally a much poorer choice, however, for desensitizing reinforcing stimuli, since that requires heavy usage of aversives. To reduce the distracting effects of reinforcing stimuli in the animal's environment, redirection, exposure through habituation (satiation) and/or requiring an increased effort to obtain the competing reinforcer are the optimal methods. For punishing stimuli, beware of sensitization which may cause an increased reaction to the stimulus in the future. To reduce this risk, lowering the stimulus strength using systematic desensitization is the safest choice. Flooding works well for environmental stimuli that are not too severe in value, and to help conquer irrational phobias after systematic desensitization has familiarized the animal with the stimulus. Combining counter-conditioning with systematic desensitization is optimal for reducing the effects of frightening stimuli. A proactive approach to desensitization, anticipating problems with changes in context and preparing an individual to accept a variety of stimuli and environments, will result in a well-balanced and confident animal.

CHAPTER 8
AGGRESSION

THE DEFINITION OF AGGRESSION
IN THIS TEXT

The subject of aggression, as it pertains to the concepts of this text and my organization of behavior modification techniques, relates centrally to animal aggression towards humans. It is a type of motivation problem. The definition of aggression for our purposes is *any behavior performed by the animal that they intend to physically harm, or threaten to harm, a human or human extension*. It behooves us to include in this definition any behavior which will reliably cause harm to the human, whether or not the animal can be judged to fully comprehend this risk. This is a functional definition designed to focus on the practical matter and objectives of animal training (as opposed to a general definition of aggression, which would rightly include inter-animal aggression as well as aggression directed by humans *towards* animals).

A 'human extension'

The 'human extension' might be a target pole, piece of clothing, or a feeding pouch - anything that the animal could perceive as linked to, and in the possession of, the human. I include this extension in the definition because if an animal is willing to display aggression towards these extensions, it will quickly generalize towards the person or at least pose significant risk to the person, leaving little practical distinction between these behaviors. It is also important to note that, insofar as the animal sees these items as belonging to the trainer, aggressive behavior directed at them is intended for the human as well. For this reason, stealing food from the hand or the pouch can been seen as a first indicator sign of aggression that should be addressed in order to prevent this behavior from expanding to further displays of aggressive behavior and dominance.

Desirable aggression

I should note here that my approach is to assume that aggressive behavior directed at a human being is *undesirable*, where, of course, there are specific cases to the contrary. Animals are deliberately trained to be aggressive for law enforcement, the military, for purposes of personal defense, and for film and theatrical reasons. In these situations the six basic operant techniques are used (see Chapter 5) to condition and control the behavior.

In this chapter, we will discuss the various drives and the development of aggressive behavior. This information should be equally helpful to understanding *how to encourage or discourage* this behavior, depending on your goal, although we will discuss the material from the perspective of eliminating it, which applies in the vast majority of the cases.

Encouraging aggressive behavior is a very risky undertaking and requires expert handling to reduce the inherent risks of this behavior spilling-over to the handlers or to other innocent bystanders. Due to the effects of rehearsal, this conditioning will always pose an increased risk. Depending on how much genuine aggressive motive is used to condition these behaviors, animals that are conditioned to display aggressive behaviors may forever be limited in how safe they can be in normal situations.

Inter-animal aggression

Inter-animal aggression can also become a serious training issue in a captive behavior management program. Both issues can be seen as behaviors we would like the animal *not to do*, and also the subject of *competing motivations*. Therefore, while this chapter is focused on aggression towards humans, the same techniques could be applied to either case. Since a human will always be involved in aggression as we are defining it, it is more practical to address the behavior on *every* presentation, making both the prevention and punishment techniques more effective.

Aggressive behavior in the captive animal

One important place where aggressive behavior towards humans differs from other aggressive behavior is the damage that it does to the working relationship between the trainer and the animal. Aggression towards the trainer undermines the trust and the fundamental truth of the relationship, which is that the human must be in charge. This is necessary because a captive animal is not capable of understanding the nuances of the human world and therefore how to best make informed decisions about their lives within it. No matter how much we love and respect them, animals simply are not qualified to be the decision makers about the majority of issues surrounding their day-to-day life. Therefore, the structure and complexity of the system necessitates that the human directs and takes the responsibility for the majority of the decision making. This arrangement is not a consequence of dominance, but one of practical reality, yet it effectively obligates a hierarchical structure to the partnership between human and animal – the human must be the leader. To lead someone effectively, it is enormously helpful if they are not trying to do you harm all the while. Therefore, *the best training systems will not allow the animal to physically dominate the human.*

Aggressive behavior limits many of the best opportunities provided by training outlined previously in Chapter 3. Aggression changes the priorities of how the trainer can proceed with the animal, since it prevents or hinders many of the best training options, and the trainer must be somewhat preoccupied with worry over their personal safety. It is for this reason that I would recommend that limiting aggressive behavior towards humans should be the *first priority of any program of animal management,* especially for an animal that has the potential to cause harm. All other problems, including inter-animal aggression, low motivation, or poor understanding should be addressed second to aggressive behavior displayed toward the trainer, in order to maximize the available techniques and potential goals.

As Konrad Lorenz famously points out in his landmark treatise "On Aggression" (1981), aggressive behavior is certainly normal and healthy in all species. It is one of the most fundamental ways that animals interact for a variety of reasons including out of fear, for play, and for control. This is a basic element of life that we must all accept. Aggressive behavior does not make the animal a 'bad seed' or even a bad seal. ☺ Nevertheless, *in the optimal captive scenario, animals should have a choice in most everything except to be aggressive,* which should ideally be prevented and eliminated expeditiously.

By making this the first priority of the training program, the trainer is reminded to be on the alert for problems of this type. This focus will enable the trainer to better anticipate and prevent aggression, which is one of the best techniques to eliminate unwanted behavior (see Chapter 6). Hopefully, this alert attitude may also protect the trainer from harm!

Once aggressive intent is detected, all other objectives should be minimized to focus on addressing the aggressive situation or problem until it is resolved (assuming that the animal poses any practical harm to the trainer). Trainers who are unwilling or unable to make this the top priority will undoubtedly allow aggressive behavior to be rehearsed, and it will become very difficult to ever fully eliminate. As we have discussed, rehearsal inherently increases the likelihood of similar future behavior, an undesirable outcome for any unwanted behavior.

Since aggression is among the most important of all behaviors to be discouraged, the techniques in this chapter can be used as examples of how to approach *any behavioral problem that needs to be eliminated.* While some of these approaches are specific to aggression problems, the reader should be able to modify these concepts for other situations of undesirable behavior. Most of these issues were previewed in the chapters covering motivation and desensitization, and it is recommended that these be reviewed, as needed, for further details on these techniques (see Chapters 6 and 7).

WHY ARE ANIMALS AGGRESSIVE?

There are many disparate and often overlapping drives that may lead to aggressive behavior. Therefore, as we seek to overcome this behavior, it is first very helpful to evaluate these various drives. Slightly different approaches to reducing the behavior and minimizing the value of the drive are warranted depending on the nature of the drive in question. Following the discussion of why animals are aggressive, we will discuss the methods of how to cope with these various drives. Although the trainer may not always be certain which of these drives is most prominent, it is often possible to make a well-informed, best-guess based on the particulars of the individual, the species and the situation.

Aggressive drives are primarily based on instinct; however, aggressive behavior can definitely be learned and developed based on experience and outcome. Handling instinctive behavior can be more difficult and less effective than addressing behavior that is learned, for reasons of instinctive drift that we have already discussed. It is possible, however, to safely address all aggressive motives using a variety of preventative and operant techniques.

INSTINCTIVE AGGRESSION

Pain or fear

Perhaps the *most fundamental means to provoking an aggressive response* is through pain or fear. This is the 'fight' aspect of the 'fight or flight response,' and it is one of the most powerful instincts that drive any animal. Within a particular distance, a frightened animal may easily attack if they feel their life or well-being is at stake.

This distance is called the *critical distance* or the *fight distance* – the distance at which an animal will fight, outside of which, they will instead flee. This critical distance can be quite different between species. For example, the fight distance of a lion or a bear is much greater than that of an antelope. As a result, it is generally necessary to stay much farther away from a bear to confidently scare him away than it is when encountering hoof stock. It is not that bears will always attack; mostly they *do* prefer to flee, but only if sufficiently warned in advance. In the Alaska wilderness, I can remember singing merrily wherever I went in hopes of warning away any possible unsuspecting grizzly bears, prior to catching them by surprise up-close.

The distance at which an animal will start to flee is called the *flight distance* (or 'flight instigation distance'). The flight distance represents the outer point of a larger 'flight zone' that surrounds the animal and its 'fight zone'. The nearest point to the animal of its 'flight zone' will be the fight distance. The advanced trainer will pay careful attention to this critical juncture, where the animal resorts to fighting over fleeing. For example, staying outside the fight zone, but inside the flight zone, is necessary for the successful use of the negative reinforcement technique. Furthermore, the nuanced use of the flight zone will enable the trainer to finesse the desired response, based on how much stimulus strength they wish to use, since stimulus strength equates to proximity (see Chapter 7).

The innate tendency to aggress from fear occurs regardless of any predilection or previous experience. Anyone can exhibit full-blown lethal aggression, without any learning or approximations, if they are afraid for their safety. Even the most naturally mild-mannered individual should not be considered safe if pushed to severe fear or pain.

The classic example of this is a mother protecting her young. A mother fearing for the life of her offspring will often react nearly as defensively as if her own life was threatened (more in some cases).

Biologically, reproduction is the central reason for life, and for many species the maternal investment can be considerable. Thus, it is quite natural for a mother to respond dramatically to any potential threat to her young. Humans are a great example of this, with one of the highest levels of investment, and as a result, a significant defensive reaction to any threats to their children. Typically, a human mother (or father) will readily die to save their children.

Aggression that is motivated by fear or pain can only be *addressed through careful desensitization* (see Chapter 7). The previous chapter detailed these techniques associated with reducing the reaction to fear-provoking stimuli. A strongly positive relationship with the trainer will also act to counter-condition the effects of fear and is another important reason to guard and develop this tool. It cannot be stressed enough, that novel stimuli or situations should be approached with caution and thoughtfulness to avoid eliciting this type of aggression. **Fear is by far best prevented and assuaged, since there is little hope of altering it otherwise. It is, in my view, the most powerful of all motives.**

Natural history

Aggression that is based on the natural history of the animal, most typically involves *territoriality and predatory behavior.* Many animals are hardwired to defend areas or hunt and attack. Sexual rivalry is very similar to territorial aggression although this particular type of intra-species behavior less frequently generalizes to humans, though it certainly can. These instinctive drives will usually manifest in particular situations and seasons based on their natural history point of origin. *Keen understanding of the particular species* will guide an informed understanding of these tendencies.

If you think of the most dangerous animals, these are usually predators whose adaptations and instincts make a lethal combination. For my money, polar bears are the apex group of all the dangerous instinctive predators. Despite their outwardly cuddly appearance, these hunters will eat just about any other animal, including members of their own species. These animals are so hard-wired to aggress that there is no longer any program that I am aware of where humans work with adult animals in free contact. In my early years working at a zoo, I once met a Russian circus trainer of polar bears who regaled us with horrifying stories of near-miss attacks. This included one where she was forced to hold in her own gutted abdomen after a bear swiped her during a routine workout. The fear-less trainer emphasized the importance of not reacting with intimi-dation to the attack, lest she encourage further predatory behavior to develop and overwhelm the situation. She endured countless min-utes holding her gutted middle, while gating the animal back to its enclosure, before being able to seek medical treatment. The number of serious scars this woman wore still haunts my memory.

Play behavior in predators is frequently linked to develop-ing and practicing hunting behavior. For this reason, big cat and bear trainers must walk a fine line between affectionate rough housing and lethal instinct. These animals can quickly turn from one drive to the next if they end up in a dominant, predatory stance or mood. Understanding and avoiding the critical lines of play and predatory behavior with these animals is vital to remaining unharmed working with them in free contact. For some animals, play behavior is just as dangerous as full blown aggression and must be managed similarly in order to protect the trainer from harm.

Roy Horn (of Siegfried and Roy) was reportedly respond-ing to such a turn of instinct when he was later attacked, after his intervention brought the behavior's focus to himself. Apparently the tiger responded with heat and agitation to someone in the crowd with large hair in the front row. Sensing this dangerous aggression developing in the animal, Roy attempted to distract the animal from the crowd. The result was that the animal's attention then became focused on him and eventually led to the tiger dragging Roy offstage by his neck - the same manner in which a big cat drags its prey. I was told by an inside source that this particular animal had been display-ing aggressive and agitated behavior in several training sessions prior to the incident. If this is true, it demonstrates the important aspect of individual past history as a warning indication of future behavior. These stories are important cautionary tales; always remember to think of the animal as the species first and the individual second (see Chapter 5). Nowhere should these warnings be heeded more seriously than with aggressive behavior in large predators!

Predatory behavior will frequently be seen to arise from hunger, a particular attack posture, or prey behavior such as running away. Conversely, territorial behavior will take place around boundaries or areas of an environment. Sea lions, for example, exhibit territoriality to defend mating or pupping areas in the wild. In captivity this behavior is routinely demonstrated by guarding and defending doorways or high ground areas in the enclosure. Understanding these tendencies makes it easier to predict and therefore redirect or avoid aggressive behavior.

Instinctive natural behavior of this type is best understood from a species-specific viewpoint. Learning from an authority on the particular species in question is invaluable to predicting, and therefore redirecting or avoiding, this type of behavior before it is rehearsed. In some cases of instinctive aggression, a person can place themselves in an *alpha position* to address this issue, such as is commonly done with dogs, for example. Whether or not it is possible to behaviorally usurp the alpha position within a group of animals will depend greatly on if there is a linear hierarchical social dominance structure, and if it is practical to present species appropriate behavior to demonstrate this position. The natural history of most species does not offer this opportunity. Regardless of this rare possibility, it is important to remember that in most cases, instinctive behavior, by definition, cannot be eliminated but only avoided and redirected at best.

Physiological factors

Physiological factors often accompany other drives for aggressive behavior. Hormonal conditions, especially adrenaline, are common examples of physiological factors that may increase aggressive response or predispose it. There are a variety of physiological mechanisms that may operate to protect an animal under stress which can also lead to a heightened aggressive tendency. For example, there is an association between rapid changes in weight and increased aggressive behavior in sea lions, as well as during certain times of year in many animals. These changes are in part physiological predispositions toward aggression.

The most important of these hormones is adrenaline, which is associated with any aggressive incident. Adrenaline is the hormone that controls the 'fight or flight' response, making the animal more reactive and alert. As we are all aware, adrenaline causes powerful physical effects, such as increased heart rate and blood flow. Many animals can learn to enjoy the feeling of this rush. The thrill of adrenaline can become a habit forming drug regardless of the reason that the animal first experienced it. This developing enthusiasm for adrenaline is a kind of learned aggressive behavior that can develop from past aggressive experiences (see Learned Aggression, in this chapter). In a sense, the animal learns to act out in order to feel the excitement brought on by the adrenaline. If this sounds unlikely, it is a very common motivation among human thrill-seekers and even those seeking careers in the military. It can be similarly valued in a captive animal's life, especially if the environment does not offer enough stimulation for the animal.

Learned adrenaline-seeking behavior is one important reason to limit aggressive behavior in general and make this an issue of first concern. Additionally, since the adrenaline rush tends to last over 20 minutes post-event, it is highly prudent to avoid contact with an animal that has been through an adrenalizing experience for a period of time while this chemical leaves the blood. Otherwise, the floating adrenaline will make the animal more reactionary and aggressive than normal, and predispose the situation to further aggressive or undesirable behavior.

LEARNED AGGRESSION

Any of the previous motives can be a gateway to developing further learned aggressive behavior. *Learned aggression or instrumental aggression typically progresses in steps as the individual develops confidence and receives reinforcement for the first tested actions.* Learned aggression does not materialize with full confidence on first presentation and can be moderated by operant conditioning. Therefore, this type of aggression is the most malleable to direct teaching if it is altered before it becomes rehearsed and reinforced.

We have already discussed the motive of adrenaline seeking as a secondary drive born from any past aggressive incident (including other cases of learned aggression), but most learned aggression occurs as a mechanism for the animal to take control over its environment.

Control over the environment

It is natural for all animals (in captivity or not) to want to dominate and control resources when possible. Goldblatt, Tennson, Markowitz and others have variously demonstrated that control over the environment is a basic need. When choices are limited, aggressive behavior is one of few options in the repertoire of the captive animal, and thus a reasonable choice.

Typically, this type of aggressive behavior is born from *frustration* or a lack of control. For that reason, frustration can be seen as a frequent precursor to learned aggression. Watching for signs of this and preventing the unnecessary development of too much pent-up frustration is a wise training decision. Frustration can be built from unsatisfied desires or even from confusion. Lack of sufficient reinforcement can easily lead to aggression, so it is best to try to maintain a productive training session. 'Schedule-induced aggression' is a special form of frustration-based aggression where a past history of a continuous reinforcement has led the animal to expect this as a type of 'promise.' Thus, if reinforcement is not delivered or is latent, the animal may aggress in frustration to get what they feel is their due (see Chapter 6).

Attraction-type *aggression occurs to acquire things that the animal wants* and, in so doing, control its environment. This is aggressive behavior aimed to get something you don't have such as food, attention, or toys. (Predatory behavior can be seen as an instinctive attraction-type aggression.) This type of aggression is relatively easy to effectively redirect through providing choices and other means to get what the animal seeks. A balanced and fulfilled life, with healthy ways to get what is needed, is an excellent way to limit and eliminate this form of aggression if it crops up.

Conversely, **avoidance-type** *aggression occurs to prevent things from happening* that the animal does not want. This type of aggression provides a means to control something undesirable that is happening to them. (Territorial aggression can be attraction or avoidance instinctive aggression depending on if the animal is acquiring or defending. Similarly, maternal defensive aggression is generally avoidance-type by nature.) Once rehearsed and reinforced, avoidance aggression can be *very hard to eliminate*. A common example is with the ineffective use of restraint.

When restrained by force, an animal will almost certainly aggress from fear. Even if no harm comes to the animal, they often will continue to aggress in an attempt to avoid the restraint. If, through these actions, the animal is *ever* permitted to be freed from the restraint, this reinforcement will encourage this behavior tenfold in the future (thanks to the lottery principle and other properties of intermittent reinforcement). *The animal that has learned it is possible to break through a cage door, herding boards, restraining nets, or human hands will, in the future, be considerably more dangerous and dedicated to this approach, even to the extent of doing themselves great personal harm in the process.* Therefore, once restraint has been chosen as the technique, it is vitally important that all necessary effort be committed to enforcing this objective, in order to insure that the lesson the animal learns does not haunt the trainer for the rest of the life of the animal! Similarly, experienced trainers understand to proactively prevent an animal from ever pushing open the door of their enclosure, lest you will endure repeated attempts to destroy their environment in an effort to repeat the feat, especially if there is anything desirable on the other side of the door.

Avoidance-type aggression often begins with fear and so fear should be addressed most assiduously so it does not blossom into this type of learned aggression. This is where the term 'fear-biter' comes from: the animal that bites preemptively is preventing and controlling any possible action you might take toward them. Fear-biting often develops from inexpert, initial, tactile conditioning, where the trainer has taken insensitive approximations towards the introduction of being touched. This is another cautionary warning since fear-biting is nearly impossible to totally eliminate.

Avoidance aggression is, in my mind, the most undesirable of all aggressive motives, because it can be an overwhelming drive and very tricky to suppress sufficiently. The most effective method yet demonstrated to truly eliminate avoidance aggression was determined by Tortora (1983) to involve the use of negative reinforcement in the form of shock collars on dogs. Unfortunately, to make this 'safety training' technique work, the animal must first be subjected to an unrelenting aversive stimulus (like a shock from a shock collar) and then the shock is released by the stimulus that the animal is trying to avoid (such as being petted) while they instead perform a DRO (such as targeting). As long as aggressive behavior is suppressed, the aversive is neutralized by the presenting of calm behavior (targeting) instead of avoidance aggression. This technique is very tricky to apply however, and subjects the animal to aversive stimuli that most trainers would not be comfortable utilizing. Short of negative reinforcement, avoidance-type aggression is at best avoided but never truly eliminated. For this reason, great care should be taken to prevent *ever developing* this type of aggressive behavior in the first place.

Control-based aggression fundamentally works against the relationship and is a danger to the entire training system by attempting to work around the framework that the trainer has developed. As a learned form of aggression, it is eminently avoidable and possible to condition against if done proactively, and especially if the animal is young, and has little history of rehearsed aggressive behavior (see below).

TECHNIQUES FOR COPING WITH AGGRESSION

Now that we have outlined the various motives for being aggressive, let us turn to understanding better how to use the techniques available to reduce or eliminate aggression. Aggression by its nature is a motivation problem that should be addressed by *using the methods to discourage behavior* outlined in Motivation (see Chapter 6). Since it is also the subject of alternative or competing motivations *some techniques from Desensitization* will also be helpful particularly to address fear-based and avoidance-type aggressive behavior. In this chapter we will focus on how to apply these techniques as they pertain to eliminating aggressive behavior, for general comments on the benefits and drawbacks of each technique please return to Chapter 6.

It is important to recognize that aggression *is a training problem*. Many people simply try to ignore it, which frequently allows it to be rehearsed and developed. While there is some reasonable argument for ignoring undesirable behavior, as we will discuss further below, using *only* this technique is neither proactive nor sufficient for many situations. Risking the development of aggression through blind hope and inattention generally demonstrates a lack of expertise that will, with enough opportunity, eventually result in permanent behavioral problems. For this reason, I recommend making aggression the top priority of any training program. Ultimately, it is very hard to accomplish any behavioral engineering objective if you must be worried about potentially being hurt by your animal.

The most powerful method of having a well-adjusted, unaggressive animal is to never allow that animal to practice and rehearse aggression in the first place. Methods of *prevention* are typically far preferable to those associated with the alternative, *punishment*, for reasons of the effect on the relationship and the psychological health of the animal. However, for the sake of comprehensiveness, we will cover both the tools of prevention and the tools of punishment, as they specifically apply to eliminating aggression.

PREDICTING AGGRESSION

In order to prevent the antecedent conditions to aggression it is most helpful to be able to predict where outbreaks of violent behavior may erupt. Predicting aggressive behavior boils down to an understanding of species and individual.

Aggression can show up full blown with lethal intent or it can present with more mild outbursts and threats. Full blown aggression comes out primarily in fear-related scenarios, where the animal may believe its life is on the line, or in situations where the animal has a long history of practicing aggression that has built up to a confident maximum. Even in predatory or territorial aggression, there is some learning and exploration as the animal becomes confident and increasingly bold. Learned aggression also typically starts small, with threats and tests. If the animal is reinforced and feels comfortable with the outcome, the aggressive behavior will go into the next phase and keep increasing in magnitude.

While an animal is in the developing phase of aggression, it will typically exhibit threat behavior that is particular to each species.

Species specific characteristics

With animals, we call the first indicators of aggression *primary aggressive signs or aggressive precursors*. These are species-specific threat displays intended as warnings (see Figure 21). They demonstrate that the animal has aggressive intent. They may be used within the species for communication, or intended to increase the animal's apparent stimulus strength to any would-be attacker.

By reading the animal for precursor signs directed at the trainer, the trainer has advanced warning of potential aggressive incidents forthcoming. I recommend addressing the aggression as soon as a primary sign is demonstrated. *It is best to stop the problem at the precursor stage before ever allowing it to develop into full blown aggression.* This early reaction will stave off any further development including adrenaline-seeking motives. *Much of the development of aggressive behavior that apparently "came out of nowhere" is a result of the trainer failing to recognize the significance of precursor warning signs.*

Figure 21: Various primary aggressive signs across animal taxa.
(Photo credit: ©iStock.com.)

Animals that have developed full blown aggression may or may not continue to demonstrate these primary signs, but in many cases these primary signs will provide important information about drives developing in the animal. Each species has its own unique primary aggressive signs, and it behooves every trainer to learn these signs for each species they interact with. If for some reason an expert is not available to provide this insight, it is possible to learn much of this language from careful observation of several members of the species interacting with one another.

I make the important distinction that, in order for these precursors to constitute aggression (as defined in this text), the precursor must be *directed at the trainer*. Directing any of these behaviors obliquely or at another part of the environment, I take as a sign of frustration, or maybe fear, but not an actual threat to the trainer.

Examples of a few distinct primary aggressive signs include: hackle raising in dogs, head darting in sea lions, hissing in sea otters, striking out with hooves in horses, and flattened ears in cats. In each example, these behaviors would have to be focused on the trainer for the intent of harm to be communicated. Many primary aggressive signs are similar between species, for example, baring of teeth is often intended as an aggressive threat (especially in predatory species), as is lunging at someone. Many forms of vocalizations can be intended to warn or threaten. Some primary signs can be very subtle, such as a front paw raised by a dog or a sea lion rushing to a doorway, so it is very important to learn the full language of the species you work with to really understand what each animal intends by its behavior.

In general, any action that the animal does which may have the potential to cause harm to the trainer, such as pushing into a person, stepping on a person, or stealing things held in the hands (where careless teeth may catch flesh), are best considered as primary aggressive signs. Depending on the social structure of the species, these actions would rarely be tolerated by the dominant animal and may develop into a problem if left to increase, although this may depend greatly on how large and dangerous the species is.

It is important to note that *signs of fear or interest are not primary aggressive signs* in that they do not carry the meaning that the animal intends to threaten the trainer. Primary aggressive signs are species-specific language in which the animal is in effect saying, "I am considering harming you (if you don't give me that, stop that, etc.)." Whereas signs of fear such as avoidance or wide eyes are an indication that says "I am worried about or afraid of that." This is a small but significant difference in my opinion. However, since fear can easily lead to aggression, it is very important to recognize and take the necessary desensitization precautions at any sign of fear, lest they quickly become aggressive signs. It is also worth noting that in prey species, where flight is usually the first choice, signs of fear may overlap considerably more with aggressive precursors.

Individual past history

Enough cannot be said about the importance of an animal's past history of aggression as a keen indicator of potential future behavior. Even if the animal has not presented any aggressive behavior in some time, a past history of aggression will always indicate it to be a likely future option for that individual more than for others. *The effects of repeated rehearsal of aggressive behavior are, for all intents and purposes, permanent haunting aspects of the animal's behavior and failure to remember this can be deadly.* I know of many cases where violently aggressive animals failed to show any sign of aggressive behavior for many years in between events, thanks in good part to careful proactive training regimes. Nevertheless, in moments of strain or opportunity, the preventative measures taken were not up to the task of changing the effects of past rehearsal.

Personal history is even more telling than species-specific behavior, but both should provide ample incentive to avoid risky behavior with dangerous species or individuals. Understanding the past history of an animal measured against the potential of that individual to cause harm should help dictate training protocols necessary to eliminate fatalities or serious injury. In many cases the only prudent training option is to avoid direct contact with dangerous individuals (or species) altogether.

PROTECTED CONTACT (PC)

Using a protective barrier or environmental distance of some kind is one of the best ways to interact with dangerous animals, especially in cases where the individual past history makes them a high risk. Where unfettered access is called 'free contact' or FC, conversely this technique is called 'protected contact' (PC) or 'closed contact' (CC) work.

In *protected contact - barriers, distance or other protective measures are used to minimize the risk to the trainer while still allowing some contact to occur between the trainer and the animal* (see Figure 22). This can involve safely occupying the dangerous parts of the animal (using a device held in the mouth), but more typical protected contact scenarios involve fences or bars restricting the animal's access to the trainer while providing the trainer controlled access to the animal's body through small periodic openings or trap doors. The amount of contact permitted by the size of the openings generally depends on how dangerous the species or individual is. Holes or slots in the barrier allow body parts to be manipulated and touched by the trainer. Training an animal that is restricted to the water while the trainer remains at the surface would be another example of PC. This works because requiring the animal to lunge up and out of the water in order to cause harm severely limits their ability to do so.

Closed contact is distinguished from protected contact in that there is essentially no contact allowed between the animal and the trainer. CC training can occur from across a moat, over a wall or through a transparent barrier. Closed contact work is necessary in the extreme cases where life threatening injury could be inflicted should the animal manage to attack the trainer through the barrier in some way (adult polar bears are typically trained primarily through closed contact, for example).

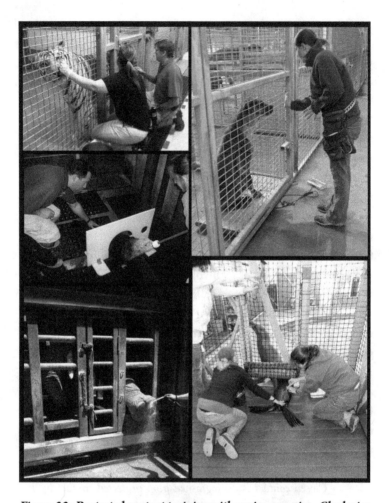

Figure 22: Protected contact training with various species. Clockwise from upper left: a tiger at the Downtown Aquarium receiving a voluntary rabies injection, a hyena at Moorpark College sitting for a weight on a platform scale, a California sea lion at Moss Landing Marine Laboratories cooperating in a blood sampling procedure, an elephant presenting its foot for a cleaning at the Oakland Zoo, and an otter at the Aquarium of the Pacific being desensitized to tactile examination.

(Photo credits: Patti Shoemaker, Gary Wilson, ATR International, and Michele Sousa.)

➤ *The benefits and drawbacks of protected contact*

For many animals protected or closed contact may be the only viable option available due to the dangers that any aggressive behavior could pose to the trainer. I cannot think of a training goal that requires free contact that I would value over the risk to my life. *Certainly most of the benefits of training can be accomplished using protected contact* including husbandry, medical, performance and even most research. This issue is the subject of much disagreement between trainers. Some believe that the *risks of contact are worth the benefits to the relationship and what can be accomplished* while others feel that it is foolish to continue to risk death or serious injury when protected contact work can be used for any desirable type of training except *riding the animal.* Indeed, *free contact is necessary in cases where the human and the animal cannot accomplish the goal without unfettered access,* such as the case where the human is to ride the animal for example. Nowhere is this more controversial than with elephant trainers, who fall into two distinct camps.

The traditional elephant training systems have for millennia been based on similar constructs to horse training, in which negative reinforcement and trainer dominance is used to emulate an alpha position in the herd and create this type of relationship between the animal and trainer. In elephants, this is a particularly risky option since the size of the animal means that they can, if motivated, overwhelm nearly any aversive stimulus the trainer chooses to employ to cause behavior. Plus, although elephants could be seen as prey animals, they are nowhere near as prone to flight as horses, making negative reinforcement much trickier. Thus, this system seems doomed to failure periodically, and good evidence of this is the fact that elephant training used to be the most deadly (per capita) occupation in the world. More recently, positive reinforcement in PC training has developed as a popular alternative to traditional elephant training regimes.

Interestingly, it is the subject of much debate how dangerous or plausible it would be to work with elephants in free contact using only positive reinforcement methods. To my knowledge, so far this has not yet been truly and purely accomplished. Clearly, the animals would have less incentive to react adversely when no aversive stimuli are used. However, just as clearly, the humans would be *completely at the mercy of the huge mammals* and, especially for animals who had previously experienced negative reinforcement methods, aggression is likely to occur 'spontaneously' as Konrad Lorenz put it, since it is a natural behavior. Time will tell whether the free contact, positive-reinforcement-only elephants will be completely harmless to their trainers. It will take a considerable number of examples before any conclusion can be drawn since, as it is, most negative reinforcement trained free-contact elephants do not harm their trainers.

The decision to use protected or closed contact is typically based on the level of danger posed by that particular species (such as bears, big cats, or elephants) and/or the past history of the individual's aggressive behavior. Protected contact *can also be an excellent method of beginning a training relationship,* regardless of any risk factors, simply as a prudent preventative measure. I often start animals in protected contact to prevent rehearsal of aggression and move to free contact when it is safer to do so, after I have established basic behavior and communication tools (such as the bridge and the target) that can be used to redirect any likely potential aggression. Since rehearsal of aggression has a damning effect on behavior, true prevention of the opportunity to aggress will establish the highest chance of any animal developing the right habits.

IGNORING BAD BEHAVIOR

Most positive-reinforcement-based instructional systems suggest the best reaction to aggressive behavior is no reaction at all. This avoids the possibility of inadvertently reinforcing the aggression by your actions. This is a valid, although un-nuanced, approach that prioritizes for prevention of further reinforcement or mistakes, rather than teaching the animals not to be aggressive. Animals in these situations may or may not even be aware that their behavior is undesirable, since no punishment or redirection stimulus has been used as a consequence.

➤ *The benefits and drawbacks of ignoring aggressive behavior*

Of course, the idea of ignoring aggressive behavior can be more easily said than done. In real life, when you have an otter's jaw clamped on your arm, it is highly unlikely that 'no response' will be manageable! Very few people I know could sit quietly and wait with an otter hanging from their forearm. The reality is that a person will instinctively respond with the use of some physical punishment to free themselves from the situation. Depending on the type and the size of the animal, this can make the situation better or worse. If the animal is small or easily deterred (like a prey species) then the use of physical punishment will likely successful terminate the encounter and reduce it in the future. If the animal is a top predator, like a lion or a bear, this reaction may inspire an increase in aggression that could result in the trainer's death (which may be imminent in either case). For this reason, having a safety trainer nearby, possibly with a tranquilizing gun, watching all free contact work with top terrestrial predators is a minimum safety requirement for me personally. Safety and safety protocols should be the first consideration of any system working with dangerous creatures (see Chapter 9).

With many species, serious aggression is likely to occur at some point. Therefore, it is advisable to decide in advance what realistic reaction you intend to have. In this case, choosing from among the other techniques in combination with any use of ignoring the behavior may provide a more honest reflection of what will occur in dangerous aggressive events. (This is one of the primary reasons I choose to have a redirection stimulus (RS), use TOs, and work in PC.)

A percentage of animals in systems with a blanket policy to ignore aggressive behavior will become 'training school dropouts' and be relegated to safe or non-training environments, especially for species with a significant tendency towards aggression. This is because their bad behavior cannot be eliminated by ignoring it alone, and *ignoring the behavior has allowed for repeated rehearsal that becomes habit.* If the animal is reinforced by anything internal, or external but not the trainer, ignoring the behavior will not necessarily withhold reinforcement and cause extinction (see Chapter 6). As we have already discussed, sufficient rehearsal of any behavior will make it almost impossible to eliminate. If these animals are truly dangerous and they have rehearsed aggression, it is irresponsible to allow them to continue in free contact. Therefore, *the strategy of ignoring aggressive behavior is best used in conjunction with other techniques like redirection or with relatively-safe non-aggressive species. This technique could be considered optimal, in the particular case, where it is likely that the animal's primary aggressive objective is seeking attention from the trainer.*

If ignored, some animals will drop the un-reinforced bad behavior and go on to become well-adjusted members of society. Whether an animal goes one way or another largely depends on species-specific tendencies toward aggression, the results of individual rehearsal history, and how self-motivating the behavior is. Ignoring the behavior works best with precursor signs of aggression and not full blown aggression. However, once precursors are noted, it is best to take future pro-active measures, especially using redirection to prevent these precursors from developing further into full blown aggression.

Being caught unaware, this technique is still one of the better reactions, especially if you have no RS, but it is not a sufficient strategy alone to cope with the problem of aggressive behavior, since it is an *entirely reactive* and not a proactive conditioning approach.

PROACTIVE CONDITIONING TO REDUCE AGGRESSIVE BEHAVIOR

Many deliberate conditioning techniques that we have already discussed can be used to reduce aggressive behavior. Some of these techniques will be more effective than others, depending on species and type of aggressive motive, so, as in all behavioral decisions, it is important to take each situation on a case-by-case basis.

Systematic desensitization

Systematic desensitization (as described in Chapter 7) is the best method to reduce the fear caused by aversive stimuli, without risking sensitization, thus minimizing the chances of fear-based aggression. Wherever possible, *any situation that involves novel stimuli or a stimulus with high stimulus strength* should be approached with considerable caution, using systematic methods to lower the possible resultant fear. It is critical that this should involve *any scenario in which the animal is touched or learning to accept touch,* as these are the most frequent avoidance-aggression motives.

Progressive training programs, of any type with any species, should involve proactive preparatory training for basic medical procedures such as routine physical examinations by a veterinarian or training to accept inoculations. Animals should be prepared in advance of need, in order to be well desensitized when the time comes. Similarly, any probable situation should be addressed proactively, through training, in order to avoid the use of force and the resultant likely aggressive reaction. Preparation for transport in a cage is another common scenario that frequently requires force if not properly counter-conditioned and systematically desensitized in advance. Each situation is unique, and it is important to thoughtfully evaluate the expected needs of the individual in question, and use systematic methods to prepare them for the eventualities of their lives.

Body posture

There can be an advantage to understanding certain rules of body posture in order to reduce or dispel possible aggressive behavior. Generally in the animal kingdom, the louder, bigger animal which does not retreat has the least chance of being attacked and may also be the dominant animal. How this understanding is applied will depend greatly on the species and the scenario. For example, turning your back or running away from a lion that is showing primary aggressive signs may result in escalating this behavior to full blown attack. Similarly, remaining standing during anti-aggression training is an important element of maintaining dominance working with dogs for example. Conversely, minimizing your stature by kneeling may reduce anxiety and associated aggression in animals that are or may be frightened, so novel stimuli introduction might be best attempted with more slight and moderate postures to maintain the lowest stimulus value possible.

Maintaining an 'alpha position'

As was discussed in the section on negative reinforcement in Chapter 5, in some very particular species (not most), there is an arguable advantage to maintaining a 'leadership' role in order to reduce aggressive behavior. This controversial idea is part of the rationale maintained by the proponents of negative reinforcement in free contact training in elephants (and the resultant lack of confidence to proceed to free contact without the use of negative reinforcement methods). This technique is primarily helpful for very particular species that naturally maintain organized or highly linear dominance systems such as horses, dogs, elephants, sea lions, and wolves.

It is important to note that dominance hierarchies are, fundamentally, about controlling access to resources (for example, food or mates) and maintaining safety. However, these social systems have evolved in order to ultimately increase reproductive success. The arrangement(s) of social organization within a species can be empirically demonstrated. They are not merely based on an individual's learning history, although learned behavior can certainly be directed at the same goals (to obtain food or mates, for example). For this reason, people can easily confuse basic operant behavior with more instinctive and organized social structure. Arguably these two are co-occurring, and learned behavior dramatically effects how an animal will respond socially. However, some in the animal training field have recently suggested that there is "no such thing" as a natural system of social organization and dominance in certain species (like dogs or horses). This assertion is incorrect.

The difference between training a cat and training a dog can easily demonstrate the intrinsic value of a native organized social leadership system. Domestic cats do form colonies and wher-ever groups of animals reside, dominance systems will be in place. However, the instinctive, pack-mentality of the dog (or wild dog) establishes a roaming, tightly-cohesive group that works collabora-tively for territorial defense as well as hunting. Pack affiliation and linear hierarchy makes dogs inherently more positively responsive to dominance-based leadership than cats, where leadership is less rel-evant to the social structure and is not implied by dominance. Thus, dogs respond differently to nuanced dominance behavior than do cats, although they both have dominance relationships. This differ-ence makes dogs easier to train, since their native social disposition makes them more likely to follow a leader, and the same can largely be said of horses. Therefore, the use of the technique of maintaining an 'alpha' or dominant leadership position is based on a keen under-standing of the species in question.

Displacement training

In most species, *the dominant animal is the animal that is capable of displacing the others.* This idea is controversially used by many dog or horse trainers. This is typically accomplished by negative reinforce-ment and repeatedly driving the animal in a desired direction using light (but effective) aversive stimulus. The lighter the applied stimu-lus strength, the lower the chance of causing inadvertent aggression in response (a distinct possibility). In 'horse whispering,' for example, this is done using a lunge whip or the human's body.

It is worth noting that whenever people describe themselves as 'using body language,' they are typically referring to some form of this technique. In many cases, so-called 'body language' used by a trainer to condition behavior in an animal will be based on extremely light negative reinforcement, linked to the species natural social tendencies. For example, the trainer will step forward or raise his/her energy level, influencing a displacement behavior in the animal.

It is also possible to use positive reinforcement to condition a redirected displacement behavior. These redirected 'displacements' help increase the chance that the animal will yield, understands to yield, and will do so without displaying aggressive behavior (see later in this chapter for more on redirection in aggressive scenarios). In these cases, the animal is taught to displace when the trainer moves forward and then reinforced repeatedly and lavishly for doing so, developing the tendency to give way over time and in a variety of scenarios of relevance to that species and situation. For example, I routinely teach animals to back away from food containers I place on the ground. Eventually this repetition makes this action an S^D to move away, thus discouraging the animal from stealing or charging the container.

Depending on the sensibilities of the trainer, the animal may also be encouraged simultaneously with negative reinforcement, since these are not mutually exclusive. It is *possible to use a combination of negative reinforcement and positive reinforcement to develop the displacement behavior.*

Nevertheless, as I have repeatedly pointed out, *the use of aversives can easily backfire and cause aggression.* Displacement or other alpha-type behavior can result in reducing or increasing aggressive behavior depending on the skill of the trainer, as well as, the past history and species of the animal. For those who use these techniques successfully, the rewards are improved safety and flexibility. Others fear the possible downside of increasing aggression, especially if the situation involves novice trainers who could easily apply the wrong level of pressure and exacerbate the situation. In those cases, simple positive reinforcement based displacement training can still be used to great effect.

Positive relationship

Associated with the various motivational advantages, *a positive relationship history between the trainer and the animal can help buffer against fear and avoidance-type aggressive motives,* especially in situations that require trust. To a certain extent this happens through counter-conditioning, where the relationship counteracts the aversive value of the situation or the aversive stimulus. Thus, the defensive mother is more likely to mildly accept the handling of her offspring by someone with whom she has a long positive history.

For animals that have little history with the trainer, protected contact can be a method of allowing this relationship to develop, all the while creating necessary tools of communication such as the bridge, targets and behaviors that can be used to redirect any possible aggressive behavior.

Redirection

As we have already discussed, redirection, either through differential reinforcement of other behavior (DRO) or differential reinforcement of an incompatible behavior (DRI), is the most relationship-friendly method of discouraging unwanted behavior, while simultaneously preventing the rehearsal of undesirable behavior (see Chapter 6). In order to use this excellent technique to stave off aggressive behavior, it is necessary to be able to both predict where aggression might occur, and to have adequate behavioral options to divert the animal from the undesirable behavior *prior* to its onset. The best methods to predict aggressive behavior were discussed earlier in this chapter and should be used to anticipate and devise a way to thwart possible violence before it develops. Behavior that can be used as a means of redirection can be developed in PC first. In FC, baiting is often a good first option until further behavior has been developed. Once the trainer has the ability to predict where aggressive behavior will manifest, it is prudent to immediately begin to use DRO or DRI in any likely aggressive context.

For example, a good deal of sea lion aggression occurs around boundary areas. Sea lions very commonly choose to charge at the doorway when a trainer is entering or exiting. This primary sign of aggression can quickly develop to biting the trainer to insure the right of passage and to dominate the boundary. Understanding this, it is possible to redirect this behavior by conditioning the animal to stay in the water or on a target whenever the door is opened. Obviously, it is incompatible to be both staying in the water (or on target) and rushing for the doorway at the same time. These behaviors can first be conditioned in PC and rehearsed through small approximations of the trainer opening the doorway increasingly, until the behavior is well established in the context of the trainer coming and going through the doorway. If practiced and reinforced sufficiently, eventually the trainer preparing to enter or exit will become an S^D for the water or target behavior. This example generalizes well to many species and represents proactive preventative training that should optimally be done in any situation where aggression is known to or likely to occur.

Using redirection with punishment

Although redirection alone can be successful at eliminating behavior, there is evidence that *DRI or DRO can work best in concert with punishment for optimal suppression of particularly difficult behavior* (see Chapter 6). This combination of techniques tends to stack the motivational decks strongly in the favor of the desired behavior by using both the carrot and the stick. On the one hand, the animal should be lavishly rewarded for performing the desired incompatible behavior, but as the choice remains theirs, they are alternatively punished or disincentivized for misbehavior. This approach creates a loaded drive toward the desirable behavior as the motives combine to make it the best option.

In order to be best prepared to react correctly and in a timely manner, this type of conditioning is optimally accomplished using what can be called an *Anti-aggressive training scenario*. These deliberate training sessions provide careful planning and preparation allowing the trainer to be highly alert to the smallest indication of aggressive precursor, and react proactively instead of reactively to the situation. Similar to straight redirection, a likely aggressive scenario is carefully chosen and created to provide the option of the redirected behavior or the aggressive choice. These scenarios are best accomplished with some initial history of DRI or DRO to help guide the animal towards the correct reinforcing option. However, should the animal even begin to choose to display any precursor or behavior indicating the possible aggressive choice, punishment (usually a TO) is the delivered consequence.

Anti-Aggression Scenario

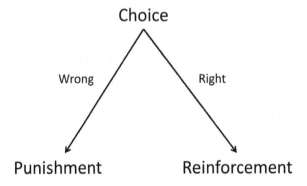

During the initial phases of redirection rehearsal, care should be taken to severely limit the possible rehearsal of successful aggression by using back-up safety measures. Examples of which would be covers over food containers placed on the ground, assistants to help provide a safeguard, or distance protecting the trainer from the animal. If the animal chooses to begin to make the aggressive choice (say by leaving the water in the previous DRI example), optimally the trainer would tag the inappropriate behavior with an RS, if such a tool has been trained. This allows the trainer to actually explain to the animal that the behavior is wrong and hopefully encourage redirection. If they change their behavior or back away, as in all cases with the RS, the trainer should bridge for choosing not to be aggressive. (This is actually a very good type of scenario in which to train an RS.) Alternatively, an LRS (least reinforcing scenario) may be helpful to bring the animal's attention to the misbehavior. *Reinforcement can be used after a correct reaction to either the RS or the LRS, however this should be kept to a minimum lest the animal learns to aggress only to halt and then receive reinforcement. The DRI should always be considerably higher paying than the correct response to the RS or LRS.*

If the animal fails to respond correctly to the RS and LRS, less mild forms of punishment can be used depending on the severity of the aggression and the trainer's comfort with these techniques. In particular, the use of time-outs may be strongly warranted to reduce any possible adrenaline motive, as long as the animal desires the presence of the trainer.

➢ The benefits and drawbacks of anti-aggression scenarios

Anti-aggression training scenarios are the most deliberate *method to identify and directly train out aggressive behavior; however, they are highly risky and require considerable skill.* The downsides of punishment cannot be stressed enough (see Chapter 6 for more on the drawbacks of punishment), and these techniques can easily be *dangerous if used by inexperienced trainers.* This training works *best with young, smaller, or inexperienced animals* who are relatively safe to punish. These animals learn the rules and grow up behaving accordingly, due to a long history of rehearsal and redirection. On the other hand, animals with a history of aggression generally will always carry a significant aggressive risk, and punishment can frequently make that risk greater due to the inherent downsides to the use of aversives.

USING PUNISHMENT

Negative punishment

To the extent that the trainer can be reasonably confident in the motivation of the animal, especially if a strong positive relationship has been cultivated, *negative punishment can be the optimal form of punishment for aggressive behavior*. Time-outs and extended time-outs allow the use of punishment without the trainer associating with aversive stimuli; as such, negative punishment has the *least potential to cause avoidance aggression*. Negative punishment *may still incite attraction-type aggression* if the animal is strongly covetous of the reinforcer being withheld. Time-outs have the significant advantage of allowing the animal time to cool down after an aggressive response (or precursor), *enabling the adrenaline rush to subside* and thus limiting the immediate risk of further aggressive behavior and rehearsal.

On the other hand, if the animal feels fear or avoidance-type aggression, it may aggress in hopes that the trainer backs off or departs. In this case, the trainer leaving on a time-out will effectively reinforce the animal and encourage this type of behavior in the future. This is the delicate line that must be walked with negative punishment, and much of the successful use of this technique depends on the astute perception of the trainer. Many trainers avoid the use of negative punishment out of fear of *potentially reinforcing the avoidance behavior* or alternatively inciting attraction-type aggression when the trainer tries to leave with all the reinforcement. The first risk may be minimized by a careful attention to the relationship and general motivation of the animal. The attraction risk, that the animal will aggress to prevent the reinforcement from leaving, will be equally concerning should the trainer choose to stay or go. The animal will be hyper-responsive from the adrenaline and therefore more reactionary, making either option a potential hazard. *If the risks are so great as to make the trainer's departure challenging, the ani-*

mal might better be trained using some form of PC at least until further behavioral control can be managed.

Positive punishment

Inherently, most forms of positive punishment associate the trainer with an aversive consequence. In this sense, this technique of addressing undesirable behavior carries with it the most perilous prospects.

Communication

Information that reduces the frequency of the behavior that it follows can be one of the least aversive forms of punishment. The RS in particular is relatively innocuous since it may result in a path to reinforcement. Stimuli that help tag or pinpoint behavior that may result in punishment can functionally warn the animal away from the behavior and prevent the ensuing punishing consequence. These signals can be effective for trainers who wish to deliberately train the animal to understand and avoid particular behaviors, but they can also present challenges to the novice trainer or in large training systems with trainers of various levels of experience. In large training systems, where oversight and consistency present difficulties, conditioning such communication devices poses inherent problems. As a result, some systems choose to use only the LRS, to provide what they feel is the best compromise of risk/reward communication.

Physical punishment

Physical punishment is undoubtedly one of the most controversial techniques in this text. It involves *any level* of aversive physical contact with the animal as a consequence (in this case) of aggressive behavior. Similar to the human example of hitting a child, most people can easily agree that this technique is unconscionable. However, it is less clear that a parent should not grab their child by the arm or spank them, both of which would be considered forms of physical punishment.

I am not recommending this method; however, as I have stated upfront, I intend to document all possible methods of addressing behavior (see Chapter 6 for more on the general benefits and drawbacks of punishment).

I have already pointed out that in many cases of aggressive attack, some response of this type, by the trainer, may be both natural and necessary, since few people will sit by idly and fail to respond if they are in direct danger. A person in danger will generally act out to protect themselves and discourage the animal. Choosing to do this in the right situations and the right way may be the difference between life and death.

Although most are opposed to this approach, I will point out again that it is widely used during unconditioned medical or restraint procedures both of which can be considered physical and aversive. In these cases, the animal may develop an aversion to the veterinarian or other aspects of the procedure. In the case of punishment for aggression, the animal can learn to develop an aversion to aggressive behavior (but also possibly to the trainer!). It is equally important to note that, *as the most profound of aversives, physical punishment can easily and frequently cause further aggression,* for this reason it must be well understood to be best managed.

Physical punishment can be very intimidating and, as such, may interact with the animal's dominance system, for better or worse. All forms of physical punishment will be *optimized if generalized directly from physical contact within the species.* Thus, it may not be safe to use any form of physical punishment with large animals in free contact. Furthermore, many species do not have a social context which is conducive to accepting physical punishment. For example, birds generally react very poorly to physical punishment. In these situations, if aversive physical contact is used to reduce aggression it should be done in such a way as to limit the association and access to the trainer (such as with nets or other devices).

By using physical contact that mimics dominance behaviors of the species, it is possible to use less force and to engage a certain amount of instinctive behavior. For example, grabbing a young cat by the scruff of the neck will instigate a submissive posture as the kitten yields to being carried by its mother. If this technique is maintained periodically, this reaction will persist into adulthood and may present an effective punishment. Cesar Millan, the dog whisperer, regularly uses a small grabbing pinch to the neck of a dog that he is trying to correct. This slight nip mimics the dominant dog's correction to a submissive. Each of these cases represents a species-specific form of mild physical punishment.

Whatever form of physical punishment is used it is *critical that the trainer not become angry, vengeful nor intend any harm to the animal.* These objectives are emotional and counter-productive. The intent must be to teach the animal about undesirable behavior; taking things personally is fruitless, abusive, and unprofessional. *Hysterical or severe usage of physical punishment will almost invariably backfire* and result in a variety of unhealthy behavioral responses: including aggression, avoidance, self-mutilation, learned helplessness, depression and fear. For these reasons, most physical punishment is more harmful than helpful. In the case of large animals, any physical punishment can cause the incident to escalate and may lead to the trainer's death.

It is also important to recognize that physical punishment tends to be *most effective with attraction-type aggression motives.* It is generally counter-productive to use physical punishment with an animal that is afraid, as more fear will certainly result, just making matters worse. When it is used, physical punishment should be used as a last resort mechanism with appropriate species, and optimally only after the animal has had the chance to learn alternative desirable behavior options to avoid the punishment.

AGGRESSION, *IN SUMMARY*

Aggressive behavior in this text denotes any behavior intended to threaten or to do harm to a human. It is recommended that this behavior be the default first priority in any species with the potential to do harm to the trainer. There are both instinctive and learned aggressive motives. Understanding the variety of motives that combine to drive aggressive behavior can help determine the best methods to discourage (or encourage) aggression. Pain and fear can be the most dangerous and powerful of all the aggressive motives and should be addressed using the principles and techniques discussed in Desensitization (see Chapter 7). Understanding of natural history as well as individual past history can identify likely aggressive scenarios and primary warning signs of aggression. Coping with aggression by means of predictive insight and redirection is the best method of preventing rehearsal and avoiding difficult avoidance-type aggressive behavior. Use of protected contact will permit safe handling for dangerous animals or those with limited conditioning history.

CHAPTER 9

PRACTICAL TRAINING

Figure 23: Trainer Stefani Skrovan using target training to train a horse to rear.

(Photo credit: ATR International.)

We have covered the basic techniques and principles of behavior modification by breaking down the issue into methods of communicating to someone how to do a behavior (Chapters 4 and 5) and also methods of convincing them to want to behave how you would like (Chapters 6, 7 and 8). To pull it all together now, this chapter will discuss the practical application of these ideas and *how to use this framework to plan, implement and troubleshoot a training program.* This chapter will draw information and theory from throughout the text to focus on the practical implementation of this material. I recommend however, that the reader rely heavily on the relevant chapters for important details and concerns regarding any particular approach.

PREPARATION AND PLANNING

Whether you are engaged in a training program for a single individual or for an entire zoological park, proper preparation and planning will help to create the optimal healthy learning environment for your animals. Investing thoughtfully in a deliberate behavior modification system will yield exponential rewards over the lifetime of the animals and facilities involved. This section highlights some of the most basic and critical foundational elements related to fostering well-adjusted and well-behaved animals (the first step being to study this book, of course ☺).

KNOW THE SPECIES

It goes without saying that an understanding of one species does not make someone an authority on others. Even for advanced trainers, it is wise to study any new species carefully to grasp the unique complexities of each as much as possible. *The natural history of a species provides considerable insight into how the animal might view and respond to situations, what might motivate them, and how to interpret their body language.* The perspective of a species expert is a valuable resource. This knowledge is particularly useful to equipping the trainer with adequate insight to 'read' the animal and understand their half of the training 'conversation.' Being able to detect and respond to primary signs of aggression or fear can also be lifesaving. Considering the animal first, as a member of its species, and second, as an individual, may provide the necessary caution and planning to prevent catastrophic development of undesirable behavior patterns.

KNOW THE INDIVIDUAL

As much variability as can be found among different species, is also present between individuals of the same species. Animals are as unique and distinct in their personalities and past histories as humans are. They have been shaped by distinct genetics and most especially by singular life histories. Therefore, trying to learn as much as possible about the individual animals you will be working with in terms of their past behavior, experiences, desires and fears will be invaluable in creating a training plan for that particular creature. To the extent that the teacher can design the instructional process directly to the sensibilities of the student, the process will be more successful for everyone. Learning is not a one-size-fits-all type of undertaking, and *the best trainers have the flexibility and savvy to react and plan differently for each distinctive creature and situation.*

I recommend creating daily training logs that record each animal's progress and experiences. This idea is especially important in large facilities with multiple trainers working with the same animals. These logs will help current trainers stay in contact and future trainers understand better the history of each animal. Even in small or private programs, some record of what the animal experienced, and when, will help preserve what may otherwise be lost to time and memory.

FACILITIES

The environment in which the animal resides can offer both opportunity and hindrance to a variety of possible training options. *A complete survey of the facilities and options available to the animal and the trainer, before engaging in the training program, is highly advised.* The facilities may dictate if it is possible to work in protected contact, whether or not you can separate animals for training, where animals might be hiding, as well as safety hazards and risks of working in certain areas of the environment.

To operate safely in any environment, it is important to understand the escape routes and where the trainer might be vulnerable to being cornered or limited in movement. It is vitally important to consider the worst case scenarios and have in place well-thought out *safety protocols* to enact in case of danger. Deliberately building species-appropriate protected or closed contact environmental options is one method of creating safety for the trainer. Increasingly, professional training systems also have written plans and employee training to make certain that everyone understands how to react in various cases of disaster, since no situation is absolutely without risk.

THE IMPORTANCE OF CONSISTENCY

A deliberate behavior modification program will have a planned and clear communication system in place. This should ideally evolve to include a written description of the behaviors, cues and behavioral criteria. Such an operational manual will help to guide and trouble-shoot behavior modification issues as they develop. *The importance of being consistent with one's approach to an animal's training program, behavioral criteria, appearance of S^D, rules of conduct, meaning of stimulus and general communication system cannot be understated,* regardless of whether or not it is actually put in writing.

It is vital that an animal can 'believe in' what the trainer says and does, and can trust what he/she learns to be the truth. This confidence is necessary to form the very fiber of the relationship between the trainer and the animal. Symbolic language depends on consistency of meaning. To the extent that the rules or symbols are variable and changing, the animal can easily become frustrated with the lack of believability and much of the empowering benefit offered by a developing understanding can be lost. Inconsistent systems or groups of trainers are identifiable by the animal's tendency to guess instead of listen and show a general lack of trust. Even private trainers can benefit enormously from a written plan of behavior and criteria. Often, once this is deliberately established, it can be the key to troubleshooting problems with a behavior. A written criteria enables and encourages the trainer to take an honest look at the specific training description, and compare that to what has been happening in the training sessions to identify possible inconsistencies.

However, *consistency should not be confused with monotony. Variability is a key to motivation, but inconsistency in communication can be disastrous and, at minimum, disabling.*

BUILDING RELATIONSHIP

Throughout this text, I have repeatedly stressed the importance of motivation as the most critical element to accomplishing any goal of behavior modification. Nothing compares to someone wanting to cooperate with you. *I believe that a well-developed positive relationship provides the added essential magic to conquer many troubling hurdles.* It can bend 'no' into 'maybe' and turn fear into acceptance. I have benefited from this precious added margin of victory more times than I can count, the most treasured of which enabled me to provide life-saving treatment or prevent injury and harm.

This relationship enabled me to convince a cherished, dying animal to move calmly into a safe environment and accept a voluntary injection that ended his suffering. Although he was not eating for several days, nor could he see well, this trust, this relationship, afforded him (and me) a peaceful, dignified ending. That we could accomplish this under these circumstances has always struck me as a lasting tribute to what can be achieved through a beautiful lifetime together. The relationship enabled me to take another animal, who, after a thirty-hour transport to a new zoo, cooperated dutifully, learning to accept an x-ray of a broken tooth, so that anesthesia was not necessary for the diagnostic procedure. The relationship caused an animal who was once lost at sea to find his way back to me and his home, though his 'natural' environment was the alternative. And these are but a few of the many stories I have to testify to the value of a positive relationship. I would not trade it for anything. Not for my sake and especially not for the sake of what peace it may provide to the animals in my care.

Every interaction between a human caregiver and their animals can potentially affect the training relationship bank account. Simple everyday events can add up to considerable benefit or harm. For this reason, I always try to come bearing gifts and offer positive reinforcement at the beginning, middle, and end of every interaction, wherever possible, so long as the animal's behavior warrants this and before it has the chance to change for the worse. Deliberately choosing primarily positive reinforcement techniques is another basic plan that ultimately produces a high relationship net worth, if it is done rigorously.

Certainly working in a system that plans to emphasize positive reinforcement techniques is a major step to developing this bond, but it is just the surface of what can and should be done. In order to truly develop a positive relationship with an animal, one must do more than merely provide positive reinforcement for behavior. Creating the relationship with an animal involves every aspect of how humans are relating to that animal. *The choices that are made to clean enclosures, conduct medical treatments, and transport animals are just as much a part of their lives as the moments of the training sessions deliberately planned to create behavior.* **Training systems should be designed to take responsibility to interact with a limited use of aversive stimuli under ALL situations,** *even when such stimuli are a component of the training technique or are necessary to the care of the animal.* Forming a positive relationship means choosing the training tools according to their effect on the relationship bank account and compensating properly when a withdrawal will be necessary. Advanced and thoughtful planning can prevent such withdrawals by deliberately creating necessary behavior and utilizing proactive desensitization practices. By actively evaluating the costs and benefits of each technique used, and maintaining a careful focus on the total relationship development, the thoughtful trainer can effectively use many techniques to expand their options while taking *honest* responsibility for the net effect on the animal.

PREVENT REHEARSAL OF BAD BEHAVIOR

The best training systems will be designed to prevent the rehearsal of foreseeable undesirable behavior. This is critical since it is much easier to prevent something from happening than to un-train something that has already been learned. Eliminating unwanted behavior becomes nearly impossible to accomplish completely, once the behavior has been rehearsed sufficiently.

Expert trainers make advanced decisions to pro-actively modify the environment (for PC, for example) and redirect behavior where aggression may occur. I routinely avoid problematic situations altogether until solutions can be found. Systematic desensitization of novel stimuli and circumstances are further examples of where advanced preparation can prevent adverse reactions from the animal. Evaluating where such interventions are warranted relies again on a thoughtful consideration of individual and species.

PREDICTING PROBLEMS

Being able to anticipate potential upcoming problems is a distinguishing quality of expert trainers. Knowing where an animal might falter gives advance warning and allows extra care to be taken to prevent, redirect, or augment the situation. This prevents disadvantageous rehearsal and even, in some cases, disaster. This section highlights some of the more typical areas where difficulties may manifest or be predictable.

LISTEN TO YOUR ANIMAL

The trainer on an inflexible agenda is most often his/her own worst enemy. Most of the situations where my trainers get themselves into trouble are from having a firm intention in mind going into a training session, and failing to change that to suit the landscape.

As much as we humans must guide and develop the training plan, trainers must always recognize that the animal always determines the starting point. This is particularly true for motivation related issues. No matter what the trainer has in mind for the day or the moment, they will not be able to ignore the animal's feelings on the subject. To the extent that the animal feels strongly, the trainer may have the entire session unravel if they attempt to push through without listening to the animal's sensibilities. For this reason, I always begin training sessions with a determined 'reading' of the animal's behavior - searching for any signs of disinterest, discomfort or distraction. Actively listening to the animal and adjusting to address their needs is absolutely critical to any successful training venture. Force-of-will alone will only get you so far, and quickly, this type of obstinance will earn outright rebellion if not aggression.

INDIVIDUAL PAST

The importance of any individual's past history, as a key element of determining their future behavior, cannot be overstated. Any situation in which an animal has previously demonstrated a problem, be it one of distraction, fear, confusion or aggression, is highly likely to result in difficulties in the future. The prudent trainer will anticipate this and have a new, alternate plan in mind to address these issues as they present, or ideally, redirect them even before they are demonstrated.

SPECIES

Similar to individual history, I have outlined the many nuances of species natural history that may infer problems or distractions. These issues again should be anticipated, prevented and redirected as much as possible.

Understanding dominance

One particular area of species-specific behavior that is common among various species is the issue of dominance behavior between individuals. Handling and understanding dominance is critical to working with groups of animals successfully. While each species may have a social system that requires a unique understanding, there are some general approaches to dominance that are helpful.

Figure 24: Trainer Wendy Lewis working with two harbor seals simultaneously.

(Photo credit: ATR International.)

When dealing with multiple animals simultaneously, it is prudent to prioritize developing and maintaining behavioral control over the dominant animal first and foremost. By controlling the dominant animal, you control the situation, because a subordinate animal generally cannot displace the dominant animal. But a dominant animal, out of control, can displace a subordinate animal that is otherwise well behaved and attempting to be compliant. Without the cooperation of the dominant, the subordinate animal is at risk and they may choose to refuse in order to protect themselves. This puts the subordinate between-a-rock-and-a-hard-place and sets the situation up for failure through the conflicting motivations of the reinforcement offered by the trainer and the aversive offered by the dominant. This can undermine confidence in the trainer by the subordinate. By instead concentrating on developing behavioral control over the dominant animal, the trainer can then begin to reward the dominant for allowing the subordinates to participate, and slowly, each animal can begin to enter the training relationship.

What follows should develop mostly from systematic desensitization (see Chapter 7). Keeping animals that are likely to conflict with each other at a distance from one another is an excellent first step in the process. Slowly through counter-conditioning and specific compliance criterion imposed on the dominant, the situation will develop to increasing manageability. Many trainers create the criterion that the dominant animal must allow the subordinates to eat before they themselves are reinforced, although, this criterion should be phased in carefully, and the dominant reinforced lavishly each time such an event occurs (at least initially). This eventually conditions the motivated dominant to think eagerly about the subordinate receiving reinforcement, since the reinforcement history demonstrates a likelihood of forthcoming reinforcement for themselves. Even once this system has been established however, focusing and maintaining the behavior of the dominant will be necessary in order for any semblance of order to be maintained.

'Group reinforcement contingencies' are another way to address dominance issues. These contingencies require correct behavior from the entire group of animals before any individual is reinforced, insuring it is in everyone's best interest to cooperate and not to conflict.

NOVEL STIMULI

Recognizing and predicting problems associated with novel stimuli or novel environments is another sign of an experienced trainer. Not doing so amounts to random, thoughtless flooding. Any given animal may or may not react adversely to any particular stimulus; however, it is reasonable to take small precautions before the animal's behavior has had a chance to indicate their appraisal of the situation. A little caution in the beginning is well worth the effort if sensitization, and its associated problems, can be avoided.

    A well designed training program will preemptively desensitize its animals to a wide variety of situations and stimuli, and this will develop an animal whose confidence should generalize to many new situations. These animals will be more calm and well-adjusted in captivity through a greater comfort with whatever may come.

TRANSITION POINTS

Trainers should also anticipate problems at what I would call 'transition points.' These are places of distinct changes in the environment of the animal, as well as moments where the animal may have to decide to commit to a given behavior or activity. *Thresholds or commitment points may engender a finalistic evaluation of the animal's true motivation for the activity, since, beyond that point, they may lose the chance to refuse the behavior.* These transition areas are often entrances or exits to enclosures or cages, or a particular spot on the path or trail. They can also be a point in a behavior where the animal becomes vulnerable, such as the moment when they must lie down, or separate from or enter a group. Hesitation at these transition points can indicate lower than optimal motivation for the task. Operant techniques with built-in motivators like baiting or negative reinforcement can assist in momentarily increasing the drive of the animal enough to punch through these critical areas, although this is only one way of increasing the drive needed.

CONTEXT SHIFTS

Changing environments can easily result in the 'loss of a learned response,' called a context shift. Typically this is a memory phenomenon and primarily applies to communication issues; however, I think it is important to recognize functionally that context changes interfere with all categories of behavior both communication and motivational in nature. Even small, local environmental shifts can cause difficulty, such as moving to a different part of the enclosure, but more substantial changes are generally more commonly associated with problems.

In a new context, an individual can have difficulty recalling a conditioned behavior or they can no longer feel inspired to perform one. Changing motivations can occur because of new environmental stimuli that compete with that offered by the trainer (either a distraction or a fear-provoking stimulus). New environments can also lead to aggressive motives over territory or fear, among other reasons. However, if an animal has been well desensitized, and has become experienced with many previous context shifts, smooth transitions occur more easily regardless of the situation. Deliberately preparing an animal to function in a variety of environments staves off problems and increases behavioral flexibility.

TROUBLESHOOTING PROBLEMS

The format of this text provides a mechanism for categorizing techniques and solutions to behavior modification issues. This allows the trainer to locate the training tools that may address the behavioral objective in question. In order to use this system, however, the trainer will need to focus on the type of problem they intend to address.

DETERMINING THE CATEGORY OF PROBLEM

Before addressing a particular problem, the first step is to attempt to determine what type of behavioral issue(s) it is. The answer will affect how you deal with the problem and which 'tool bag' of training techniques to apply. To use this text properly, the trainer with an objective or a training issue should first ask themselves the question, "Do I have an aggression, desensitization, motivation, or communication issue?"

Determining the difference between these behavioral issues relies on an understanding of the definitions of each. At the center of a communication issue is whether the animal understands what to do or how to do a behavior. A motivation issue revolves around if the animal wants to do a particular behavior that the trainer would want to either encourage or discourage. The category of motivation can be general, but also breaks down further into special issues of either desensitization or aggression. A desensitization issue asks if the animal has conflicting motives about performing for the trainer either because they are scared to do something or they are completely captivated by an alternative. Finally, an aggression issue is one in which the animal is attempting to physically threaten, physically dominate, or harm the trainer. This is further recognized if anything in the behavior is representative of a primary aggressive sign, or a past scenario in which aggression had previously occurred. It is worth noting that many of these issues can in part overlap, particularly the issues of aggression and desensitization, since fear can easily cause aggression, in which case, elements of each category may be involved in the solution.

One way to attempt to determine where the issue is falling is to consider the history of the particular animal in question. If it is a new behavior, the issue is likely to be that the animal does not understand (communication), or possibly, some element of the behavior is uncomfortable (desensitization). Conversely, if it is a behavior the animal knows well and has performed on many previous occasions, it is less likely to be a communication problem and instead probably some form of motivational issue. If something about the environment is novel, the trainer should consider desensitization or a context shift effect which would invite further analysis to determine which category is being affected. An animal that is purely unwilling to cooperate is suffering from a motivational problem. Past history or species-specific precursors may infer aggression related concerns.

DEALING WITH EACH CATEGORY OF PROBLEM

Once the category of behavioral issue or issues has been determined, I recommend addressing behavior modification goals in the following order of precedence: 1) aggression, 2) desensitization, 3) motivation, and finally, 4) communication. It can definitely be practical to undertake several areas at once, so long as the trainer recognizes and defaults to the order of importance when making decisions, and focuses primarily on the issue of most importance. This order is recommended to prevent the most damaging issues of behavioral difficulty from being rehearsed, and becoming relatively fixed, or at least, severely problematic. This is also a purely practical suggestion. If you have not prevented the animal from harming you, the entire process of addressing either fear related issues (desensitization), disinterest (motivation) or misunderstanding (communication) becomes unmanageable and more perilous as these different issues combine to create further and larger difficulties. Similarly, attempting to get an animal to focus on learning a specific new operant, when they are distracted by alternative desires, is a losing battle unless you address what has captivated their interest. A similar argument can be made if any attempt is made to reverse the prioritization of any of these categories.

For each category of behavioral issue, an entire chapter (or more) has been dedicated to a conceptual understanding of the subject as well as a review of possible solutions and training tools. I would maintain that each situation is unique and there are potentially many successful roads to any desired outcome. Here, as a brief final compilation, I will provide a very simplified summary and analysis, as an example of troubleshooting each of the four primary behavioral issues.

Aggression- the animal is threatening the trainer

Aggressive behavior is optimally *prevented in advance* by a thorough knowledge of the individual's previous history or the species' natural proclivities. Proactively redirecting aggressive behavior by using anti-aggressive training scenarios to teach healthy choices, or preventing likely scenarios where aggression may occur are, by far, the most effective methods of dealing with aggression. Various forms of protected contact are excellent opportunities to prevent aggression while continuing a healthy training program.

Responding to active aggressive precursors or fully developed aggression can take a variety of paths. Some trainers default to ignoring all signs of aggression to prevent further reinforcement. A different approach would be to punish aggressive behavior by first identifying it using an RS or LRS, followed potentially by some form of time-out, if the trainer is confident that the behavior will not be rewarded by the trainer's absence. Other forms of punishment can be considered (with extreme caution) depending on species-specific availabilities and the practicality and safety of administering the punishment relative to the risk of disadvantageous backlash.

Desensitization – the animal is afraid or distracted

For situations in which novel environments or stimuli are involved, the trainer is wise to predict potential problems. Approaching these situations with a slow, deliberate and distant approach will always minimize competing motivations and their associated stimulus strength.

If *the animal exhibits fear,* it is wise to increase the distance, reduce exposure and attempt to lower the stimulus strength until the animal demonstrates habituation to the stimulus. Desensitization can take considerable time and exposure to be effective. To accelerate the process, it is helpful to present the stimulus associated with positive reinforcement while carefully avoiding reinforcing undesirable behavioral reactions. For this reason, it can be useful to introduce reinforcement slightly in advance, as well as throughout the exposure. Stimuli should optimally not touch the animal until other sensory aspects are desensitized. If the trainer decides to commit to flooding the stimulus, then the process should not abate until no further reaction is observed from the animal, or else risk possible sensitization from the exposure.

If the *animal is distracted by a desire* for an alternative motivator, the trainer could choose to satiate that desire by exposing the animal to the reinforcer, increase the value of the reinforcers and activities being offered (overshadowing), or make the ability to acquire the competing motivator discouragingly difficult (increased response effort).

Motivation - the animal doesn't want what is being offered enough to cooperate fully

Basic motivational problems are probably the most common issues that trainers face. These problems boil down to the cost/benefit analysis of the animal - *the trainer simply has not made cooperation worthwhile to the animal relative to other considerations.* Another way to consider these types of issues is to ask what is driving the behavior in question. Is an undesirable behavior being positively or negatively reinforced? Is the desirable behavior being offered sufficient incentive? Altering the animal's drive state accordingly will change the motivational status and the resultant cooperation.

Often for basic motivational problems, it can be best to *ignore bad behavior* and move on to a different agenda that might be more motivating and "live to fight another day." Consider if there are enough competing motivators to warrant the use of some desensitization techniques. *Try something else to develop cooperation.* This may enable reinforcement delivery and can also begin to set the path for success. Changing things up will also offer the opportunity to provide alternative, potentially more desirable, reinforcement options that might increase the animal's drive. Maintaining sufficient reinforcement and cultivating a variety of interesting reinforcers is another key to developing sustainable motivation. A deliberate change in environment or waiting for a period of time (including the use of time-outs) may also increase the value of reinforcers being offered. Ultimately, associating with a long history of reinforcing techniques and situations will develop a strong relationship that can provide the needed buffer against the "slings and arrows" of outrageous motivation.

Communication - the animal doesn't understand

When *training a novel behavior* the trainer should follow the basic process of operant conditioning and select from and/or combine from the six basic operant techniques. The successful training process will generally involve much repetition, the development of stimulus control and ultimately a confident navigation of discrimination and context changes. If trouble develops during this process, the trainer should attempt to explain the behavior using different techniques and/or smaller approximations focused on a single criterion at a time.

If a problem develops with *confusion over an already completed behavior*, the trainer should first make sure that they have *the attention of the animal* before repeating the S^D, to clarify if the animal was distracted at the time the cue was originally offered. Alternatively, if the environment has changed from the context in which the behavior was originally established, it is possible that a context shift is interfering with the animal's recall in the moment. Returning to the original context and orientation to request the behavior, then shifting more slowly once it has been reestablished, will usually address this issue. Finally, if all else fails, retracing some of the steps used to condition the behavior may be necessary to assist the animal in regaining the operant. In these cases, using a training aid, such as a target or bait, can rapidly recapture the behavior, once a few reminder trials retrace the movement for the animal.

The "three-times-and-you're-out" guideline

Regardless of the type of problem or behavioral issue, by the time you get to trial number three of failure, it is generally wise to stop, evaluate, and make a change. This guideline is not set-in-stone, of course, but it is a useful idiom to remember and guide the trainer to react to a developing problem (you may alternatively wish to stop on trial 2 or 4 depending on the circumstance). Modifying in some way what is being done by trial three will help mobilize alternative options, prevent a pattern of frustration, avoid rehearsal of bad behavior, and counteract the development of an unsuccessful situation. A beautiful quote of uncertain origin (erroneously attributed to Albert Einstein), sums up this concept succinctly, "the definition of insanity is doing the same thing over and over and expecting different results." **The art of skillful training is reactive with an astute flexibility; the best trainers will be fluidly responsive to the changing needs of the moment.**

PRACTICAL TRAINING, IN SUMMARY

Training programs of all types will benefit from a deliberate and proactive behavioral plan and clear system of communication. The most successful systems will properly predict and prevent potential training hurdles before allowing major problems to develop. Troubleshooting behavior modification issues depends on accurately identifying the root behavioral issue (communication, motivation, desensitization and/or aggression) and choosing from among the training tools offered in the appropriate section of this text. Trainers are encouraged to react quickly to training challenges to avoid developing more permanent problems and to prioritize first for aggression problems, second for desensitization issues, thirdly for general motivational problems, and finally for issues of communication.

CHAPTER 10
CONCLUDING REMARKS

(**Photo credit: Animal Training and Research International.**)

A comprehensive approach guided by motivation

With this text, I have tried to provide an *inclusive* and informative summary of the complex art and science of animal behavior modification. To guide the reader, I have provided an advantages and drawbacks analysis of each technique, from the critical standpoint of the motivation of the animal to perform for the trainer. I hope that this text will be only a first edition, and welcome constructive criticism and/or suggestions from any in the industry to help me to expand and improve on the ideas and techniques of this field.

My preference for a comprehensive approach stems in part from my perception of what it takes to be a truly skilled 'Dr. Doolittle.' The best trainers have the flexibility and savvy to react and plan differently for each distinctive creature and situation. They will be fluidly responsive to the changing needs of the moment. To do that, they will need a *deep* understanding of how to communicate, how to listen and, most especially, how to motivate. I believe a greater comprehension of these techniques provides a trainer with greater finesse, even if this only means he/she will be better able to avoid certain approaches altogether.

I hope that my framework will allow the reader to make *informed personal judgments* based on their individual needs and beliefs, as well as, to make the most of any given training tool, while minimizing the disadvantages.

I strongly suggest that guarding the motivation provided by an excellent relationship 'bank account' should be factored highly in all choices about how an animal is handled and trained. The process of relationship development is a very complex one. It is not usually the result of a single associative event, but the cumulative result of all of the meaningful associations between any two individuals (or between the animal and the 'training system'). All interactions between the animal and the trainer have an impact on the animal's learning and viewpoint. Therefore, training systems should be designed to take responsibility to interact with a limited use of aversive stimuli under *all* situations, even when such stimuli are a component of the training technique or are necessary to the care of the animal.

Highlights

Having chosen to provide an overarching treatise on the subject limits any particular suggestions I might make regarding a selection of techniques. Also, any specific suggestions I would make would, to a great extent, depend on the skill level of the particular trainer, the species of animal in question, and even an understanding of the individual animal(s) involved.

Nevertheless, in concluding, I will review and highlight some of the approaches and techniques that I have found to be the most reliably successful.

The task of animal training involves techniques that both describe and persuade (communication and motivation). However, the real challenge is to be optimally persuasive. To this end, there is no technique more promising to promote well-adjusted, cooperative animals than the use of *positive reinforcement*.

Associating yourself with desirable stimuli and scenarios will result in a motivated animal and an excellent relationship. One of the simple strategies to help maintain your best relationship value is my personal philosophy to always "come bearing gifts!" This is a reminder to include positive reinforcement, whenever and wherever possible. Positive reinforcement can help mitigate the downsides of other less friendly techniques and situations, and can generally be used in combination with most other training strategies. Conscientious application of reinforcement according to the merits of behavior, called *differential reinforcement*, is a critical element to the most successful use of positive reinforcement. Meritorious reward is fundamental to the basic tenant of operant conditioning: that behavior is determined by its consequences.

At the pinnacle of positive reinforcement techniques is the **bridge stimulus**. Of all the training tools available, the bridge stimulus provides the most powerful means to both communicate with *and* motivate an animal. It is really the ultimate trainer's tool. The bridge pinpoints in time the moment when the animal has performed the correct behavior, and bridges the gap between that moment, and when they will receive reinforcement. The security and confidence provided by a bridge stimulus cannot be overstated as a form of clear communication to an otherwise guessing animal. I cannot recommend any single technique more highly.

There are six basic operant techniques used to teach behavior, each of which is optimal for different behaviors and situations. However, overall, **target training** offers the most advantages. Target training teaches an animal to operate confidently and thoughtfully on their environment as the animal chooses deliberately to touch a specific area of their body to a designated place. Training even a single targeting behavior will allow the trainer to pursue most other critical training goals necessary to any animal's optimal care. Targets can be effortlessly used to move animals around or from one area to the next. They offer an easy 'recall' to instruct an animal to come to the trainer. They provide a means to have the animal stay or to teach them to enter a cage. All of these behaviors are central to the repertoire of any healthy captive animal.

A good trainer will always engineer environmental antecedents to influence the desired behavior to occur. This *sets the animal up for success* making the entire process faster and more effective. Repetition of successful behavior is at the center of all learning. Rehearsal is the key to mastery. For the same reason, rehearsal of undesirable behavior must be studiously avoided.

The effects of repeated rehearsal of undesirable behavior are, for all intents and purposes, permanent haunting aspects of the animal's behavior, and failure to remember this can sometimes be deadly. Thus, understanding where an animal (according to species) might make mistakes, and *preventing them from rehearsing disadvantageous behaviors,* is one of the most sophisticated demonstrations of training expertise. Well-behaved animals are almost always a product of a proactive training program that has astutely avoided problem scenarios.

Redirection is one of the most powerful techniques to prevent unwanted behavior by reinforcing incompatible or alternative behaviors. Redirection manages to use reinforcement to eliminate bad behavior, while simultaneously suppressing its rehearsal. Of all the techniques associated with the putting an end to undesirable behavior, redirection has the most advantages.

As an animal trainer, at the top of my list of things to prevent would be the problem of sensitization, or a heightened reaction to fear-provoking stimuli. Once sensitization sets in, "forever shall it dominate your destiny." Fear is by far best prevented and assuaged, since there is little hope of altering it otherwise. It is, in my view, the most powerful of all motives. The technique of **systematic desensitization** provides a reliable means to condition an animal to accept even painful and frightening situations by reducing the stimulus to smaller, less frightening components and sequentially increasing the strength. This allows animals to be trained to accept even complex medical procedures such as blood sampling, wound sutures, and tooth removal. This type of training, which directly benefits the animal's welfare and peace of mind, is the most sacred responsibility of a truly humane training system. It represents the future of what can be increasingly expected for all captive animals' welfare and care, especially those in professional organizations.

With proper understanding and dedication I believe it is possible to work *in cooperation* with animals to our mutual satisfaction and benefit, regardless of the purpose of that collaboration. I believe we have an obligation to pursue this honorable end. I hope this text helps to expand the promise of this vision for the future. My dream is for a world where fewer animals are forced, afraid or confused and more are engaged, comfortable, and cooperative. I believe both humans and animals alike will find the advantages of that world far outweigh the drawbacks.

"In the long history of humankind (and animal kind, too), those who learned to collaborate and improvise most effectively have prevailed."

~ **Charles Darwin**

Train well, my friends.

TRAINING AND BEHAVIORAL TERMS GLOSSARY

A

Accidental Reinforcement • Accidental reinforcement describes a coincidence between a performance and a reinforcer. Even though there is no intentional connection between the organism's performance and the reinforcer, there is still an increase in frequency of the performance. With a deliberate reinforcement contingency, the organism must emit a particular performance before the reinforcer is presented. Accidental reinforcement is synonymous with spurious or superstitious conditioning and adventitious reinforcement.

Active Desensitization: See Counter-conditioning

Aggression • Any behavior performed by the animal by which it intends to physically threaten a human or human extension or any behavior which can be reasonably predicted to reliably do so.

Antecedent • The situation under which the behavior is first emitted, or the scenario and its associated causal properties. This evolves to become the S^D in cases of conditioned behavior.

Approximation • One of many progressive steps from simple to more complex behavior, all leading to a finished desired behavior by gradually raising the requirement for reinforcement (successive approximation). • A single step in the refinement process of shaping. Comes from the idea that each differential or selective reinforcement selects a behavior that is a closer approximation of the end-point behavior than the previous response. • One of a series of stages, measures or units calculated to achieve a desired goal.

Aversion Conditioning • A type of counter-conditioning in which punishment is used in order to associate negative feelings with an undesirable response. • A technique in which a painful or discomforting stimulus is paired with another stimulus in order to extinguish the undesirable response to that stimulus.

Aversive Event or Stimulus • A stimulus whose termination increases the frequency of the performance is called an aversive stimulus. Such an increase in frequency is called negative reinforcement. An aversive stimulus which increases the frequency of a performance through the termination of the aversive is called a negative reinforcer. It may decrease the frequency of the performance it follows, in which case it is called a punisher.

Avoidance Learning • Learning that occurs when the subject makes a particular response in order to avoid an aversive [unpleasant] stimulus. • The process of learning to emit a behavior in order to prevent an aversive event, e.g., children learn to duck an oncoming ball in order to avoid being hit by it.

B

Baiting • The use of food or other strong positive reinforcer as an antecedent technique to guide operant behavior to be emitted. • Luring.

Baseline • The frequency that behavior is performed prior to initiating a behavior modification program. The rate of performance used to evaluate the effect of the program. • In experimental work, the term is often used to refer to the control group which serves as a basis for evaluating data from the experimental group.

Behavior • Any observable or measurable response or act. [The terms behavior and response are used synonymously]. Behavior occasionally is broadly defined to include cognition, psychological reactions and feelings, which may not be directly observable but are defined in terms that can be measured using various assessment strategies. • A specific action created by an animal. For the purposes of training, an animal action defined and named by the trainer.

Behavioral Enrichment • Stimuli and methods used as tools to increase interest in the environment and decrease the frequency of stereotypical behaviors. • Stimuli presented to an animal to enrich the environment and discourage stereotypical and/or injurious behavior. Training is a major form of BE.

Blocking • A phenomenon in which an organism fails to learn a new conditioned stimulus because the new stimulus is presented simultaneously with a stimulus that is already effective as a signal.

Bridge • A stimulus that pinpoints in time the precise moment of a desired response and bridges the gap in time between that point and when the animal may receive further reward. • A signal that is conditioned to be reinforcing because it is paired with other reinforcers which evolves to pinpoint an instant in time for the animal in training. Intermediate Bridge signals the animal that at that instant it is on the path to success, but it has not completed the behavior yet. Terminal Bridge signals the instant at which an animal successfully completes a requested behavior. • A stimulus which signals the delivery of a reinforcer. Often called a secondary or conditioned reinforcer because it acquires its effectiveness through a history of being paired with primary reinforcement, such as food to a hungry animal.

C

Chain or Chain Behavior • A series of behaviors which are linked by stimuli that act both as conditioned reinforcers and discriminative stimuli.

Chaining • The process of learning a sequence of behaviors that proceeds semi-automatically in a determinate order; the last previous response provides the necessary cue that determines which behavior comes next.

Classical Or Respondent Conditioning (Sometimes referred to as Pavlovian conditioning) • A form of conditioning in which stimuli associated with naturally meaningful stimuli tend to become substitutes for the stimuli themselves and to elicit similar responses. Technically, the pairing of a conditioned stimulus (CS) with an unconditioned stimulus (US) elicits a conditioned response (CR) similar to the unconditioned response (UR) originally elicited by the US. • A basic form of learning in which stimuli initially incapable of evoking certain responses acquire the ability to do so through repeated pairing with other stimuli that are able to elicit such responses.

Closed Contact (CC) • Training which occurs in a completely protected manner where no contact is permitted between the trainer and the animal, such as through an opaque barrier.

Conditioned Reinforcer • See Secondary Reinforcer • A learned reinforcer that derives its value as a result of its association with other reinforcers.

Conditioned Response (CR) • In classical conditioning, a reflex response elicited by a conditioned stimulus alone in the absence of the unconditioned stimulus after a number of pairings of the conditioned stimulus with an unconditioned stimulus. • A conditioned response is the change in the organism's behavior elicited by a conditioned stimulus. In a reflex, the buzzer (conditioned stimulus), which precedes food in the dog's mouth (unconditioned stimulus), comes to elicit salivation (conditioned response) after a sufficient number of pairings.

Conditioned Stimulus (CS) • A stimulus which has the property of producing a response through pairing or association. • A stimulus which acquires the property of eliciting a previously unconditioned response.

Conditioning • The term conditioning is used to describe both operant and respondent behavior. It refers to a change in the frequency or form of the organism's behavior as a result of the influence of the environment. Functionally, conditioning and learning are synonyms. In operant conditioning the frequency of a performance changes as an organism interacts with the environment. In respondent conditioning, a neutral stimulus comes to elicit a response as a result of pairing it with an unconditioned stimulus.

Context Shift • The loss of a learned response originating from a change in environment or context.

Continuous Reinforcement • Continuous reinforcement is a schedule of reinforcement in which each performance is followed by the reinforcer. Continuous reinforcement is distinguished from intermittent reinforcement, which refers to schedules of reinforcement in which some performances go un-reinforced.

Counter-Conditioning (Active Desensitization) • Process whereby normal defense reactions elicited by an aversive stimulus are modified by association with a positive reinforcer. • To expedite the desensitization of a novel stimulus by associating it with a reinforcer or to nullify the value of a reinforcer by association with a punisher (aversion conditioning).

Cue • A signal which will elicit a specific behavior or reflex - as a result of a learned association • See Conditioned Stimulus and Discriminative Stimulus

D

Delta • See No Reward Marker

Deprivation • Reducing the availability of, or access to, a reinforcer in order to drive up its value or salience.

Desensitization • Exposing an animal to a stimulus using time or experience to drive the stimulus value towards neutral. • A process of changing an animal's perception of an event, negative or positive, but usually negative, to a neutral perception, as evidenced by the animal's lack of response to the event when compared to a previous baseline. • See Habituation and Counter-Conditioning.

Differential Reinforcement • The occurrence of reinforcement on selected occasions at or after one topography of a performance as opposed to another topography is called differential reinforcement. For example, one may differentially reinforce performances which exert a great deal of force on the lever as opposed to performances which operate it lightly. • Reinforcement is offered for behavior only in the presence of the S^D.

Differential Reinforcement of Incompatible Behavior (DRI) • Delivery of a reinforcer after a response that is incompatible or competes with a target response that is to be suppressed. The effect is to increase the frequency of the incompatible response (e.g. cooperative play) and to decrease the frequency of the undesirable target response (e.g. fighting).

Differential Reinforcement of Other Behavior (DRO) • The DRO schedule refers to a procedure in which a reinforcer follows any performance the animal emits except a particular one. Thus, the DRO schedule specifies the performance that is to go unreinforced rather than the one which is increased in frequency. The result of such a schedule of reinforcement is a decrease in the frequency of the particular performance that is specified. This decrease in frequency usually results from an increase in frequency of an incompatible performance.

Differential Reinforcement Stimulus • A differential reinforcement stimulus is a conditioned stimulus that indicates differential reinforcement ratios, typically a variant of a bridge stimulus.

Discrimination • Discrimination frequently refers to the control of an operant performance by a discriminative stimulus (S^D). Thus, discrimination has occurred when the discriminative stimulus controls the frequency of an operant performance. • Discrimination is the ability to differentiate between stimuli attempting to have control over operant behavior, an element in both classical and operant conditioning. • The ability to reliably produce behavior according to the associated stimulus descriptive.

Discriminative Stimulus (S^D) • A conditioned stimulus which has the property of producing a specific behavior by offering the opportunity of reinforcement for that particular behavior. • A stimulus which has a specific meaning. In animal training, this usually denotes a stimulus which elicits a specific behavior, also called a cue or a command.

Drive • An aroused condition of an organism resulting from deprivation of the means of fulfilling a physiological need. • An incitement to action that has its origin in an internal bodily state (e.g. hunger), or that has been learned (e.g. the drive to obtain approval). Something which produces directed behavior.

E

End of Session Stimulus • A stimulus that indicates that the training session is over and that the animal is released from focusing attention on the trainer.

Environmental Enrichment • A dynamic process for enhancing animal environments within the context of the animal's behavioral biology and natural history. Environmental changes are made with the goal of increasing the animal's behavioral choices and drawing out their species-appropriate behaviors, thus enhancing animal welfare.

Emit • Emitted behaviors produce a change in the environment. Operant behavior is emitted. Emitted behavior is produced through willingness. • We speak of operant behavior as emitted because the main variable controlling the frequency of the performance is the way in which the performance changes the environment. The emitted nature of operant behavior is to be contrasted with the elicited nature of reflex behavior. In operant behavior, the main emphasis is on the stimulus which follows the performance in contrast to reflex behavior where the main emphasis is on the stimulus which precedes the response and elicits or evokes it. Because operant behavior is emitted, it has the quality of purposefulness, in contrast to the highly determined nature of the reflex.

Escape or Escape Behavior • The term escape describes a relation between a performance and an aversive stimulus in which the performance terminates the aversive stimulus. Escape is to be contrasted with avoidance, where the aversive stimulus does not occur at all as long as the avoidance performance continues to postpone it.

Escape Learning • The process of learning to emit a behavior in order to escape an aversive event in progress, e.g., if a room is too hot, a person will leave it to escape the heat. If the person or animal can predict when the room will be too hot, they can then avoid the room when it becomes hot. Thus, avoidance learning can directly follow escape learning.

Extended Time-out (ETO) • A prolonged period of absence of opportunity of reinforcement from the trainer. A type of negative punishment.

Extinction • A procedure where the reinforcement of a previously reinforced behavior is discontinued. A behavior which has undergone extinction will decrease in frequency. When a previously conditioned performance is extinguished (no longer reinforced), it generally occurs initially with a high frequency and then falls continuously until its rate reaches near zero. Occasionally, the rate of a performance may actually increase (although temporarily) when the performance is no longer reinforced (extinction burst).

Extinction Burst • An increase in the frequency and intensity of responding at the beginning of extinction.

F

Fading • A term used to describe a procedure for gradually changing a stimulus controlling an organism's performance to another stimulus. For example, consider a pigeon which pecks at a green key and not at a red one. If a cross is superimposed on the green key and the green color is faded out, the new stimulus will control the bird's behavior without the occurrence of any un-reinforced pecking. If the rate of change of the stimuli is properly paced with the organism's behavior, the control may be shifted from one stimulus to another without any instances of the bird's pecking inappropriately.• The gradual removal of discriminative stimuli [S^D] including prompts such as instructions or physical guidance. Yet, it is important in most situations to fade the prompt. Fading can also refer to the gradual removal of reinforcement, as in the progressive thinning of a reinforcement schedule.

Fixed-Interval Schedule • The application of reinforcement on a systematic time basis. • In a fixed-interval schedule of reinforcement, the first performance that occurs after a fixed period of time elapses is reinforced. The interval of time is measured from the preceding reinforcement. Thus, on an FI 5 schedule, reinforcement is given after the first performance which the animal emits at least five minutes after the preceding reinforcement.

Fixed-Ratio Schedule • A schedule of reinforcement in which the organism is reinforced after a set number of non-reinforced correct responses. • In a fixed-ratio schedule of reinforcement a fixed number of performances (counted from the preceding reinforcement) are required for reinforcement. Thus on a FR 50 schedule, the fiftieth performance after the preceding reinforcement produces the next reinforcement. The term ratio refers to the ration of performances required for each reinforcement.

Flooding • Flooding is an extreme method of stimulus exposure where the animal is heavily and unrelentingly exposed to a frightening novel stimulus or environment until it stops reacting. It was originally developed to treat phobias.

Free contact • The animal and the trainer are in unfettered access to one another.

G

Generalization • The phenomenon of an organism's responding to all situations similar to one in which it has been conditioned. • Generalization is when a stimulus acquires control of a response due to reinforcement in the presence of a similar, but different stimulus.

Group Contingencies ("Team behavior") • Contingencies of reinforcement in which the group participates. There are two major variations: 1) An individual's behavior can determine the consequences delivered to the group. 2) The behavior of a group as a whole determines the consequences that each member receives.

H

Habit • A recurrent pattern of behavior acquired through experience and made more-or-less permanent by various reinforcing events including the act of rehearsal.

Habituation (Passive Desensitization) • The lessening or disappearance of a response with repeated presentations of the stimulus. • The relatively persistent waning of a response as a result of repeated stimulation which is not followed by any kind of reinforcement.

Husbandry • Long term physiological and psychological management ensuring the viability of a captive animal. • A branch of agriculture concerned with the breeding and feeding of domestic animals.

I

Immediacy of Reinforcement • A critical feature of conditioning. The act of reinforcing, exactly following the behavior, which is intended to increase in frequency. If reinforcement is delayed as much as a couple of seconds, it may follow some other behavior.

Imprinting • The process by which a young animal forms a lasting attachment to and preference for some object, usually a parent. • The very rapid development of a response or learning pattern to a stimulus at an early and usually critical period of development, particularly characteristic of some species of birds.

Incompatible Behavior • A performance is incompatible with another when it is impossible for both performances to occur at the same time. For example, the behavior of clasping the hands behind the back is incompatible with reaching for an object on a table.

Innovative Training • Learning by which an animal is reinforced for successfully reaching appropriate approximations through a self-experimental or self-inventive process. Reinforcement is contingent on producing a novel or different response than the one previously reinforced.

Instrumental Conditioning See Operant Conditioning.

Inter-Stimulus Interval (ISI) • In classical conditioning, the time elapsed between the conditioned stimulus and the unconditioned stimulus. • In habituation, the inter-stimulus interval (ISI) is defined as the time between exposures to a stimulus.

Intermediate Bridge • A series of continuous and instantaneous signals marking a progression of successful instances advancing toward a successfully completed behavior. • A tertiary reinforcer that allows a trainer to give continuous encouraging feedback to an animal as they near the completion of a requested behavior.

Intermittent Reinforcement • A schedule of reinforcement in which a response is not reinforced every time it is performed. Only some occurrences of this response are reinforced.

J

Jackpotting • See Magnitude Reinforcement

K

Keep Going Stimulus (KGS) • A signal given in the middle of a behavior to indicate to the animal that the behavior it is engaged in is correct and should be continued to eventual reinforcement. This signal is typically given in the middle of a behavioral extension.

L

Latency • The extended duration of time between an event and its response, either a stimulus and a behavior or a behavior and its consequence.

Learned Helplessness • A condition created by exposure to inescapable aversive events. This can retard or prevent learning in subsequent situations in which escape or avoidance is possible. • The state of considering oneself helpless because of the failure of attempts to control a situation. Some animals will eventually quit trying.

Learning • The process in which relatively permanent changes in behavior are produced through experience.

Learning Plateau • A period in which early progress in learning appears to have stopped and improvement is at a standstill; the plateau is followed by a new period of progress. • An interval in which no improvement is observed in learning followed by further improvement as practice continues.

Least Reinforcing Scenario (LRS) • A 2-3 second period of no attention or reaction from trainer in response to an undesired behavior to reduce its frequency. If the animal reacts to this non-stimulus form of stimulus with attentive behavior, this attentive behavior may be followed by reinforcement on a variable schedule.

Luring • See Baiting

M

Magnitude Reinforcement • Large quantity of reinforcement delivery after a single behavior, also called jackpotting or bonusing.

Manipulation Training • The use of touch to form operant behavior. • Any time tactile contact between the trainer and animal is used to create novel behavior. Also called sculpting.

Matching Law • Principle that states the effort expended on any given behavior will be matched with its history of reinforcement (in a given environment).

Matching-to-Sample • A procedure in which the choice of a stimulus that matches a sample stimulus is followed by a reinforcer. Typically, in the matching-to-sample procedure, the organism touches a key in which the sample stimulus appears. The performance on the sample stimulus is reinforced by the appearance of two stimuli on two other keys. The final reinforcement occurs if the organism chooses the key on which the stimulus corresponding to the sample stimulus appears.

Mimicry • The act, practice or art of copying the manner or expression of another- a form of observational learning. • An operant technique that uses the behavior of one individual to stimulate behavior in another, also called imitation.

Motivation • The comparatively spontaneous drive, force, or incentive, which partly determines the direction and strength of the response of a higher organism to a given situation; it arises out of the internal state of the organism. • A general term referring to the forces regulating behavior that is undertaken because of drives, needs, or desires and is directed toward goals. • The non-stimulus variables controlling behavior; the general name for the fact that an organism's acts are partly determined in direction and strength by its own nature and/or internal state.

Motive • Anything that initiates behavior. • A desire for a goal or incentive object that has acquired value for the individual. • A drive, force, or tension state within the organism that impels it to act.

N

Negative • Removed from the environment.

Negative Punishment • In operant conditioning, the removal of a reinforcing stimulus -- something the organism seeks to encounter -- from the organism's environment following an undesirable response, thereby decreasing the frequency of that response (e.g. a time-out).

Negative Reinforcer • The frequency of the behavior is increased by the subtraction of something the animal does not like, as an immediate result of the behavior. Negative reinforcement is not the same as a punishment • Negative reinforcement refers to an operant performance whose frequency increases because it has terminated an aversive stimulus. Both negative and positive reinforcement increase the frequency of the performance. In the case of negative reinforcement, the increase comes about because of the termination of the stimulus, while in the case of positive reinforcement, the increase occurs as a result of the addition of a reinforcing stimulus. • In operant conditioning, any stimulus that, when removed, reduced, or prevented, increases the probability of a given response over time.

Neutral Stimulus or Cue • Any stimulus that has no effect on behavior before conditioning.

No reward marker/ Delta • A punishing signal that indicates that as a result of previous behavior, no reinforcement will be provided. This signal is a consequence of behavior.

Novelty Affect • Innate fear-provoking response associated with exposure to novel stimulus.

O

Observational Learning • Learning by observing another individual [a model] engaged in a behavior. To learn from a model, the observer need not perform the behavior nor receive direct consequences for his or her performance. • A type of learning in which the behavior of another organism is observed and imitated.

Operant or Operant Behavior • Emitted behavior that is controlled by its consequences. • Operant behavior acts on and produces a change in the environment. It is voluntary, and it is produced through willingness.

Operant Conditioning (Instrumental Conditioning) • The process by which, through learning, free operant behavior becomes attached to a specific stimulus. • A form of conditioning in which the persistence of a response emitted by an organism depends on its effect on the environment. The conditioning procedure involves presenting an organism with a reinforcing or punishing stimulus immediately after the occurrence of a given response to affect the frequency of the behavior in the future. The fundamental principle of operant conditioning is that behavior is determined by its consequences.

Orienting Response • The initial phase of an organism's response to a novel stimulus, a component of the novelty affect. • A response to a stimulus in which the organism turns toward the source of the stimulus.

Overshadowing • When two stimuli are present and one stimulus produces a stronger response than the other because it is more salient.

P

Passive Desensitization • See Habituation

Positive • Added to the environment.

Positive Punishment • In operant conditioning, the addition of an aversive stimulus -- something the organism seeks to avoid -- to the organism's environment following a response, thereby decreasing the frequency of that response.

Positive Reinforcement • Presentation of a reinforcer following the performance of a correct response which increases the probability that a response will reoccur in the future. • Frequency of the behavior is increased by the addition of something the animal desires, immediately after the behavior.

Precursor Stimulus • An event that comes before another that signals its arrival.

Premack Principle • A principle that states that of any pair of responses or activities in which an individual freely engages, the more frequent one will reinforce the less frequent one. • Desirable behaviors can act as reinforcers.

Primary • Any innate or self-maintaining perception that does not require continual association. • A quality that an animal responds to innately in a certain way. A primary reinforcer might be food, sex, water, or sleep. A primary punisher might be the deprivation of any of the above, fear, or pain.

Primary Reinforcement • Reinforcement provided by a stimulus that the organism finds inherently rewarding-usually stimuli that satisfy biological drives such as hunger or thirst. • Defined by some psychologists as any stimulus that reduces a need or motive.

Protected Contact (PC) • Handling of an animal when the trainer and the animal do not share the same unrestricted space. Typically, in this system, the trainer has contact with the animal through a protective barrier or mechanism of some type.

Punisher or Punishment • Anything which decreases the frequency of the behavior it immediately follows. • Presentation of an aversive event or removal of a positive event contingent upon a response which decreases the probability of that response.

R

Ratio strain • The disruption of responding that occurs when a fixed ratio response requirement is increased too rapidly. • Describes the dampening effect on motivation as reinforcement becomes less predictable and associated with the behavioral effort.

Recall • The process of sending or retrieving an animal from one point of station to another through the use of a conditioned stimulus, or to bring back to station.

Redirection • The use of one of several types of differential reinforcement strategies to refocus behavior from undesirable to acceptable by increasing the frequency of alternative behaviors.

Redirection Stimulus (RS) • Signal which pinpoints in time when an animal has done something incorrectly and is not on the path to reinforcement, in order to provide information which will allow the animal to succeed more rapidly. The RS cues the animal to change behavior. The animal correctly changing behavior to terminate the undesirable behavior can be followed by a bridge and/or other reinforcement on a variable schedule at the discretion of the trainer. Used in conjunction with a bridge stimulus has the effect of providing "hot and cold" information to the animal.

Reflex • A reflex is a relationship between an eliciting stimulus and an elicited response such as the contraction of the pupil of the eye as a result of shining light on it, the jerk of the knee as a result of tapping the patellar tendon, the excretion of sweat as a result of warm air, or the constriction of blood vessels in response to a loud noise. The reflex describes both the behavior of the organism (response) and its environment (stimulus). This response is controlled by the spinal cord rather than the brain. • An automatic and unthinking reaction to a stimulus by the organism. A reflex is inborn, involuntary, not learned, and depends on inherited characteristics of the nervous system.

Refusal • A lack of response.

Reinforcement • The event which increases the frequency of the behavior it follows. • An increase in the frequency of a response when the response is immediately followed by a particular consequence. The consequence can be either the presentation of a positive reinforcer or the removal of a negative reinforcer.

Reinforcement Contingency • Refers to the relationship between the reinforcement and the exact properties of the performance which it follows.

Reinforcement Schedule • The rule denoting how many or which responses will be reinforced.

Reinforcer • Anything that increases the frequency of the behavior it immediately follows.

Respondent Behavior • Behavior that is elicited or automatically controlled by antecedent stimuli. Reflexes are respondents because their performance automatically follows certain stimuli. The connection between unconditioned respondents and antecedent events which control them is unlearned. Respondents may come under the control of otherwise neutral stimuli through classical conditioning. Respondent behavior is not produced willingly.

Response Effort • The "cost" of the amount of effort required to produce a particular behavior.

Reward • A return given to an animal for a correct response to a stimulus (see reinforcer).

S

S^D • See Discriminative Stimulus

Salience • The *relative* value of a particular stimulus to a given individual at a particular moment in time. The index of the effectiveness of a stimulus.

Satiation • Refers to having a certain reinforcer being used excessively to the point where it no longer has reinforcing value. • The point at which an animal no longer continues to consume an object or engage in an activity that is related to some primary need.

Scan and Capture Technique • The operant antecedent technique consisting of the act of seeking and then reinforcing desired behavior. Scanning refers to the trainer's active searching for a desired behavior or, more typically, its earliest approximation to occur. Capturing refers to the act of timely reinforcement being delivered following the production of the target operant. Since reinforcement ultimately increases the frequency of the behavior it follows, the operant will begin to occur more frequently and therefore it has been "captured."

Schedule Of Reinforcement • The type, amount and frequency of the reinforcement that will be given when a task is completed. There are generally considered to be two basic schedules: continuous and intermittent. • Refers to the various plans for applying reinforcement. • Rules governing the delivery of reinforcement. When a given schedule is in effect, reinforcement can be attained only by meeting its requirements.

Sculpting Technique • See Manipulation

Secondary • An initially neutral perception that an animal comes to respond to because its perception has been conditioned or learned by association with a primary.

Secondary Reinforcer • Any stimulus that acquires reinforcing properties through repeated, predictable association with a primary reinforcement. • An event which becomes reinforcing through learning. An event becomes a secondary reinforcer by being paired with other events [primary or conditioned], which are already reinforcing. Praise and attention are examples of basic secondary reinforcers; the bridge stimulus is an example of a secondary reinforcer that is also a conditioned communication stimulus.

Selective Reinforcement • See Differential Reinforcement.

Sensitization • The enhancement of a response solicited by a stimulus with repeated presentations of that stimulus. • The intensifying of an organism's response to stimuli that did not originally produce such strong reactions.

Shaping • The entire process of selectively reinforcing responses that approximate the desired response to an increasingly greater degree. A method of modifying behavior. • Developing new behavior by reinforcing successive approximations toward the terminal response. • The learning of complicated tasks through operant conditioning, in which complex actions are built up from simpler ones.

Station • An assigned position for an animal, designated by a trainer.

Stereotypic Behavior • A repetitive response that is without variation for extended periods of time. Stereotypic behavior is usually brought about through lack of stimulation.

Stimulus • Any environmental condition which impinges on the animal's sensory perception.• Any physical event or condition, including the organism's own behavior.

Stimulus Control • The predictability of a behavior performed in the presence of one stimulus which is not evident in the presence of another.

Stimulus Delta • Represents the particular occasion on which a performance will not be reinforced, in contrast to other occasions (discriminative stimuli) during which the performance will be reinforced. • An antecedent stimulus under whose presence an operant will not be reinforced, the stimulus precedes the circumstance.

Stimulus Generalization • Transfer of a trained response to situations or stimulus conditions other than those on which training has taken place. The behavior generalizes to other situations. • When an organism is trained to make a response in the presence of one stimulus, there is a tendency to make the same response to other stimuli resembling the training stimulus. The amount of responding decreases as the similarity of the stimuli decreases.

Successive Approximation • Successive approximation is used to condition performance which is not currently in the organism's repertoire. Some performance which is an approximation to the desired behavior and which the organism is already emitting is first reinforced. Thereafter, reinforcement occurs after those performances, which are in the direction of the desire performance. Conversely, performances that are most distant from the desired behavior go unreinforced.

Superstitious Behavior • Behavior which results from misunderstanding. It is produced where there is no intended relation between response and reinforcement. • Behavior resulting from the chance or inadvertent reinforcement of unwanted behavior which then comes under stimulus control.

Systematic Desensitization • Systematic desensitization refers to the practice of reducing stimulus strength and using incremental steps of exposure to increase an animal's tolerance of a frightening or aversive stimulus in an approximated and non-aversive manner.

T

Tactile Reinforcement • Any reinforcer discernible by touch.

Target (Noun) • A prop which pinpoints a critical location for an animal in training. This location may be a body contact point on the stationary animal, it may be a destination point, or it may be a place where other critical information will appear. The target can be an extended finger or fist, the end of a pole, a mark on a wall or a paper, a plaque, a matt or anything else that the trainer indicates.

Target (Verb) • The operant antecedent technique of stimulating an animal to touch a particular object and using a sequence of these contact points to form more complex behaviors.

Team Based Contingency • A group contingency in which members earn reinforcers on the basis of performance of the group. Every member of the group must succeed in completing their correct behavior in order for any member to receive reinforcement. In addition, subgroups or teams can be used so that there is competition to earn the reinforcers between the teams.

Tertiary reinforcer • A reinforcer conditioned through its association with a secondary reinforcer.

Threshold • The point at which an animal's understanding of a behavior is uncertain or incomplete. • The threshold is the magnitude or strength of a stimulus which is just sufficient to elicit a respondent behavior or emit an operant behavior.

Time-out • The cessation of stimulus or response from the trainer, for some interval of time. In essence, the animal receives no cues from the trainer, but also cannot influence the trainer to produce a consequence such as food or praise until the "time-out" or TO has passed. • Removing the situation in which an organism can get reinforcement; used to suppress incorrect responses correlated with non-reinforcement. A type of negative punisher.

Training (Animal) • Behavior modification brought about by direct interactions (usually intended) with people.

U,V,W,X,Y,Z

Unconditioned Reinforcer • See Primary Reinforcer.

Unconditioned Response • A response that is elicited by an unconditioned stimulus without prior training. Any display of instinct is an unconditioned response. • An automatic, unlearned reaction to a stimulus. • In classical conditioning, this is the response that the animal manifests prior to the beginning of the conditioning procedure.

Unconditioned Stimulus (US) • Any stimulus possessing the capacity to elicit reactions from organisms in the absence of prior conditioning. • An environmental event that automatically elicits an unconditioned response.

Variable Interval Schedule • A schedule of administering reinforcement. In a variable interval (VI) schedule, the first occurrence of the target response after a given time interval has elapsed is reinforced. However, the time interval changes each time, that is, it is variable. The schedule is denoted by the average time which must elapse before a response can be reinforced. • A reinforcement schedule in which a reward is available after a varying amount of time has elapsed after the last reward.

Variable Ratio Schedule • Variable-ratio reinforcement is a schedule of intermittent reinforcement in which reinforcement follows after a variable number of performances. The schedule is specified by the average number of performances required for reinforcement. Therefore, variable ratio 10 (VR 10) means that ten performances on the average are required for each reinforcement. • In all VR schedules, a number of occurrences of the target response is required for reinforcement. The number of required occurrences varies each time reinforcement is delivered.

REFERENCES AND SUGGESTED READING

Ahern,W., & Hineline, P.N. (1992). Relative preferences for various bivalued ratio schedules. Animal Learning and Behavior. Vol. 20, No.4, pp.407-415.

Bailey, R. E., & Bailey, M. B. (1980). A view from outside the Skinner box. American Psychologist, 35, pp. 942-946.

Bassett, L., & Buchanan-Smith, H.M. (2007). Effects of predictability on the welfare of captive animals. Applied Animal Behaviour Science. Vol. 102, pp. 223-245.

Bindra, D. (1959). Stimulus change, reactions to novelty, and response decrement. Psychological Review. Vol.66, No.2, pp.96-103.

Bishop, P.D., & Kimmel, H.D. (1969). Retention of habituation and conditioning. Journal of Experimental Psychology. Vol.81, No.2, pp.317-321.

Bodnoff, S.R., Suranyi-Cadotte, B.E., Quirion, R., & Meaney, M.J. (1989). Role of the central benzodiazepine receptor system in behavioral habituation to novelty. Behavioral Neuroscience. Vol.103, No.1, pp.209-212.

Bouton, M.E., & Peck, C.A. (1992). Spontaneous recovery in cross-motivational transfer (counter-conditioning). Animal Learning and Behavior. Vol.20, No.4, pp.313-321.

Bouton, M.E. (1993). Context, time, and memory retrieval in the interference paradigms of Pavlovian learning. Psychological Bulletin. Vol.114, No.1, pp.80-99.

Breland, K., & Breland, M. (1961). The misbehavior of organisms. American Psychologist. 16, pp.681-684.

Breland, K., & Breland, M. (1966). Animal behavior. New York: The Macmillan Company.

Burgoon, J.K., Johnson, M.L., & Koch P.T. (1998). The nature and measurement of interpersonal dominance. Communication Monographs. Vol 65(4), pp. 308-335.

Carey, J. R., & Gruenfelder, C. (1997). "Population biology of the elderly." In KW Wachter and CE Finch (eds.) *Between Zeus and the Salmon*. Washington, D.C.: National Academy Press, pp. 127-160.

Carlstead, K., Seidensticker, J., & Baldwin, R. (1991). Environmental enrichment for zoo bears. Zoo Biol. 10, pp. 3-16.

Carson K., & Wood-Gush, D.G.M. (1983). A review of the literature on social and dam-foal behaviour. Applied Animal Ethology, 10, pp.165-178.

Crook, J.H., Ellis, J. E., & Goss-Custard, J.D. (1976). Mammalian Social Systems: Structure and function. Anim. Behav. 24, pp. 261-274.

Crowell-Davis, S.L., Curtis, T.M., & Knowles, R.J. (2004). Social organization in the cat: a modern understanding. Journal of Feline Medicine & Surgery. 6(1), pp. 19-28.

Davison, G.C. (1983). Systematic desensitization as a counter-conditioning process. Journal of Abnormal Psychology. Vol.73, No.2, pp. 91-99.

Dawkins, M. S. (1990). From an animal's point of view: Motivation, fitness, and animal welfare. Behav & Brain Sci. 13, pp. 1-61.

Dickson, A.L. (1977). Wolpe's reciprocal inhibition principle: An animal analogue. Psychological Reports. Vol.40, pp. 395-401.

Domjan, M., Gillan, D., & Trent, J.M. (1976). Reinforcing properties of novel and familiar solutions of saccharin for rats. Bulletin of the Psychonomic Society. Vol.7, No.2, pp. 151-153.

Droppa, D.C. (1978). The application of covert conditioning procedures to the outpatient treatment of drug addicts: Four case studies. The International Journal of the Addictions. Vol.13, No.4, pp.657-673.

Duncan, I.J.H., & Hughes, B. O. (1972). Free and operant feeding in domestic fowls. Animal Behaviour 20, 775-777.

Elsner, R.W. (1965). Heart rate responses in forced versus trained experimental dives in pinnipeds. Hvalradets Skrifter. Vol. 48, pp. 24-29.

Friend, T. (1989). Recognizing behavioral needs. Appl. Anim. Behav. Sci. 22, pp.151-158.

Glavin, J.P., & Moyer, L.S. (1975). Facilitating extinction of infant crying by changing reinforcement schedules. Journal of Behavioral Therapy and Experimental Psychiatry. Vol.6, pp.357-358.

Goldblatt, A. (1993). Behavioral needs of captive marine mammals. Aquatic Mammals. Vol.19, No.3, pp.149-157.

Goldstein, A.J. (1969). Separate effects of extinction, counter-conditioning and progressive approach in overcoming fear. Behavioral Research and Therapy. Vol.7, pp.47-56.

Grings, W.W., & Uno, T. (1968). Counter-conditioning: Fear and relaxation. Psychophysiology. Vol.4, No.4, pp.479-485.

Groves, P.M., & Thompson, R.F. (1970). Habituation: A dual-process theory. Psychological Review. Vol.77, pp.419-450.

Hall, G., & Honey, R.C. (1989). Contextual effects in conditioning, latent inhibition, and habituation: Associative and retrieval functions of contextual cues. Journal of Experimental Psychology: Animal Behavior Processes. Vol.15, No.3, pp.232-241.

Hanley, G.P., Piazza, C.C., Fisher, W.W., & Maglieri, K.A. (2005). On the effectiveness of and preference for punishment and extinction components of function-based interventions. J. Appl. Behav. Anal. 38(1),pp. 51-65.

Hanson, J.P., Larson, M.E., & Snowdon, C.T. (1976). The effects of control over high intensity noise on Plasma Cortisol Levels in rhesus monkeys. Biol. Behav. 16, pp. 333-340.

Harris, J.D. (1943). Habituatory responses decrement in the intact organism. Psychological Bulletin. Vol.40, pp.385-422.

Hinde (1970). *Animal Behavior:* A synthesis of ethology and comparative psychology. pp. 577-579.

Hothersall, D. (2004). History of Psychology. McGraw-Hill.

Hughes, B.O., & Duncan, I.J.H. (1988). The notion of ethological 'need'. Models of motivation and animal welfare. Anim. Behav. 36, pp. 1696-1707.

Hurley, J.A., & Holmes, N.H. (1998). A review of the psychological principles and training techniques associated with desensitization. Marine Mammals: Public Display and Research. 3(1), pp. 16-26.

King, A. J., Johnson, D.D.P., & Van Vugt, M. (2009). The origins and evolution of leadership, Current Biology, 19 (19): R911-R916.

Lorenz, K. (1942). Here I am- where are you?: The behaviour of the greylag goose. London: Harper Collins (with M. Martys and A. Tipler, translated R.D. Martin).

Markowitz, H., & Woodworth, G. (1977). Experimental analysis and control of group behaviour. Pp. 107-131 in H. Markowitz & V. Stevens (eds.), The behaviour of captive wild animals. Nelson Hall, Chicago.

Matson, J.L., & Taras, M.E. (1989). A 20-year review of punishment and alternative methods to treat problem behaviors in developmentally disabled persons. Research in Developmental Disabilities, 10, pp. 85-104.

McFarland, D. (1989). Problems of Animal Behaviour. Longman Scientific and Technical, Essex, England.

Menzel, E.W. Jr. (1991). Chimpanzees pan-troglodytes problem seeking versus the bird-in-hand least-effort strategy. Primates 32, pp. 497-508.

Mineka, S., Gunnar, M., & Champoux, M. (1986). Control and early socioemotional development: Infant rhesus monkeys reared on controllable versus uncontrollable environments. Child Dev. 57, pp. 1241-1256.

Myers, W.A. (1977). Applying behavioral knowledge to the display of captive animals. Pp. 133-159 in H. Markowitz & V. Stevens (Eds.), The behavior of captive wild animals. Nelson Hall., Chicago.

Neuringer, A.J. (1969). Animals respond for food in the presence of free food. Science 166, pp. 399-401.

Osborne, S.R. (1977). The free food (contrafreeloading) phenomenon: A review and analysis. Anim. 5, pp. 221-235.

Pavlov, I.P. (1960). Conditioned reflexes. An investigation of the physiological activity of the cerebral cortex (G.V. Anrep. Trans.) New York: Dover. (Original work published 1927).

Pfungst, O. (1911). Clever Hans (The horse of Mr. von Osten): A contribution to experimental animal and human psychology (Trans. C. L. Rahn). New York: Henry Holt. (Originally published in German, 1907).

Pierce, W.D & Cheney, C.D. (2008). Behavior Analysis and Learning (4th edition). New York: Psychology Press.

Pryor, K. (1999). Don't shoot the dog: The new art of teaching and training. (Rev. ed.) New York: Bantam Books.

Rohr, J. J., Fish, F. E., & Gilpatrick, J. W. (2002). Maximum swim speeds of captive and free ranging delphinids: critical analysis of extraordinary performance. Marine Mammal Science 18(1),pp.1-19.

Runyan, A. M., & Blumstein, D. T. (2004). Do individual differences influence flight initiation distance? The Journal of Wildlife Management. 68(4), pp.1124-1129.

Schulz, R. (1976). Effects of control and predictability on the physical and psychological well-being of the institutionalized aged. Journal of Personality and Social Psychology. 33(5), pp.563-573.

Singh, D. (1970). Preference for bar pressing to obtain reward over freeloading in rats and children. J. Comp. Physiol. Psychol. 73, pp. 320-327.

Skinner, B.F. (1938). The behavior of organisms. New York: Appleton-Century-Crofts.

Tenneson, T. (1989). Coping with confinement - features of the environment that influence animals' ability to adapt. Appl. Anim. Behav. Sci. 22,pp. 139-149.

Tortora, D.F. (1983). Safety training: the elimination of avoidance-motivated aggression in dogs. J. Exp. Psych.: General, 112(2), pp.176-214.

Van Houten, R., Axelrod, S., Bailey, J.S., Favell, J.E., Foxx, R.M., Iwata, B.A. et al. (1988). The right to effective treatment. Journal of Applied Behavior Analysis, 21, pp.381-384.

Wingfield, J.C., & Ramenofsky, M. (1999). Hormones and the behavioral ecology of stress. In: Balm, P.H.M. (Ed.), Stress Physiology in Animals. Sheffield Academic Press, Sheffield, UK, pp. 1–51.

INDEX

ABOUT THE AUTHOR

J enifer A. Zeligs, Ph.D. is the owner of Animal Training and Research International, which oversees a small "teaching aquarium" at California State University. She is the author of numerous articles and award winning presentations on animal behavior modification and its uses.

Dr. Zeligs has been working with animals since she got her start at the Smithsonian's National Zoo in Washington, D.C. while still in grade school. Since that time, she has worked with dozens of species of terrestrial and aquatic animals. She has also worked as a training consultant with exotic and domestic animals, as a veterinary technician, and with domestic and exotic animals trained to assist the handicapped. She has collaborated with and consulted for a large number of private and public facilities and organizations, and has trained animals for research, free release in the open-ocean, feature films and documentaries, public display, and veterinary purposes. Dr. Zeligs has been featured in dozens of documentaries and television shows including National Geographic Explorer, the Tonight Show with Jay Leno, and Dateline, NBC.

Of all of her accomplishments, Jenifer is most proud of her students, and finds the greatest joy in teaching and working with those passionate about their interests in conservation, animal care and training. Jenifer currently teaches at California State University, Monterey Bay and mentors students from all over the world in cutting-edge animal behavior and husbandry.

CPSIA information can be obtained
at www.ICGtesting.com
Printed in the USA
BVHW061202270620
582324BV00002B/3

9 781634 130660